Changema

Changemakers reveals a startling new perspective on the family as it focuses on the largely unconscious factors that determine the use and abuse of power. Louis H. Stewart explores the many aspects of the family, looking in particular at the relation between birth order and political genius. He takes up the four basic sibling positions, shows how each is related to a corresponding style of political leadership, reviews the literature on birth order, and presents a study of American presidents and British prime ministers over some two hundred years.

Stewart describes a fourfold cycle of creative change that occurs in every field of endeavour. It requires the contribution of individuals of genius who embody the viewpoints inherent in each of the four basic sibling positions: the last born is the rebel, finely tuned to the winds of change; the intermediate born is also frequently a rebel but, because of the vantage point between older and younger, a master of accommodation and mediation; the first born is the preserver, the extender and developer, the carrier of tradition; and the only child is the synthesizer, the carrier of the opposites, being both first and last. Stewart's exploration takes place in the context of depth psychology and leads him to develop a new hypothesis about the nature and function of the emotions, which he sees as motivating and transformational forces that shape every kind of human development, creative and destructive alike.

Stewart extends his study to look at the lives and family background of leaders who have been in the news, including Mikhail Gorbachev and Saddam Hussein. Of special interest to psychotherapists, psychologists, political scientists and sociologists, *Changemakers* will also have a wide general appeal.

Louis H. Stewart is an analyst member and former President of the C. G. Jung Institute of San Francisco. He is Professor Emeritus of Psychology, San Francisco State University, and is a Clinical Professor of Medical Psychology at the University of California at San Francisco.

Changemakers

A Jungian perspective on sibling
position and the family atmosphere

Louis H. Stewart

London and New York

First published in 1992
by Routledge
11 New Fetter Lane, London EC4P 4EE

Simultaneously published in the USA and Canada
by Routledge
a division of Routledge, Chapman and Hall, Inc.
29 West 35th Street, New York, NY 10001

© 1992 Louis H. Stewart

Typeset by Witwell Ltd, Southport
Printed and bound in Great Britain by
Biddles Ltd, Guildford and King's Lynn

British Library Cataloguing in Publication Data
A catalogue record for this book is available from the British Library.

Library of Congress Cataloging in Publication Data
Stewart, Louis H.
  Changemakers: a Jungian perspective on sibling position and the family
  atmosphere/Louis H. Stewart.
      p.   cm.
  Includes bibliographical references and index.
  1. Birth order.   2. Social change—Psychological aspects.
  3. Politicians—Psychology—Case studies. 4. Psychoanalysts—
  Psychology—Case studies. 5. Jung, C. G. (Carl Gustav),
  1875–1961. I. Title.
  BF723.B5S74   1992
  155.9'24—dc20   92–1050
                                                                      CIP

ISBN 0–415–07443–6
     0–415–07444–4 (pbk)

To Joan Marie Chodorow

Contents

Tables and figures

TABLES

FIGURES

Preface

My younger brother, my only sibling, was born when I was six and a half years of age. I had prepared myself for the event by coming down with the measles, and had been restricted to the murphy bed in the dining room where the window shades were drawn. On the day my brother was brought home from the hospital I was wearing my red bandana around my neck, had my toy pistol on my belt and my uncle's marine hat on my head. My mother and father came into the room. My father (himself a firstborn) was carrying the baby. In a jovial voice he said, 'This is your brother; see, he has no chin, he looks like a fish!' I could only agree with my father.

C. G. Jung had a similar reaction to the birth of his only sibling when he was nine years of age. When his sister Gertrude was born,

> My father brought me to my mother's bedside, and she held out a little creature that looked dreadfully disappointing: a red, shrunken face like an old man's, the eyes closed, and probably as blind as a young puppy, I thought. On its back the thing had a few single long red hairs which were shown to me – had it been intended for a monkey? I was shocked and did not know what to feel.
>
> (Jung 1961: 25)

For many years after the fateful day of my brother's birth, I did my best to ignore and neglect him. However, after I left home for college I began to undergo a conversion to more humanitarian attitudes. When I returned, my brother and I began a process of rehabilitation which evolved into a lifelong friendship and collaboration in our closely related fields.

I have no reason to doubt that this indelible early memory reflects one of the impulses to my interest in this subject. As I have been writing this book, many other memories of my childhood have floated

up from the dark well of unconsciousness and have informed my
understanding of the inescapable consequences of family life in its
lasting imprints on children.

One of these other memories is from my early teenage years when I
came across in the local library a book entitled *Satan Sanderson*. All that I
remember of the book is a very dramatic moment in the story when the
hero calls out in bitter agony, 'Am I my brother's keeper!' This age-old
'tale of two brothers' touched a deep chord in my unconscious. The
story leads back to the ancient biblical tale of Cain and Abel. Yahweh
accepted Abel's sacrifice, but rejected Cain's. And in a rage, Cain
killed his brother Abel. This ancient biblical tale reveals the depth of
sibling rivalry of the sons for the love of the father. This is the context
of this book: rivalry and hatred and love, the deep chords of sibling
relationships and the family atmosphere. I hope I have been able to
convey the significance of these complex family situations and their
impact on the destiny of the individual and the future of society.

Acknowledgements

My great appreciation is due to Andrew Samuels for his early interest and support in seeing the manuscript move towards publication. My brother, Dr Charles Stewart, took on the task of reading the rough drafts throughout, and provided me with many clarifying suggestions, for which I am immensely grateful. Many friends and colleagues from the C. G. Jung Institute of San Francisco contributed helpful comments during the progress of the book: Doctors James Yandell, George Hogel, Neil Russack, Paul Kaufman, Wayne Detloff and others expressed lively interest in the ideas of the book and gave me a feeling of support over the long haul. Dr Joseph L. Henderson became interested in the book at a critical moment in relation to aspects of his own writings on the cultural attitudes, and helped to clarify my related writings on the family. My appreciation also to Dr Gerold Post, Professor of Political Psychology at George Washington University. His profile of Saddam Hussein (Post 1990) as well as the additional background material he made available has been invaluable. Above all I am deeply grateful to my beloved wife, Dr Joan Chodorow for her constant support and assistance in every phase of the writing, editing and promotion of the book – all of this at a time when she herself was engaged in the publication of her own book, *Dance Therapy and Depth Psychology–The Moving Imagination*, published by Routledge.

Portions of some of my previously published papers are interwoven throughout the book: 'Birth Order and Political Leadership' in *A Psychological Examination of Political Leaders*, © 1977 The Free Press; 'Affect and Archetype in Analysis' in *Archetypal Processes in Psychotherapy*, © 1987 Chiron Publications; and 'The World Cycle of Leadership' in the *Journal of Analytical Psychology* (1991), 36, 449–59. I want to express my appreciation to the editors for publishing these parts of my study and for their editing.

Acknowledgements are due to the publishers of the following works for permission to quote extensively: *Memories, Dreams, Reflections* by C. G. Jung, translated by Richard and Clara Winston; translations copyright © 1961, 1962, 1963 by Random House, Inc; reprinted by permission of Pantheon Books, a division of Random House, Inc. Excerpts from the *Collected Works of C. G. Jung*, copyright © Princeton University Press; reprinted by permission of Princeton University Press, Princeton, N.J. Excerpts from *Masks of God: Primitive Mythology* by Joseph Campbell, copyright © 1959, 1969, renewed 1987 by Joseph Campbell; used by permission of Viking Penguin, a division of Penguin Books USA, Inc.

Introduction

This book is an exploration of the fated intertwining of individual, family and society. The task is to unravel the tangled web of kinship bonds which underlies the family's influence on the individual, and determines its projection on to the plane of society. This requires an understanding of how the destiny of the individual is influenced by the family constellation, sibling position and the family atmosphere. Only then can we begin to see how the individual's fate affects society. Questions that then arise are: How does change occur? What is the process? This comes down to the question of why certain individuals are always ahead of the collective, and lead any new development. How is a particular individual 'chosen' by the spirit of change, so to speak, to embody a new development that is 'in the air'? Finally, how does the individual successfully express to the collective the essence of the change which is in the wings, and is already beginning to affect society?

This exploration takes place in the context of depth psychology, particularly the psychological theory of C. G. Jung. In the end this exploration will lead to the example of depth psychology itself which embodies one of the greatest changes taking place in society today; a change which Erich Neumann (1969) has forecast is the hope for a 'new ethic' which may forestall the disheartening uprush of evil in our times.

It is apparent that Jung's synthesis of the theories of Freud and Adler laid the groundwork for his later forays into the greater depths of the psyche. Jung saw that Freud and Adler in theory and practice had each taken up one of the two central dynamics of the psyche, the restless desires for love (Freud) and power (Adler). More than that though, he also understood that their theories were part and parcel of who they were. This insight led to his theory of psychological types from which he drew the conclusion that Freud was an extrovert and Adler an introvert; Freud's theory is focused on the other, the object, while Adler's theory is focused on the subject, the ego. Jung says that he undertook his exploration of psychological types in order to understand his own particular bias.

Since he considered himself an introvert it follows then that his theory should be focused on the subject, as it is, but not solely on the ego as he perceived Adler's theory to be, but with a broader synthetic perspective which seeks the foundation of the psyche in the concept of the Self, the centring function and the totality of the personality.

The question which arises is whence comes Jung's synthetic propensity? Freud's natural bent was analytic and reductive; he sought to explain the present through its origins. Adler on the other hand had a teleological inclination that led him to explain the present through its goals for the future. Jung also adopted a teleological perspective, but he did not reject the return to the origins, seeing it as necessary to the recovery of undeveloped aspects of the personality. The dynamic of Jung's analytical psychology rests on his theory of the tension between the opposites as the source of psychic energy. We see then that Jung's particular personal bias is not explained by his theory of psychological types. Jung is an introvert as is Adler, but his theory is not a theory of the ego and its desire for power. Rather, as I have said, Jung's theory is a broad synthetic effort which contains the opposites, the theories of love and power.

As Samuels has recently pointed out in *Jung and the Post-Jungians* (1985) and his essays in *The Plural Psyche* (1989), there is a wide diversity of focus amongst the various groups of Jungian analysts around the world. Moreover, to some extent, particularly in London where the Freudian and Jungian analysts appear to live in a reasonable state of coexistence, there is a growing interchange amongst the 'schools' of depth psychology. In a similar vein, the International Federation for Psychoanalytic Education (IFPE) includes analysts from the Freudian, Adlerian and Jungian schools. The conclusions to be drawn from this cross-fertilization depend in part on whether one focuses on the diversity or on the convergences that are also occurring, and are perhaps on the increase. But no matter which perspective one takes, the ferment is likely to prove creative. As one immersed in this period of change I cannot expect to have a perspective that stands outside this ferment. There is nevertheless evidence from other fields of endeavour that a cycle of development occurs which is essentially a dialogue over time between different points of view. Moreover, this dialogue is seen by science historian Thomas S. Kuhn (1957) to arrive periodically at a critical locus of synthesis.

What emerges, then, is the realization that the development from Freud and Adler to Jung is an example of Kuhn's cycle of creative development in science which arrives at a paradigm that for varying periods of time stands as the accepted view of things. This cycle is most clearly evident in the great transformation of the physical sciences which has taken place over the past several hundreds of years. It began with Copernicus and his revolutionary assertion that the earth moved around the sun. It was followed by Kepler's discoveries of the laws of movement of the planets in their orbits, and by Galileo's telescope and his look at the moon, as well as his further development of the laws of motion. The concepts were developed further by others, notably Huyghens with his understanding of centrifugal–centripetal force. These ideas were disputed by Descartes and his followers, but finally all of these efforts were brought together in Newton's great synthesis which laid the groundwork for all of the developments of physics for many years.

This, I believe, is how Jung's analytical psychology is to be viewed. Slowly but surely it is being accepted as the paradigm of our present understanding of depth psychology. The barriers set up by Freud between psychoanalysis and Jung's theory are breaking down as daring analysts like Kohut and Winnicott incorporate essential elements of Jung's analytical psychology. Jung's central concept of the Self appears everywhere in general psychology as well as depth psychology, albeit not always yet thoroughly understood. Introversion and extroversion have long since passed into common parlance, and the term archetype is rapidly becoming a buzz word for every kind of 'typical' experience. It is my belief that Jung's analytical psychology represents one of those moments of synthesis. This does not mean that depth psychology is now and forever to remain in the mould of Jung's synthesis. Surely another psychological Copernicus will appear, and may be among us now; parenthetically, this has already occurred in physics with Planck's quantum theory.

The view of the individual and family I am presenting here is thoroughly pluralistic in the manner of James and Jung. It is also thoroughly structural in the manner of Piaget, Lévi-Strauss, and Jung. Pluralism and structuralism are by no means contradictory ways of viewing the family or the psyche. Jung's concept of the emotionally-toned complex is a pluralistic view of the psyche, but it is also a structural view. His concept of psychological types is another example.

Here Jung speaks to the question that is raised by any theory of psychological types: Is all psychological theory purely relative to the originator?

> This book on types yielded the insight that every judgment made by an individual is conditioned by his personality type and that every point of view is necessarily relative. This raised the question of unity which must compensate this diversity, and it led me directly to the Chinese concept of Tao . . . It was only after I had reached the central point in my thinking and in my researches, namely, the concept of the self, that I once more found my way back to the world.
>
> (Jung 1961: 207–8)

Samuels notes that like Jung, Hillman's position is pluralistic but that Hillman eschews the notion of structuralism. Samuels seeks to reconcile these positions by enlarging the scope of pluralism. In the final section of his book, he asks the following questions: 'Can diversity be analyzed so as to reveal its special requirements and guidelines? And can we develop a vision of diversity that makes a place for unity?' He concludes that we must consider the moral function of psychological pluralism as it

> struggles to hold the tension between the One and the Many without making them into 'opposites.' Pluralism is engaged in the discovery of truths just as monism is engaged in the discovery of Truth. *The existence of diverse theories about people complements the psychological diversity within a person.* My concern has been that pluralism would not follow the logic of competition so fully that an ideological purity leading to tyranny is the result, nor allow its embracing of diversity to degenerate into a farrago of seemingly equal truths leading to ennui as much as chaos. I will stick my neck out and say that the *telos* or goal of pluralism is 'reform.' By reform, I do not mean something specially distinguished from revolution, as in 'liberal reform', but reform as a portmanteau term to include renewal, rebirth, spontaneous *and* well-planned evolutions, and imaginative productivity generally. Reform has its moral connotation and that is deliberate.
>
> (Samuels 1989: 230–1)

These ideas resonate with my own interest in the subject. In my view, the moral imagination is largely shaped by the archetypal emotion of contempt/shame and the archetypal symbolism of alienation with its compensatory imaginal pursuit of Utopian *communitas*. In my experience the other forms of the archetypal imagination: the aesthetic, the sacred, and the philosophic, are likewise 'reformative' in Samuels's broad sense.

The sibling positions in the family lead to a pluralism of family 'world views'. The family atmosphere leads to a pluralism of family 'ancestral views'. To illustrate the influence of these pluralistic views on the individual child I have used the image of the 'envelope' (Stewart 1976). This seemed particularly fitting when trying to describe what happens to the new-born infant. For example, along with other factors, the number of which has greatly increased now that sonic images of the infant in the womb are possible, the parents know in advance not only the infant's ordinal position amongst siblings, but the infant's gender as well. In this sense then an envelope of expectations is slipped over the infant even before birth so that in some respects the parents' reactions to the infant may be skewed in this way or that. Particularly likely to have an effect in such skewing, usually unconscious, is whether or not either parent is of the same sibling position. D. W. Winnicott's famous case of *The Piggle: an account of the psychoanalytic treatment of a little girl* (1977) is an illustration of such a situation when a mother unconsciously recapitulates with her children her own troubled sibling experience. Parental sympathies and antipathies toward one child or another can often be traced to the parental sibling complex. But with respect to the child's developing sibling complex, the greater and more continuous effects are the result of the child's ongoing experiences with siblings, or, if an only child, without siblings. The end result for each child in the family is a 'world view' that is a direct consequence of sibling position, and which presents unique expectations for each child in the family.

The way in which each child acquires a unique 'ancestral view' is somewhat more complicated and difficult to explain. It is the unconscious complexes of the parents which carry the heaviest freight. These unlived aspects of the parents' lives spring in large part from unanswered questions of the ancestors which also reflect nascent changes in the *Zeitgeist* (the spirit of the age). The child's experience is likely to be an inexplicable influx of highly-charged emotion carrying a numinous symbol. The ancient tribal peoples spoke of this as a 'seizure' by the spirit or spirits, and Jung came to adopt this way of speaking. In a mundane sense this is the question of what it may be that determines an individual's interests in which libido can be invested. We naturally must take into account varying degrees of inherited ability and the like which makes for a wide range of achievement and expectation in any particular case. What we are particularly interested in here is the fact that each child in a family may be 'called', so to speak, by very different 'voices', and with very different degrees of numinosity. It is rather the exception than the rule that individuals of great genius spring from the same family milieu. The reasons for this are exceedingly difficult to know with any degree of certainty. Some clues are to be found, as we might expect, in genetics and in the particular relationship a child has with the parents.

The central focus of this book then is on the two primary elements of the family, the family constellation and the family atmosphere, and how they affect the destiny of the individual. As I have said above, these two fundamental aspects of the family influence the individual in related, but unique ways.

In its constellation the family is a tiny kinship group of parents and children – sometimes including extended family members. Each child is dependent – body and soul – on the parents to sustain the family as a *temenos*, a safe and secure haven for the nurturance of its potentials and the testing of its abilities. From the moment of birth each child is also immersed in the family crucible, the alchemical vessel in which the fiery heat of family relationships transforms the child's innate archetypal emotional and instinctive inheritance into a sensitive matrix of feelings and complex family emotions. Finally, as a microcosm of society, the family oversees the child's initiation into the mores and the rites – the cultural values – of the society. In these ways the child gradually acquires, in tangible and intangible ways, a unique, and yet universal view of the world and the Self, which reflects its place in the family, and eventually in society.

Through its immersion in the family atmosphere, the ghostly presence of the ancestors transmitted by the parents through their behaviour, personality and values, and especially their unconscious complexes, the child acquires a specific vulnerability to an influx of the spirit whose source lies in the unanswered questions of the ancestors, the unlived life of the parents. The nature of this influx of the spirit determines the *channel* in which the child's fate will course. It is here that Jung's personal experience of the 'daemon' of creativity is most helpful to our understanding.

In the course of this exploration it will, I believe, emerge that these two aspects of the family, the sibling configuration and the family atmosphere, are inclusive of all the major influences of the family. This is so because they represent, or to say it more precisely, they *are*, the two dimensions of the family tree, the kinship tree. Along its vertical dimension we are united with the spirit of the ancestors; on its horizontal dimension we are integrated with the body social, the spirit of the society within which the family is embedded. The tree is an orienting symbol of great power. Rooted in the earth and rising toward the heavens it reaches out its branches in layer after layer of generations. As the all-encompassing archetypal symbol of the family it is the genealogical tree of the heroes and the gods and goddesses, and as such is a representation of the Self.

The history of this book is roughly as follows. Early on I had been interested in Jung's original research with the family constellation. When Jung took up his duties as a fledgling psychiatrist at the Burghölzli Clinic in Zurich in 1903, he was assigned a research study of the family constellation. Jung was deeply impressed by some of the findings of this study, and he went on to use the word association test with many of his patients while he was at the clinic. This research was the basis for his theory of the feeling or emotionally-toned complex.

One of the other findings which greatly intrigued Jung was the similarity in the profiles of word associations among family members. This finding became a cornerstone of his later theory of the family atmosphere and its influence on the development of the child. By family atmosphere he meant the influences stemming from the character and behaviour of the parents, and most particularly the unanswered questions of the ancestors which were expressed through unconscious complexes. In essence these complexes represent the unlived life of the parents, and they may also be representative of a movement in the *Zeitgeist*. In his memoirs, *Memories, Dreams, Reflections*, Jung looks back on his own childhood from the perspective of the family influences:

> I feel very strongly that I am under the influence of things or questions which were left incomplete and unanswered by my parents and grandparents and more distant ancestors. It often seems as if there were an impersonal karma within a family, which is passed on from parents to children. It has always seemed to me that I had to answer questions which fate had posed to my forefathers, and which had not yet been answered, or as if I had to complete, or perhaps continue, things which previous ages had left unfinished.
>
> Children react much less to what grown-ups say than to the imponderables in the surrounding atmosphere. The child unconsciously adapts himself to them, and this produces in him

correlations of a compensatory nature. The peculiar 'religious' ideas that came to me in my earliest childhood were spontaneous products which can be understood only as reactions to my parental environment and to the spirit of the age.

(Jung 1961: 90)

For all his interest in the family constellation, however, Jung never completed the research to his own satisfaction. Like so many of his earliest discoveries, this subject was thrust aside by the great upheaval of his confrontation with the unconscious in midlife which turned his life about and directed him into new areas of study. Yet he never lost sight of the value of his early work. Late in his life, when he delivered an address on the occasion of the founding of the C. G. Jung Institute in Zurich, he listed some of the subjects he felt warranted further study. Amongst those to which he gave high priority for further study was the family constellation.

Around the same time that I discovered Jung's studies of the family constellation, I also became acquainted with Alfred Adler's work. Adler was the first depth psychologist to recognize that each sibling position in the family carried implications for the character and personality of the child. His characterization of the differences between children of different birth order were based on his studies of children and adults in his clinical practice and in his work in the schools of Vienna where he established the forerunners of our systems of child guidance clinics. But Adler's interest in this subject had a deeper origin in his own personal experience as a child – the younger brother of an exemplary older brother. Adler's contribution to the psychology of the family constellation came from his realization that his own experiences as a younger brother were in a certain sense not at all unique; they could be shown to have certain universal characteristics for all younger brothers. In his studies of birth order Adler cited ancient Biblical stories and the classical Greek myths as evidence of the significance of the effects of sibling position in the family, and the understanding possessed by earlier peoples. It was here no doubt that he first found confirmation for his own conviction that the second son is a rebel, which he himself demonstrated when he proposed to Freud's psychoanalytic group in the early days of psychoanalysis that aggression was as important a motivating drive as sex. This led eventually to his expulsion from the group and was the spur to his creation of his own school of individual psychology.

With these complementary views of Jung and Adler in mind, I then engaged in some studies of the family constellation, focused particularly on the sibling position (Stewart 1961, 1962; Smelser and Stewart 1968). I began then to cast about for an appropriate area of study in which to further test the ideas this research had stirred up. I found that political leadership offers an especially apt area for study (Stewart 1970, 1976, 1977b). The individual leader stands at the interface of family and society – a creative amalgam of family influences, the individual's own striving for power, and the collective's equally strong desire to be led.

In what follows I have elected to take the reader more or less along the same course I myself followed in the development of my perspective. Chapter 1, 'The family and the destiny of the individual', explores briefly the many aspects of the family as *temenos*, alchemical crucible, and microcosm of society, and speculations are entertained about the family's origins in prehistoric times through the development of marriage proscriptions and the incest taboo. Chapter 2, 'The Sumerian revolution', details the great transformation of family and society which took place in Sumer around 3200 BC, that is, some 5,200 years ago. In Chapter 3, 'Political leadership and the sibling complex', I shall take up the four basic sibling positions in the family and relate each position to a corresponding style of political leadership. I close this chapter with a discussion of research methodology and a review of the literature on the sibling position – often referred to as birth order. Chapter 4 presents a study of the American presidents and the British prime ministers, covering a period of some two hundred years of history. A consistent pattern is found that shows a congruence between the sibling positions of the leaders and corresponding shifts in the social-political *Zeitgeist*. In Chapter 5, 'The world cycle of creative change', I describe a fourfold creative process through which any and every great innovation in any field of endeavour appears to proceed. This creative cycle seems to require the contributions of individuals of genius who embody the viewpoints inherent in each of the sibling positions. Chapter 6, 'The innate affects and the complex family emotions', takes up the motivating and transformational forces that shape every kind of human development, creative and destructive. Chapter 7, 'The spirit chooses', looks at how an individual is 'chosen', so to speak, by a joining of the spirit of the ancestors and the spirit of the times, to carry forward an idea or task. Chapter 8, 'Depth psychology and the world cycle of creative change', explores the development of depth psychology with particular attention to the contributions of the four major pioneers: First-born son, Sigmund

Freud; second-born son, Alfred Adler; last-born son, Otto Rank; and only son, C. G. Jung. In Chapter 9 I look at Jung's synthesis of the stages of psychotherapy and try to illustrate how his theory is gradually becoming recognized as the contemporary paradigm or exemplar for depth psychology. Chapter 10, 'The family of nations', is an epilogue that explores questions regarding the nature of good and evil. I look at certain historical and contemporary events and compare the lives of some political leaders, with particular attention to sibling position and the family atmosphere. This leads to a discussion of the sources in the psyche of democracy and dictatorship. I close with the question: What if anything can depth psychology contribute to understand better the nature of the spirit, and what are the implications for good or for evil, democracy or dictatorship, in the world?

Chapter 1

The family and the destiny of the individual

For better or for worse, to greater or lesser degree, an individual's destiny rests in the laps of the gods and the milieu of the family. For the ancient Greeks this amounted to the sense of destiny evoked by the fated accident of birth, as witness the myth of the fates: the three sisters, Clotho, Lachesis and Atropos spinning out the linen thread of our destiny from which we are suspended at birth. Underlying this myth, Robert Graves thought he could detect vestiges of the ancient custom of swaddling the new-born infant in a linen band 'on which his clan and family marks were embroidered and thus assigned to him his destined place in society' (Graves 1955: 204). It is no longer so, of course, that the clan determines our 'destined place in society', but depth psychology has revealed just how important early childhood may be for the life of the child. The *Zeitgeist* as well as inherited factors play a role, yet even the child's unique 'fingerprint' of inherited deoxyribonucleic acid (DNA) is dependent for its realization upon the child's containment in a nurturing environment for a prolonged period following birth.

Whatever the influence of any such factors may be, they coalesce for every individual at the crossroads of the family. This is not to say that the family is the sole determinant of the individual's personality or destiny. Nevertheless the family is the *temenos*, or alchemical vessel within which the new-born child's innate inherited potential is contained and first tested in relation to the world and society, since in the beginning, for the infant and very young child, the family *is* world and society. The far-reaching consequences that the family foreshadows for the individual, and for society as well, can hardly be exaggerated. Our most formative years are spent in thrall to the mysterious family which 'took us in' at birth, and which is our entrée to society and the world. The rest of our life is spent seeking to make our peace with the myth of the 'family' which we have internalized in our bodies, in our memories, our complexes and fantasies. To move closer now to the central theme of these studies; to the family in its mediating function between the innate archetypal affects of the self and the multiplicity of demands of the world.

All in all the family is a tangled web of kinship bonds, an indescribable amalgam of feelings and emotions: love-hate, dominance-submission, jealousy-envy, admiration-dislike, and so on. The better part of life – psychotherapy and analysis as well – may be spent in freeing the kinship libido which has been invested in the family and which now manifests as what may be called the emotionally-toned 'kinship complexes'. Jung describes the need for the withdrawal of this 'kinship libido' from the family of origin, which can only be accomplished 'through a whole-hearted dedication to life':

> All the libido that was tied up in family bonds must be withdrawn from the narrower circle into the larger one, because the psychic health of the adult individual, who in childhood was a mere particle revolving in a rotary system, demands that he should himself become the centre of a new system. That such a step includes the solution, or at least some consideration, of the sexual problem is obvious enough, for unless this is done the unemployed libido will inevitably remain fixed in the unconscious endogamous relationship to the parents and will seriously hamper the individual's freedom . . . For if he allows his libido to get stuck in a childish milieu, and does not free it for higher purposes, he falls under the spell of unconscious compulsion. Wherever he may be, the unconscious will then recreate the infantile milieu by projecting his complexes, thus reproducing all over again, and in defiance of his vital interests, that same dependence and lack of freedom, which formerly characterized his relations with his parents. His destiny no longer lies in his own hands: his . . . (fortunes and fates) fall from the stars. The Stoics called this condition Heimarmene, compulsion by the stars, to which every 'unredeemed' soul is subject.
>
> (Jung 1956: 414–15)

We live out our lives between the two great mysteries of birth and death. As a child we come into this world from who knows what distant shore and after the time allotted to us by the fates pass on to another distant shore, or return, perhaps, to the same one. Mythology may be understood as the unceasing human effort to understand and come to grips with these two all-absorbing mysteries. First is the need to recognize and foster the innate process of psychological development. This is perhaps a meaning of Plato's admonition that we must put back in order the circuits of the mind that were disrupted by birth:

> The motion akin to the divine part in us are the thoughts and revolutions of the universe; these, therefore, every man should follow, and correcting those circuits in the head that were deranged at birth, by learning to know the harmonies and revolutions of the world, he should bring the intelligent part, according to its pristine nature, into the likeness of that which intelligence discerns, and thereby win the fulfilment of the best in life set by the gods before mankind both for this present time and for the life to come.
>
> (Plato n.d./1952: 354)

This is accomplished, again as Plato suggests, through a continuing effort to live life the way it is meant to be lived, in accord with the spiritual needs of the human soul. Collectively these needs are met by the rites and rituals of initiation and transformation.

All mythologies accordingly are historical in the sense that they go back to the 'beginnings', to 'creation'. Usually it is the world and the cosmos that is created first and in the earliest known mythologies, world and cosmos are goddesses and gods. These gods and goddesses are then, themselves, 'creative'. They have offspring who have offspring until at some point a solidification takes place and the latest generation becomes 'the' goddesses and gods, and 'creation' ceases. These solidifications of mythologies are usually the point at which 'religions' have differentiated themselves from the creative stream of myth, as Cassirer (1955: 239) suggests, and henceforth become dogmatic and institutionalized.

Of particular interest is the way in which the development of mythology is a reflection of similar developments in the consciousness of human beings (Neumann 1954, 1973). At birth the infant's consciousness is but slightly developed; then between one to three months of age comes the first clear-eyed smile of recognition of the mother's face and voice which is followed very rapidly by the first laughs of recognition of the self when observing rhythmic movement or most frequently itself moving rhythmically. The next major shift in consciousness comes when the infant between six to nine months of age recognizes the permanent existence of the mother and father and the other people and things around it. The hallmark of this period is the game of peek-a-boo, as well as throwing toys and recovering them, and the like. At this point the child has not yet developed a truly conscious recognition of itself as the source of 'things'. What is required for that recognition is the separation of consciousness and unconsciousness which occurs between fourteen and eighteen months of age when the child becomes aware of being able to 'pretend'. Very frequently this occurs in the daytime when the child discovers its 'sleep ritual', that is to say, the purely unconscious behaviours it has developed at bedtime to ease the way into sleep. Common features of the sleep ritual are thumb-sucking, rubbing the silky edge of a blanket between the fingers, twisting a strand of hair, or cuddling in a particular way with a stuffed animal. The importance of this increase in consciousness cannot be exaggerated. In mythological terms it may be compared to genesis, that is, the stage of the separation of the world parents, heaven and earth. It is our earliest experience of self-reflective consciousness.

To recapitulate, the infant develops consciousness in predictable stages just as it develops biologically. These universal developmental stages are presumably laid down in the code of DNA. But this is not to say that development is purely innate whether it be biological or psychological or spiritual. In all cases the child's development is an interaction between an innate inheritance and the circumstances of its life in the family, society and the world at large.

One of the influences of the family on the child's development is the comparison of the infant with family members. These comparisons are frequently along partisan lines and reflect attitudes of the parents which are often at odds. For example, one parent may say of a child that it behaves just like its mother, or father, or grandparent, with the intent of casting aspersions on child and referent. Willy-nilly, no matter what the attitudes expressed, no matter whether expressed openly or held in secret, parents do indulge in comparisons with relatives. Whether such comparisons hold positive or negative meanings, they always come from a more-or-less conscious belief that heredity is something to be reckoned with.

The child gradually acquires a sense of the family that is built upon an amalgam of its own impressions, the attitudes of family members, and the 'stories' that are told of the 'ancestors'. In large part this is a family myth, portions of which have been passed down the generations; almost every family can point to its skeleton in the closet, as well as its 'noble' heritage, and a good deal of time and energy are devoted by many individuals to tracing their ancestry. A knowledge of one's 'roots' satisfies the need to keep in touch with the mystery of birth; the mystery of our presence and increase on this earth. Perhaps the greatest fear of humans is to be left alone in the dark. Knowing about one's ancestry is a way of transforming that ultimate fear into an unbroken human ladder, or better yet a tree, the family tree of humankind, to which we are all attached.

By remembering its origins and history, the human race keeps in touch with the great mystery of creation and honours its ancestors. This is also a way in which the human soul is in-spirited. It is not enough to trace one's roots, for the mystery of the original creation remains. Here is where mythology takes on its greatest importance. Where history ends, mythology takes over. Thus the human family tree reaches back to a time, the 'dream time' in the words of the Australian tribal societies, which is the realm of the gods and goddess who live as immortals in 'eternal' time. Throughout history this place and these times have tended to migrate to the heavens, and to the 'holy mountain' which is the connection, the lightning rod, that safely conveys to humans the infinite powers of the gods and goddesses.

The ultimate mysteries of birth and death are the sources of the rites of passage. The human family is a mysterious affair as well. Like all mammals, humans are social creatures for whom intimate, affectionate relationships are the norm. Depending upon the exigencies of the ecological niche, this innate sociability has evolved in many degrees of co-operativeness, ranging from the ultimate 'groupiness' of the Kalahari desert meerkats to the relative 'standoffishness' of the leopard. Care and nourishment of the young of the species is a universal characteristic of mammals no matter what the degree of closeness of group relationships may be. The family life of elephants, and wolves, as well as many other species of mammals, is exemplary. These species usually live in packs or groups of one kind or another; small societies in which kin are spread throughout. There is apparently no systematic ordering to the kinship relationships, but there is no question but that some kin relationships are sustained by these groups. This is clearly apparent amongst the chimpanzees, our closest mammalian cousins (Goodall 1990).

When humans came to the ordering of tribal society through a systematic manipulation of kinship, they were building upon their innate social nature. It appears that in the formation of the early pre-literate societies, the transition from separate families or small bands to organized tribes and clans, was apparently arrived at by a compromise in which some degree of intimacy of relationship among members of the immediate family was sacrificed for an improved relationship to other families, through the establishment of marriage alliances which provided the basis for a co-operative social order. The additional gains from this sacrifice were realized in the psychological realm of soul and spirit; for in the process men and women discovered a deeper sense of themselves.

Those early tribal peoples must have come to recognize the adhesive power of kinship and capitalized upon it by devising patterns of preferred, actually proscribed, marriages between specified kin. Perhaps the earliest form of these marriage patterns was the sharing of brothers and sisters with each other. This form moved to the first-cousin marriage along the matrilineal line. A great advantage, presumably, of these marriage systems was the avoidance of more intimate incestuous relationships within a family, while at the same time insuring the spread of kin throughout the group and the introduction of new blood. As group size increased these marriage patterns became increasingly complicated leading to as many as twelve sections, remnants of which may still be seen in rural Chinese communities. For aeons of time this was the preferred marriage arrangement in early tribes and societies. It still continues in the tribal peoples of Australia, New Guinea and other areas which have been isolated from the influences of the industrialized world (Jung 1945, 1946a; Layard 1945; Fox 1967).

At first entwined in this web of kinship sections, the family over time emerges as a microcosm that is more separate from society – a tiny universe within a larger universe – held together by the bonds of kinship libido. Reflection on the family as a social system leads to a deeper appreciation of the family's vital function in the mediation of past, present and future in the life of the individual and in the life of the community. This mediating function brings into sharper focus the mythological form of the genealogy of the gods and heroes as an archetypal family image which in the unity of its vertical and horizontal dimensions simultaneously defines relationships with the ancestors and relationships among members of the immediate family and the larger society.

On the whole Jung's interest, and that of the majority of Jungian analysts early on, gravitated to the archetypal images underlying the family roles of mother, father and child. Among Jungians until very recently, interest in the family as a social system has been scant. Moreover, at times we seem to act as if the archetypes were capable of an autonomous existence without need of a mediating environment which constellates and supports inner development. We tend to lose sight of the fact that the ritual observance of the rites of passage is as important as are the archetypes of the psyche from which those rituals may derive.

Not only Jungian analysts but depth psychology as a whole has been slow to recognize the significance of the family as a co-ordinated totality; a complex system of relationships between parents and children, which mediates between the child's innate, archetypal self, on the one hand, and society and the world on the other. There has long been a need for a Jungian perspective on the family that would encompass the personal and archetypal figures of mother, father, and divine child, and accommodate as well, the structure and dynamics of the family as a microcosm of society. As with many another unfinished aspect of his analytical psychology, Jung put forth many of the elements of such a perspective, albeit tucked away in prefaces to books, in letters, or inserted into articles on related subjects (Jung 1909, 1927/31, 1948, 1973, p. 525). Nevertheless, he was deeply interested in the family as is evident in his very early research on the family constellation, and his studies of the emotionally-toned complexes that arise in the family. In that research his interest also was captured by the similar patterns of word associations among family members. This finding became a cornerstone of his theory that the family atmosphere influences the development of the child (Jung 1909).

As I have said, there are two aspects of the family which are inseparably entwined with all the others, but which nevertheless stand in a distinct relationship to each other. These are the 'sibling position' and the 'family atmosphere'. The child's sibling position is determined by the fated accident of birth. The family atmosphere is in large part determined by the parents' behaviour, attitudes, values, and particularly their unconscious complexes which carry the unanswered questions of the ancestors. These two aspects of the family determine what may be called the child's 'sibling' and 'ancestral' complexes. In turn they represent the two dimensions of the family tree, the horizontal which relates us to the body social, and the vertical which relates us to the ancestral spirit.

In this regard it is fruitful to think of the family as a living organism. The marriage of a man and a woman is the marriage of two families. Their children are the fruits of the two family trees. It is easy to see why the family is symbolized by a tree, the family tree – the tree of life itself. As a living organism, the family grows as children arrive. Each child is born into a different family. For the first child the family is mother, father and me! For the second child the family is mother, father, brother or sister and me!, and so on. The family constellation is the basic structure of the family. It is the tree itself. The two parents are the 'older' generation, the children are the 'younger' generation. The parents are the connection with the 'ancients', the ancestors. The children are the 'new' generation. From this little fantasy we can see that the family constellation is in fact the living body of the family tree in its two dimensions: the vertical which connects with the ancestors and the horizontal which links with the extended family and society.

To recapitulate: in earliest prehistoric times the human additions to the nature of family were the formalization of relationships through marriage and kinship taboos. All social species must find the means for maximizing co-operation through controls on the two major dynamisms of relationship, namely love and power. This is the purpose of the barnyard pecking orders and the dominance and submission behaviours in our mammalian ancestors which control mating between the sexes, as well as the hierarchy of leadership in the group. And it is a major purpose of the elaborate kinship marriage systems developed by our early human ancestors.

In many places in his writings, Jung draws attention to the significance of love and power as the two elemental, and polarized dynamics of the family. Often it is in the context of his efforts to place the theories of Freud and Adler in proper perspective. One of his most interesting statements on this subject appears in *Mysterium Coniunctionis* at a point where he is discussing the Aelia-Laelia-Crispis inscription – The Enigma of Bologna – which was cited by alchemists, but which appears to be as Jung puts it:

> sheer nonsense, a joke . . . but one that for centuries brilliantly fulfilled its function as a flypaper for every conceivable projection that buzzed in the human mind. It gave rise to a 'cause célèbre,' a regular psychological 'affair' that lasted for the greater part of two centuries and produced a spate of commentaries.
>
> (Jung 1963: 57)

At this point in his commentary Jung refers to an interpretation of this inscription by Veranius that strikes him as a forerunner of Freud's sexual theory of the unconscious. In reference to this, Jung gives a capsule statement about the two driving forces in life and the problem of one-sidedness:

> Now it is, as a matter of fact, true that apart from the personal striving for power, or *superbia*, love, in the sense of *concupiscentia*, is the dynamism that most infallibly brings the unconscious to light.

And if our author was of the type whose besetting sin is *concupiscence*, he would never dream that there is any other power in heaven or earth that could be the source of his conflicts and confusions. Accordingly, he will cling to his prejudice as if it were a universal theory, and the more wrong he is the more fanatically he will be convinced of its truth. But what can love mean to a man with a hunger for power! That is why we always find two main causes of psychic catastrophes: on the one hand a disappointment in love and on the other hand a thwarting of the striving for power.

(Jung 1963: 86)

Jung's discussion of kinship libido in the 'psychology of the transference' sheds some further light on this subject. In the context of a discussion of the intercrossing of anima and animus projections in the transference, which Jung notes are foreshadowed in the archetype of a crossed marriage or what he speaks of as the 'marriage quaternity', he defines kinship libido as follows:

Incest as an endogamous relationship, is an expression of the libido which serves to hold the family together. One could therefore define it as 'kinship libido', a kind of instinct which, like a sheep-dog, keeps the family group intact. This form of libido is the diametrical opposite of the exogamous form. The two forms together hold each other in check: the endogamous form tends toward the sister and the exogamous toward some stranger. The best compromise is therefore the first cousin.

(Jung 1946a: 224)

Jung's wording can be improved; first is the fact that he is obviously speaking of males. In some families there may be no sister and for the boy, the mother may well be the first resting-place of the endogamous kinship libido; for the daughter it could be the brother or the father. As we see Jung states that 'Incest as an endogamous relationship, is an expression of the libido which serves to hold the family together'. He goes on to suggest that we could therefore speak of it as 'kinship libido'. This bears some scrutiny. The statement is somewhat ambiguous, perhaps purposely so. It identifies 'kinship libido' as the psychic energy that holds the family together, and suggests that incest is an endogamous expression of this 'kinship'. Does he mean by this that incest, defined as sexual relationships with family members that are forbidden, is one of the possible consequences of the close family kinship ties? If so, this would be a simple and straightforward use of the term incest.

As for the exogamous libido, it does not, of course, ordinarily come to rest on a 'stranger'. As children move out into the wider social world, the libido – Jung's exogamous libido – is naturally invested in others – friends and lovers – who are not members of the family of origin. When there is close contact with the extended family, this exogamous libido, particularly during the adolescent period of developing sexuality, most naturally and frequently comes to rest with a first cousin. This is the underlying psychological dynamic that made the 'cross-cousin' marriage system of the tribal peoples so binding. This first-cousin marriage has persisted into modern times as both a natural marriage choice, often creating 'ideal' marriages, as in Darwin's case, or as once was quite common in the hereditary monarchies, and among the aristocratic classes, as a means of acquiring alliances for the purposes of power and the accumulation of wealth within the family.

This compromise of the first-cousin marriage is a primitive marriage pattern. It derives from sister-exchange marriages which constitute one of the earliest forms of social organization. According to Howitt, whom Jung quotes: 'It is upon the division of the whole community into two exogamous intermarrying classes that the whole social structure is built up' (Howitt, in Jung 1946a: 225).

> These 'moieties' show themselves in the layout of settlements as well as in many strange customs. At ceremonies, for instance, the two moieties are strictly segregated and neither may trespass on the other's territory.
>
> (Jung 1946a: 225–6)

These two halves of the society are, nevertheless, connected by a ritual interdependence which involves such activities as breeding and fattening animals by one side for the other, and so on. The names given to the two moieties, such as east and west, water and land, represent an antithetical feeling and thus, according to Jung, expressed an endopsychic antithesis:

> The antithesis can be formulated as the masculine ego versus the feminine 'other,' i.e. conscious versus unconscious personified as anima. The primary splitting of the psyche into conscious and unconscious seems to be the cause of the division within the tribe and settlement. It is a division founded on fact but not consciously recognized as such.
>
> (Jung 1946a: 226)

In actual practice this social split leads to a fourfold division of the tribe and settlement which, originating in a matrilineal division into two, which is then crossed by a patrilineal division, thus separates the entire population into marriage classes. Every man belongs to his father's patrilineal moiety, and can only take a wife from his mother's matrilineal moiety. To avoid the possibility of incest, he marries his mother's brother's daughter and gives his sister to his wife's brother. It was this kind of social order that required that the Biblical Jacob be sent to a distant land to his mother's brother Laban in order to find a wife. There he fell in love with his first cousin Rachel and worked seven years for the promise of her hand in marriage. In this system the son is required to marry his mother's brother's daughter. This is the cross-cousin marriage (Jung 1946a: 226–7).

This sociological development carried immense consequences for cultural development. John Layard, on the basis of his anthropological studies, sees in the endogamous tendency a genuine instinct which, if denied realization in the flesh, will realize itself in the appropriate realm of the spirit.

> The social or manifest purpose of the incest taboo is to enlarge the social horizon . . . Its latent or spiritual purpose is to enlarge the spiritual horizon by developing the idea that there is after all a sphere in which the primary desire may be satisfied, namely the divine sphere of the gods together with that of their semi-divine counterparts, the culture heroes.
>
> (Layard 1945: 284)

In 'The structure and dynamics of the self' in *Aion*, Jung speaks to these questions in the context of psychotherapy. He suggests that the Gnostic *quaternio* which he is incorporating into his model of the Self, 'took a form that derives from the primitive cross-cousin marriage, namely, the marriage quaternio'. However, with the further differentiation of marriage classes into a six-, eight-, or twelve-class system, the original cross-cousin marriage became obsolete, and this, according to Jung, led to a change in the marriage relationship.

> That is to say, an anima–animus projection takes place. This modification brings with it a great cultural advance, for the very fact of projection points to a constellation of the unconscious in the husband–wife relationship, which means that the marriage has become *psychologically* complicated. It is no longer a state of mere biological and social coexistence, but is beginning to turn into a

conscious relationship . . . The cause of the activation of the unconscious that goes hand in hand with this development is *the regression of the endogamous tendency – the 'kinship libido' – which can no longer find adequate satisfaction owing to the increasing strangeness of the marriage partner* [my italics].

(Jung 1951a: 242–3)

To summarize briefly: This situation of the 'increasing strangeness of the marriage partner', is the psychic arena within which husband and wife today seek to find an accommodation which gives a sufficiently satisfactory equilibration of the needs of each. As we have seen, societies have sought to contain the forces inherent in this situation by the arrangement of marriages and by the codification of the rights of men and women. For aeons these systems were more or less adequate as the stability of tribal societies suggests. One of the aims of these early marriage systems was to distribute power throughout the society by establishing alliances through marriage proscriptions. This was enforced by the incest taboo which defined kinship sections for the society and proscribed those into which an individual could or could not marry. These forms of marriage can be found in the still-existing tribal societies, but they have long since been given up in the contemporary societies of the industrialized countries.

Today in the western world we live with a situation in which relationships with the extended family in any form are less and less of a reality. This results in a concentration of kinship libido within the nuclear family. Inevitably this will produce a greater intensity in the strivings for love and power within the family. It is this situation that has produced the catastrophes Jung mentions above, and, coupled with the collapse of religious solutions and cultural education in general, has led to the development of psychotherapy.

Particularly relevant to this examination of the results of excessive concentration of kinship libido in the nuclear family, is the development of depth psychology. Freud discovered that incest was at the core of many of the problems that his women patients, and some men presented. Children were left in the care of unreliable nursemaids, teachers and priests, and not infrequently fathers, and occasionally mothers, who eroticized and brutalized the children. Freud and Jung were themselves exposed to this kind of misconduct by trusted caretakers. This was a major aspect of the demoralization throughout society, particularly in the western world, which led to depth psychology, and these were the first findings of the newly-developing field of psychotherapy. To be sure, these discoveries were temporarily swept under the rug, but they have now resurfaced and become a reality that is more evident every day. We shall return to these issues in later chapters in which depth psychology is discussed in detail. First an exploration of the great change in the world which prepared the way for our present situation.

It is evident that something happened a long time ago which irrevocably changed the ancient system of kinship sections. For aeons of time our ancient ancestors lived in the social order we have described above in which family and society were woven together in an almost seamless web of kinship ties. But sometime around 3200 BC, in the fertile delta lands between the Tigris and Euphrates rivers, the mysterious people who came to be called the Sumerians altered that way of life for ever. Within a few hundred years all of the fundamental elements of civilization as we know it today were created.

Chapter 2

The Sumerian revolution
(circa 3200 BC)

'We all know the convention, surely!' writes Joseph Campbell in the introduction to volume one of his *The Masks of God*.

> It is a primary, spontaneous device of childhood, a magical device, by which the world can be transformed from banality to magic in a trice. And its inevitability in childhood is one of those universal characteristics of man that unite us in one family. It is a primary datum, consequently, of the science of myth which is concerned precisely with the phenomenon of self-induced belief.
>
> (Campbell 1959: 22)

This 'convention' appears in the play of childhood as 'pretend', or 'make-believe', the earliest form of what will become the highly-differentiated function of creative imagination. But what is it that potentiates the imagination? In the extreme instance, as with Jung, it is the question of what it may be that can stir the soul of a child in such a way that a whole lifetime may be devoted to understanding it and giving expression to it.

Frobenius gives an example of a 'potentiation of the imagination' in a 4-year-old girl who is trying to get her father's attention while he writes at his desk. The father gives the little girl three used matches to play with and she begins to enact the fairy tale of Hansel, Gretel, and the Witch.

> Suddenly the child shrieks in terror. The father jumps. 'What is it? What has happened?' The little girl comes running to him, showing every sign of great fright. 'Daddy, Daddy,' she cries, 'take the witch away! I can't touch the witch any more!'
>
> (Frobenius, in Campbell 1959: 22)

In explanation of what ensued in the child's play, Frobenius makes the following observation about the interwoven relationship of the imagination and the emotions.

An eruption of emotion is characteristic of the spontaneous shift of an idea from the level of the sentiments (*Gemut*) to that of sensual consciousness (*sinnliches Bewusstsein*). Furthermore, the appearance of such an eruption obviously means that a certain spiritual process has reached a conclusion. The match is not a witch; nor was it a witch for the child at the beginning of the game. The process, therefore, rests on the fact that the match has *become* a witch on the level of the sentiments and the conclusion of the process coincides with the transfer of this idea to the plane of consciousness. The observation of the process escapes the test of conscious thought, since it enters consciousness only after or at the moment of completion. However, inasmuch as the idea is, it must have *become*. The process is creative, in the highest sense of the word; for, as we have seen, in a little girl a match can become a witch.

(Frobenius, in Campbell 1959: 22–3)

The questions raised by this child's play and Frobenius' explanation touch upon the most profound mysteries of life: the source of creativity and the origins of culture. The elements that appear in this example are the child's spontaneous 'make-believe' play, and the subsequent eruption of a primal emotion and a universal cultural image. But there remains to be considered the fundamental experience of play itself which is that it's fun. Here Campbell turns to Huizinga's *Homo Ludens: A Study of the Play Element in Culture* (1950).

As J. Huizinga has pointed out in his brilliant study of the play element in culture, the whole point, at the beginning, is the *fun* of play, not the rapture of seizure. 'In all the wild imaginings of mythology a fanciful spirit is playing,' he writes, 'on the border-line between jest and earnest.'

'By considering the whole sphere of so-called primitive culture as a play-sphere,' Huizinga then suggests in conclusion, 'we pave the way to a more direct and more general understanding of its peculiarities than any meticulous psychological or sociological analysis would allow.' And I would concur wholeheartedly with this judgement, only adding that we should extend the consideration to the entire field of our present subject.

(Campbell 1959: 23)

It cannot be contested but that the spirit of play is fundamental to the development of culture; nor can it be denied that there is an element of the play spirit in even the most elevated forms of cultural expression.

Nevertheless, it is also incontestable that play and the cultural forms are not identical. Play has a life of its own that is continuous from earliest childhood on, both in spontaneous playfulness and in the playing of games. In contrast, the cultural forms (art, religion, philosophy, society) demand more than play; each gives expression to a specific domain of the spirit. They are not 'just' for fun, as is play. An explanation of the development of culture out of the play spirit requires something other than play itself, and this is the archetypal imagination, or so I believe. And to understand the archetypal imagination it is necessary to understand the emotions.

The startling shift in the behaviour of the little girl described above is precisely what is still to be understood. At first she played happily, imagining the familiar fairy tale of Hansel and Gretel and acting it out with the three matches. Suddenly she was thrown into a state of terror. The witch was no longer 'make-believe'; she had become all too 'real' and 'alive'. 'This vivid, convincing example of a child's seizure by a witch while in the act of play', observes Campbell, 'may be taken to represent an intense degree of the daemonic mythological experience' (ibid.: 23).

And what is the daemonic mythological experience? According to Rudolph Otto it is rooted in daemonic dread, a primitive terror, which is the precursor to religious awe. Seeking to clarify the quintessential element of the religious experience, Otto adopted a new term, 'numinous', to designate the irreducible aspect of the 'holy'.

> It is worthwhile . . . to find a word to stand for . . . this 'extra' in the meaning of 'holy' above and beyond the meaning of goodness. By means of a special term we shall the better be able, first, to keep the meaning clearly apart and distinct, and second, to apprehend and classify connectedly whatever subordinate forms or stages of development it may show. For this purpose I adopt a word coined from the Latin *numen*. *Omen* has given us 'ominous', and there is no reason why from numen we should not similarly form a word 'numinous'. I shall speak, then, of a unique 'numinous' category of value and of a definitely 'numinous' state of mind, which is always found wherever the category is applied. This mental state is perfectly *sui generis* and irreducible to any other; and therefore, like every absolutely primary and elementary datum, while it admits of being discussed, it cannot be strictly defined . . . Its nature is such that it grips or stirs the human mind with this and that determinate affective state.
>
> (Otto 1923: 6–7, 12)

According to Otto these 'determinate affective states' are aspects of the *Mysterium Tremendum*. The elements of awfulness, overpowering-ness ('majestas'), and energy or urgency derive from an analysis of the term *Tremendum*. The additional elements of the *Mysterium Tremendum* derive from an analysis of the term *Mysterium*. The first of these elements is the 'wholly other', the second is the element of fascina-tion. All of these elements of the *Mysterium Tremendum* hold a significant place in the totality of the experience, but when it comes to tracing the evolution of the experience Otto finds the starting point to lie in 'daemonic dread' which is the antecedent to 'religious dread' (or 'awe').

> Its antecedent stage is 'daemonic dread' (cf. the horror of Pan) with its queer perversion, a sort of abortive offshoot, the 'dread of ghosts'. It first began to stir in the feeling of 'something uncanny', 'eerie', or 'weird'. It is this feeling which, emerging in the mind of primeval man, forms the starting-point for the entire religious development in history. 'Daemons' and 'gods' alike spring from this root, and all the products of 'mythological apperception' or 'fantasy' are nothing but different modes in which it has been objectified. And all ostensible explanations of the origin of religion in terms of animism or magic or folk-psychology are doomed from the outset to wander astray and miss the real goal of their inquiry, unless they recognize this fact of our nature – primary, unique, underivable from anything else – to be the basic factor and the basic impulse underlying the entire process of religious evolution.
>
> (Otto 1923: 14–15)

Seeking his own differentiation between play and myth, Campbell turns in the last analysis to Immanuel Kant and his efforts to explain the inescapable fact that the human reason must think about final things even though they cannot be substantiated by reason. Kant concludes that such thinking can proceed only by way of analogy. Campbell quotes Kant as follows: 'The proper expression for our fallible mode of conception would be: that we imagine the world as if its being and inner character were derived from a supreme mind' (Kant, in Campbell 1959: 28). 'Such a highly played game of "as if"', suggests Campbell, 'frees our mind and spirit on the one hand, from the presumption of theology, which pretends to know the laws of God, and, on the other, from the bondage of reason, whose laws do not apply beyond the horizons of human experience' (ibid.).

Campbell goes on to rhapsodize on the power of play from the perspective of 'secular man (*Homo sapiens*)'. Enter the 'play sphere of the festival', he says, 'acquiescing in a game of belief, where fun, joy, and rapture rule in ascending series'. Thus we remove ourselves from the limitations of 'the laws of life in time and space–economics, politics, and even morality'. And then all is 're-created by that return to paradise before the Fall, before the knowledge of good and evil, right and wrong, true and false, belief and disbelief'. The goal is to bring the 'spirit of man the player (*Homo ludens*) back into life'. By playing again as children we shall find that the 'spontaneous impulse of the spirit to identify itself with something other than itself for the sheer delight of play, transubstantiates the world in which, actually, after all, things are not quite as real or permanent, terrible, important, or logical as they seem' (Campbell 1959: 28–9).

When he comes to describe the Sumerian development, Campbell utilizes Frobenius' ideas as an explanation of the way in which this new civilization sprang into being. He notes first that there must have been a long period of 'meticulous, carefully checked and re-checked observations', to establish that

> there were, besides the sun and moon, five other visible or barely visible heavenly spheres (to wit, Mercury, Venus, Mars, Jupiter, and Saturn) which moved in established courses . . . along the ways followed by the sun and moon, among the fixed stars.
>
> (Campbell 1959: 146)

Then and then only could arise what Campbell refers to as 'the almost insane, playful, yet potentially terrible notion that the laws governing the movements of the seven heavenly spheres should in some mystical way be the same as those governing the life and thought of men on earth'. From the careful observations and the wildly imaginative vision of the heavenly spheres as corresponding in 'some mystical way', with the laws governing 'the life of men on earth', there followed a detailed working out of the relationship between the entire city and each of its inhabitants:

> The king was the center, as a human representative of the power made celestially manifest either in the sun or in the moon, according to the focus of the local cult; the walled city was organized architecturally in the design of a quartered circle (like the circles designed on the ceramic ware of the period just preceding), centered around the pivotal sanctum of the palace or ziggurat (as the ceramic designs around the cross, rosette, or swastika); and there was a

mathematically structured calendar to regulate the seasons of the city's life according to the passages of the sun and moon among the stars – as well as a highly developed system of liturgical arts, including music, the art rendering audible to human ears the world-ordering harmony of the celestial spheres.

(Campbell 1959: 146–7)

It is important to note that in Campbell's attempt to explain this development, play is not sufficient. Prior to play is curiosity; it took years of meticulous observation, 'carefully checked and re-checked'. Once the facts about the movements of the planets and the sun and moon had been recognized, this new information could be submitted to the play of imagination, from which sprang 'the almost insane, playful, yet potentially terrible notion that the laws governing the movements of the seven heavenly spheres should in some mystical way be the same as those governing the life and thought of men on earth'. In his efforts to explain further this 'life-inspiring monad that precipitated the image of man's destiny as an organ of the living cosmos', Campbell suggests that

the psychological need to bring the parts of a large and socially differentiated settled community, comprising a number of newly developed social classes (priests, kings, merchants, and peasants), into an orderly relationship to each other, and simultaneously to suggest the play through all of a higher, all-suffusing, all-informing, energizing principle – this profoundly felt psychological as well as sociological requirement must have been fulfilled with the recognition, some time in the fourth millennium B.C., of the orderly round-dance of the five visible planets and the sun and moon through the constellations of the zodiac. This celestial order then became the model for mankind in the building of an earthly order of coordinated wills – a model for both kings and philosophers, inasmuch as it seemed to show forth the supporting law not only of the universe but of every particle within it.

(Campbell 1959: 149)

Campbell notes,

It was at this moment in human destiny that the art of writing first appeared in the world and . . . also the wheel appeared. And we have evidence of the development of the two numerical systems still normally employed throughout the civilized world, the decimal and the sexagesimal; . . . Three hundred and sixty degrees, then as now, represented the circumference of a circle – the cycle of the horizon – while three hundred and sixty days, plus five, marked the measurement of the circle of the year, the cycle of time.

The five intercalated days 'represent a sacred opening through which spiritual energy flowed into the round of the temporal universe from the pleroma of eternity'. According to Campbell, the ziggurat was also 'characterized by the number five; for the four sides of the tower, oriented to the points of the compass, came together at the summit, the fifth point, and it was there that the energy of the heaven met the earth' (1959: 147–8).

Campbell goes on to say that

> This early Sumerian temple tower with the hieratically organized little city surrounding it where everyone played his role according to the rules of a celestially inspired divine game, supplied the model of paradise that we find, centuries later, in the Hindu-Buddhist imagery of the world mountain, Sumeru, whose jeweled slopes, facing the four directions, peopled on the west by sacred serpents, on the south by gnomes, on the north by earth giants, and on the east by divine musicians, rose from the mid-point of the earth as the vertical axis of the egg-shaped universe, and bore on its quadrangular summit the palatial mansions of the deathless gods, whose towered city was known as Amaravati, 'The Town Immortal.
>
> (Campbell 1959: 148)

In Campbell's view, the Sumerian model was widely disseminated. We see it in the Greek Olympus and the Aztec temples of the sun, as well as Dante's holy mountain of Purgatory with the earthly paradise at its summit. From the earliest times, humans have explored the world by land and by sea. Even the early neolithic cultures communicated with each other, traded and exchanged ideas:

> The form and concept of the City of God conceived as a 'mesocosm' (an earthly imitation of the celestial order of the macrocosm) which emerged on the threshold of history circa 3200 B.C., at precisely that geographical point where the rivers Tigris and Euphrates reach the Persian Gulf, was disseminated eastward and westward along the ways already blazed by the earlier neolithic. The wonderful life-organizing assemblage of ideas and principles – including those of kingship, writing, mathematics, and calendrical astronomy – reached the Nile, to inspire the civilization of the First Dynasty

of Egypt, circa 2800 B.C.; it spread to Crete on the one hand, and on the other, to the valley of the Indus, circa 2600 B.C.; to Shang China, circa 1600 B.C.; and, according to at least one high authority, Dr. Robert Heine-Geldern, from China across the Pacific, during the prosperous seafaring period of the late Chou Dynasty, between the seventh and fourth centuries B.C., to Peru and Middle America.

(Campbell 1959: 148)

If the foregoing facts of dissemination be true, and Campbell is confident that they are, then it is safe to say, that 'without exaggeration . . . all the high civilizations of the world are to be thought of as the limbs of one great tree, whose root is in heaven' (1959: 149). That 'mythological root' is 'the life-inspiring monad that precipitated the image of man's destiny as an organ of the living cosmos' (ibid.). Another way of saying this is: Human community is governed by the same higher law or principle that orders the cosmos.

Campbell notes that the 'Egyptian term for this universal order was Ma'at; in India it is Dharma; and in China, Tao' (ibid.). What then is the meaning of all the myths and rituals that have developed out of this idea that there is a universal order? Campbell suggests that the myths and rituals are its structuring agents,

functioning to bring the human order into accord with the celestial. 'Thy will be done on earth, as it is in heaven.' The myths and rites constitute a mesocosm – a mediating, middle cosmos, through which the microcosm of the individual is brought into relation to the macrocosm of the all. And this mesocosm is the entire context of the body social, which is thus a kind of living poem, hymn, or icon of mud and reeds, and of flesh and blood, and of dreams, fashioned into the art form of the hieratic city state. Life on earth is to mirror, as nearly perfectly as is possible in human bodies, the almost hidden – yet now discovered – order of the pageant of the spheres.

(Campbell 1959: 150)

With this conception of the 'mesocosm, the middle, sociological cosmos of the City' (Campbell 1951: 155), that is to say, 'the entire context of the body social' (1959: 150), which has been shaped by 'the pageant of the spheres' (ibid.), and the idea that the 'patterns of this mesocosm are what . . . have shaped the soul' (1951: 155), we have reached the nub of this study. The basic question is: What are the patterns of this mesocosm, the social body, and how in fact do they shape the individual soul? To answer this question it is necessary to begin with the family, for the patterns of the body social are transmitted to the individual in the alchemical vessel of the family. In order for the family to transmit the patterns of the body social, it is necessary for the family to be a microcosm of society. We do not have sufficient historical data to say for sure how the family functioned in Sumerian times, although everything suggests that it must have been patterned in the same way as the 'pageant of the spheres' (Campbell 1959: 150), that is, in a hierarchical model. Nor can we with certainty determine the nature of the family in ancient Greece, nevertheless we have good reason to believe that Greece drew on the Sumerian model. A major aspect of these changes was a new pantheon of the gods and goddesses which was structured as a hierarchal family. In his *Origins of Greek Religion*, B. C. Dietrich draws particular attention to the development of the hierarchical family among gods and humans:

> Two important features of the Mesopotamian Pantheon are firstly the integration of the city gods with their chthonic vegetation origin into a hierarchical family system, and secondly the fact that the divine 'family' reflected the organization of the human society in the city. Both features were destined to recur in the formation of the Greek Olympian family.
>
> (Dietrich 1974: 31)

Whatever the means by which this was achieved, the final result of the new ordering of society in Sumer was to free up individual initiative and creativity. No other explanation can be found for the explosion of creativity that within a few hundred years produced all of the basic elements of culture and civilization as we know it today. That this creativity had something to do with the new vision of the family which appeared at this time in the pantheon of the gods and goddesses, and which was mirrored by a similar development in the human family, seems highly probable, particularly in view of the fact that the next major explosion in creativity took place in Greece some hundreds of years following the Sumerian period when, as Dietrich points out, the pantheon of gods and goddesses was again structured along similar lines. A major feature of the new pantheon and the new family that emerged in Sumer, is the importance given to the sacred marriage as an *hieros gamos*. The life-generating union of heaven and earth was expressed in the form of the first temples. In its earliest stage, the ziggurat is a mound built of sun-dried mud bricks. In the centre and at the highest point, the energy of earth and heaven are drawn together.

The ritual marriage may have been 'enacted there by a divine queen and her spouse' (Campbell 1959: 146). This early temple is described as:

> a little height, artificially constructed, supporting a chapel for the ritual of the world-generating union of the earth goddess with a god of the sky . . . The queen or princess of each city was in these earliest days identified with the goddess, and the king, her spouse with the god.
>
> (Campbell 1951: 150)

The human marriage as an incarnation of the sacred ritual concentrated a new power in the parents. Before Sumer, as in tribes that still exist today, power was spread more widely throughout the society through the complex network of kinship ties.[1] But in Sumer, the family took on the hierarchical features of the pantheon. As a result of these changes, the individual citizen was created – to be sure, at first as a mere servant to the gods, but, nevertheless, with certain privileges and rights assured by the gods through their civil authorities, the king and his councillors. As we know in Greece these rights and privileges of the citizen were considerably increased as was creativity in the arts, science, philosophy – in fact in every field of endeavour.

Now the argument being made is that the changes in the pantheon of the gods and goddesses and the similar structuring of the family freed up the creative spirit to focus on the world and the self in a new way. This new way led to the discovery that the individual human being is the conduit of the spirit in all its creative forms. But the creation of the individual citizen is not the only element of the change in pantheon and family. There is also the hierarchical structure which in the Sumerian pantheon begins with the separation of the world parents, heaven and earth, and leads to the generations of the gods and goddesses. Following is a brief summary by S. N. Kramer of the 'cosmogonic or creation concepts of the Sumerians':

1. First was the *primeval sea*. Nothing is said of its origin or its birth, and it is not unlikely that the Sumerians conceived it as having existed eternally.
2. The *primeval sea* begot the *cosmic mountain* consisting of heaven and earth united.
3. Conceived as gods in human form, An (heaven) was the male and Ki (earth) was the female. From their union was begotten the air-god Enlil.
4. Enlil, the air-god separated heaven from earth, and while his father

An carried off heaven, Enlil himself carried off his mother Ki, the earth. The union of Enlil and his mother Ki – in historical times she is perhaps to be identified with the goddess called variously Ninmah, 'great queen'; Ninhursag, 'queen of the (cosmic) mountain'; Nintu, 'queen who gives birth' – set the stage for the organization of the universe, the creation of man, and the establishment of civilization.
(Kramer 1961: 40–1)

In Hesiod's codification of Greek mythology the origins are similar. In the beginning Mother Earth emerged from chaos and bore her son Uranus. Then Uranus fathered the Titans upon Mother Earth. Thus was the continuing generation of the gods and of humans set in motion. Other early creation myths begin with a single creature who is either divided into male and female, or who creates the opposite sex out of him/herself. In all these myths of origins the separation of the feminine and masculine principles is the source of all further creativity. This identification of the feminine and masculine principles as the life-force which permeates the universe is the great discovery which suffused human creativity. Thus the significance of its eventual formalization in the dialectical opposites of Eros and Logos, and the Yin and Yang of the Tao.

But here again we must look to a further differentiation which takes place in the new pantheon and the new family. Sibling position becomes important in a new way. The hierarchical family structure now derives from the parents as incarnations of the masculine and feminine principles. Their union produces offspring, whose order of birth now takes on a meaning stemming from the authority of either the masculine or the feminine spirit. Thence came the discovery that there are qualities of character and personality inherent in the structure and dynamics of the family.

But even more significant than that discovery is one which is yet scarcely perceived, namely, that these inherent potentials of the family for shaping the destiny of the individual also lead to the shaping of the world in ways which manifest as a fourfold cycle of creativity that has its origins in the family constellation. And this too has its counterpart in the realm of the gods and goddesses.

I shall be taking up the fourfold cycle of creativity in greater depth later on. But for the moment I shall conclude this discussion with a cautionary note regarding some of the other consequences of the Sumerian revolution. Campbell is certainly justified in his enthusiasm over the great achievements of the Sumerians and the mythological themes which united them and then spread to other regions of the world, influencing similar, albeit culturally-adapted, developments. This is the positive side. The dark side of the rise of the hieratic city-state, and then the great civilizations, is the increasing centralization of power supported by armaments and warfare. Not long after the Sumerian revolution the mighty war gods made their appearance in the mythological pantheons. The brief respite of 'democratic' principles which arose in Greece was followed by Alexander's empire. The history of human relationships as far back as we can determine, has been one of varying degrees of comity being established within the group, or tribe, or clan, and so on, but which did not extend to the 'alien', that is to say, anyone of another group or tribe, or clan, and so on. Such tribal, ethnic, and religious intolerance still exists today throughout the world. The tragic wars which have come to encompass all nations have made us all too aware of the potential for total destruction which we face.

As we continue with this study it will be important to keep in mind that the creativity that was unleashed in the Sumerian revolution has led to both positive and negative creations; or perhaps, to put it differently, the human uses of such creation have been both positive and negative. The atomic bomb is our most salient example. We now have the means for total destruction of everyone on this planet. And it is we who unleash the weapons. There is yet another dimension to this issue. In the Second World War, we saw how a leader's identification with an archaic form of an archetype can wreak such havoc, and ignite such fear, that we ourselves in the end felt obliged to create atomic weapons.

Since that time, the atomic weapons possessed by the United States and Russia have seemingly maintained peace. But now that uneasy peace is evaporating, and the possibility of a true peace in Europe is emerging. For a single moment during the meeting of Mikhail Gorbachev and Ronald Reagan at Reykjavik there apparently was the opportunity for the two leaders to agree to eliminate all nuclear weapons. It seems that only the intervention of the hardline conservative members of President Reagan's party prevented that possibility. Subsequently the two men achieved a limited degree of success in eliminating some nuclear warheads.

Meanwhile democracy is breaking out all over Europe. The question posed for us is whether there is a scarcely discernible process which has slowly, oh so slowly, been pushing us toward a new revolution beyond the one at Sumer, a revolution which must of necessity unite the whole world into a community whose new form is as yet unknown. If that is to occur it would seem to demand yet another change in the individual, the family, and society.

We shall return to these issues in Chapter 10. For now we shall explore further the intertwining of individual, family and society as it is manifest in political leadership.

NOTE

1 Before Sumer, as in tribes that still exist today, power was spread more widely throughout the society through the complex network of kinship ties. For example, the male head of a family was not the natural father of the children, but was more likely to be the mother's brother, the uncle of the children. The natural father of the children was then in turn the male authority to his sister's children, or even some more distant female relation. This spread alliances of power throughout the tribe, rather than keeping power focused within the nuclear family.

Chapter 3

Political leadership and the sibling complex
A fated symmetry

BACKGROUND

We turn now to my study of political leadership. Little did I know when I undertook the study that I would willy-nilly be swept into the maelstrom of USA and British history. I found myself reading biographies and autobiographies of all the leading presidents and prime ministers, and many of the lesser ones as well; and reliving with the participants the great and the minor wars and rebellions, along with the peaceful interludes. Always there was the thrust of expansion of the English, then the travail of the birth of a new nation, and again the westward course of expansion on the American continent, and so on and on. For me, this has been an extraordinary experience which has returned fourfold and more a deepened appreciation of the struggle of humanity, in all its follies and defeats, and occasional triumphs, to realize some ideal of a Utopian community.

This was an early attempt to understand the fateful intertwining of individual, family and society. At the completion of the study I was startled to realize that, so far as I could determine, not a single United States presidential candidate, nor a British candidate for prime minister, past or present, has attributed his or her success or failure in an election to sibling position in the family. Yet the selection of presidents and prime ministers provides convincing evidence that, in many cases, sibling position is a critical factor. In a majority of elections it turns out that by the time the party primaries are over and the two, or sometimes three, principal candidates are known, they turn out to be of the same or very closely related ordinal positions. It is as if things are 'arranged' in some unknown, or at least unconscious way, so that the state of the nation and the ordinal position of the final candidates, or, the candidate who is finally elected, have an affinity for each other and – to put it more strongly – appear to be destined for each other.

When these results first began to emerge from my preliminary observations of the current United States presidential elections I was cautiously curious. Could this be some aberration of American politics at this particular time? To satisfy my curiosity I finally undertook this study of sufficient size – all of the presidents of the United States and all of the prime ministers of Great Britain; and covering a long enough span of history – over 200 years.

The best way I know to approach the topic is to describe some of the events that early on teased me into this study. For example, in the summer of 1960 as the USA presidential election loomed on the horizon, the Democrat convention, in a close decision, chose John F. Kennedy as their standard bearer, while the Republicans nominated current president Dwight Eisenhower's vice-president, Richard M. Nixon. Neither candidate had much of a reputation at the time. Kennedy struggled with the handicap of being Catholic, and Nixon was still somewhat tainted by an illegal slush fund which had nearly lost him the vice-presidency. In fact, the public showed so little interest in either candidate, that, by the time of the election, bumper stickers appeared saying 'Kneither-Knorr'. As it turned out the election was the closest ever held, and the final results were not known until after the electoral college had met to settle disputed votes.

What particularly caught my interest in the election was that the family constellations of the two candidates were very similar. Both Kennedy and Nixon were second sons in families with four sons, and in both families the eldest son was deceased. This piqued my curiosity. I then learned that the vice-presidential running mates, Lyndon Johnson and Earl Warren, were both first-born sons. Naturally a single instance of such close matching between presidential and vice-presidential candidates could not be considered proof of anything; it might be pure coincidence. But it was a hint, and I took the hint seriously.

In the presidential elections that followed, I came to see that the matching of sibling positions among candidates is more than a coincidence. As a brief overview: Johnson and Goldwater (1964) were both first-borns; Nixon and Humphrey (1968) were both younger sons; Nixon and McGovern (1972) were both second-borns; Carter and Ford (1976) are both first-borns. The exception to this trend (1980) involved last born Reagan vs first-born Carter. The 1984 election returned to a matching of sibling positions: Mondale and Reagan are both second sons. Again in 1988, the candidates Bush and Dukakis are both second sons.

Although it may at first be difficult to understand the significance of these sibling facts in view of the issues of the campaigns and many apparently sharp differences of ideology, it is nevertheless true that more often than not, the presidential candidates have a common human bond; they both know what it is like to be first-borns (or second-borns, and so on) in a family.

Back in 1960, I wondered whether the close election results might have been in part due to the similar family constellations of Kennedy and Nixon. But I soon learned that there are landslide elections as well as close elections between candidates of the same sibling position. For example, in 1964 there was a landslide election in favour of first-born Johnson who was running against first-born Goldwater. So the question is not whether the election is won by a wide or narrow margin. Rather, the question is: What is the reason for the surprising symmetry regarding sibling positions? I concluded that there must be an understandable psychological principle that underlies these patterns.

One question led to another: Is there a readiness in the candidates which corresponds to a particular social-political situation at the time of a particular election? In other words, are the candidates of a particular sibling configuration 'destined' (in some psychological meaning of that term) to strive for leadership, and to achieve it when the 'signs' are right, so to speak? This brings to mind that old argument of historians and political scientists as to whether the times make the individual, or the individual makes the times. I propose that the 'individual' and the 'times' are simply two perspectives on the same facts: the individual and the times effect each other in ways that are deeply entwined.

For some time I pondered what it might be about the sibling positions that could account for the matching of candidates. Further, I wondered what that might mean about the nature of elections. What determines a candidate's prospects? If there is a reason why both candidates in an election tend to be from the same sibling position, what might it be? What could be accomplished by having two candidates of the same position in their families? It occurred to me then that it must be, first of all, some completely unconscious motivating factor which would be more or less identical for each candidate. Furthermore, this motivating factor must derive from the position in the family constellation.

The 'nuclear' family constellation is composed of mother, father, and children. Other members of the 'extended' family may also live in the home, grandparents, aunts, cousins, and they may need to be considered in individual cases. The terms 'sibling position,' and 'sibling configuration' are interchangeable; both include various factors such as ordinal position, age spacing and gender of the children. The entire family constellation contains key factors that determine the conditions under which a candidate of a particular position in a particular family constellation is likely to be nominated to run for the presidency, and also why the matching of sibling positions among candidates may take place.

As I have said, it must be certain constant and completely unconscious factors related to the family constellation, and especially the sibling position that accounts for the matching of candidates, as well as for the election of a candidate. But having said that, it becomes apparent that some kind of matching must occur as well with some constant features of the social-political situation which acts as a magnet, shall we say, to draw particular candidates into the political arena in a particular election year. Now what could that be? And how would it correspond with the candidate's sibling position? Obviously there must be some constant features in the family and in the society that fit together in a significant way and it would appear that these features must be socio-political in nature. This suggests that the solution must lie in understanding the family as a microcosm of the society.

Let us now turn to the imagination, and let us assume that the family, in principle, is to a greater or lesser extent a microcosm of the society in which it is embedded. It is not too difficult to come up with examples where this appears on the surface to be true. I am thinking, for example, how for centuries the ruling families in Great Britain were largely of the upper class and structured in a strictly patriarchal model which was in accord with the monarchical and parliamentary system of British government. And in America, too, there has been a coterie of old guard families which have contributed more than their share to American political life. Let us then continue our imaginative exercise and for the moment assume that such an imbedding of families in a society can and does occur.

Now comes the more difficult part. How do features of the family actually mirror the essential socio-political elements of the society? The following answer to that question is speculative and may require a temporary suspension of disbelief.

THE FOUR SIBLING POSITIONS

To begin, let us think of the 'nuclear' family as a social system made up of two generations, the parents and the children, and let us take the child's eye view of this social system. First imagine that the 'child's eye view' is that of an only child. From this perspective 'society', that is to say the family, is made up of two grown-ups who represent the previous generation and one child who represents the present generation. In other words, the only child in this imaginary scenario represents the sole, and total constituency of the current society. And so far as the infant or young child is concerned this family-society is, for a considerable period the whole 'world'. This first 'world' is internalized, so to speak, by the child.

Only gradually does the child's 'family-society-world' expand to include the outer world of society. This expansion of the child's world is always a process of assimilation of the outer world to the 'family-world' which was the first to be assimilated. The end result of development for the child is an 'inner world', partly unconscious and partly conscious, which is a layered integration of the stages of development from infancy to adulthood. Of course this process of assimilation is not a pure and simple swallowing whole of either the world of the family or the greater outer world of society. A complementary process of development sees to it that the child interacts with its world and develops in the process an adaptive sense of itself in the world. The final resultant 'world' that is internalized is a product of the dialectic of assimilation and accommodation. This dialectical process is best understood as involving the innate archetypal-affective dynamisms of play/imagination (as assimilation) and curiosity/exploration (as accommodation). Imagination and curiosity can be understood as the prototypical forms of the evolved cosmogonic principles of Eros and Logos, understood in their broadest sense as relatedness and discrimination.

This, obviously, is but the briefest psychological explanation of the process whereby the child develops a 'core' inner world which mirrors the family social system, and which is then gradually expanded to include the outer world through subsequent assimilations. It will, however, suffice for our present purpose which is to present a preliminary description of the child's eye view of its inner 'family-social' world. The following descriptions are to show that each sibling position involves a unique experience for the child.

The only child

The only child experiences itself as the sole member, and totality of the 'new' generation. In the family as a social system this 'new' generation is a single-member social system, if such can be imagined. Moreover, the only child experiences the parents as an 'older' generation whose total attention goes to their only child, the 'new' generation. The foregoing describes an experience which is unique to the only child. It is not shared by the first-born with siblings, the intermediate children, or the last-born.

The first-born child

The first-born child begins life with the same experience as the only child, and remains an only child for a period of time which can vary between about 11 months to several years. There comes a time, however, when a sibling is born and the only child is transformed into a first-born with a sibling. This means, in terms of the family as a social system, that for some period of time the child has experienced the family in the same fashion as does the only child. It is the sole member of a 'new' generation and it is the sole recipient of the attention of the 'older' generation. But all this changes with the birth of a sibling. The first-born's social world now suddenly and inexplicably expands to become a two-member sibling generation, and the attention of the 'older' generation must now be shared with the sibling. In addition the birth of a sibling introduces the experience of there being older and younger members of the 'new' generation. Thus it is that the first-born child has an experience that is uniquely different from the only child, the intermediate child and the last-born child.

The intermediate child

The intermediate child is born into a world which already contains one or more members of the younger generation. And for a period of time the intermediate child is the youngest in the family. This means that the intermediate child first experiences the social world of the family as one in which the 'new' generation is completed by its birth. But then, like the first-born child, the intermediate child's view of the social world of the family is transformed by the birth of yet another sibling; now it is intermediate between members of the 'new' generation who are older and younger than itself. Just so, a unique experience is created for the intermediate child which is not shared by the only, first-born or last-born child.

The last-born child

The last-born child is the one who completes the 'new' generation of the family, and remains the youngest member forever. The last-born's experience of the social world of the family is that one or more members of the 'new' generation are already present; the attention of the members of the 'older' generation must always be shared. Moreover, as the last-born child it is and it remains, the youngest of the 'new' generation. The last-born child thus has its own unique experience of the family social world which is not shared by the only child, first-born or intermediate born.

This completes the brief imaginative formulation of early childhood experiences of the four unique sibling positions. I cannot emphasize enough that it is the unique, yet universal aspect, of each of these sibling experiences which accounts for the matching of political candidates with one another in any election, and their match with the state of affairs in the society at large. The correlations we shall present could not have occurred if such unique experiences of each of the family sibling positions did not exist.

THE FAMILY ATMOSPHERE

Now, having outlined the four sibling positions, it is necessary to explore the other dimension of the family, the family atmosphere. It is the family atmosphere that is responsible for the psychological dynamics leading to a particular individual being 'chosen' by the spirit, so to speak, to become the particular leader at a specific moment in history. Moses was called by Yahweh from the burning bush; Joan of Arc was guided by her angels; and Gandhi listened to the voice of the people.

Seizure by the spirit does not imply that the resultant development will manifest as good or evil, as history well illustrates. Gandhi, for example, was seized by the spirit with the aim of taking back his native land from the rule of the British, and giving to his people their rights and privileges as citizens of a sovereign state. He created a non-violent revolution which in the end achieved his aim. Hitler, too, was presumably seized by the spirit with the aim of taking back his divided homeland from the allied countries that had defeated the Germans in the First World War, and giving his people their rights and privileges. Hitler created a violent revolution with a commitment to his notion of a Utopian society; a society that would breed a perfect race of blond, blue-eyed heroes and heroines; rid itself of all those who were Jewish, or weak, disabled and unfit; and then impose its rule on the rest of the world.

What makes the difference between a Hitler and a Gandhi, both of whom were younger sons engaged in revolution? Here we must look to the family atmosphere, that indescribable amalgam created by the behaviour, values, cultural development, and (perhaps most significantly) the unconscious parental complexes which carry the unanswered questions of the ancestors, and represent the unlived lives of the parents. It is to these influences of the family that we should look for the difference between a Hitler and a Gandhi, or so I believe. I shall take up this theme later on.

MYTHIC ORIGINS

In the ontogeny of the individual, the order of birth is a 'primordial' event, so to speak. It is known to the parents before birth and is slipped over the new-born infant like an invisible envelope. Inescapably, we are received into this world not just as a boy or girl infant, but as a first-born, a second-born, and so on, boy or girl. What significance this *a priori* quality has for individual development is still little known, but we cannot doubt that sibling position has been of the greatest significance to society from time immemorial. The myth and ritual of all peoples as well as the laws of inheritance and of royal succession everywhere reveal its pervasive presence. We are not yet in a position to say whether this is an expression of purely social and political expedience, as some contend (Graves 1955), or whether (as I suspect) it has deeper roots in the recognition of an underlying psychological situation. But regardless of the conclusion, the aura of mystery which surrounds birth itself extends to encompass sibling position.

It was this birth aspect of the vast reservoir of family romance found in myths and legend which first captured the attention of psycho-logists.[1] Rank's *The Myth of the Birth of the Hero*, originally published in 1909, stands as a landmark of this early interest. Intrigued by the unusual set of circumstances that surrounded the birth of the hero in many cultures, Rank isolated a characteristic pattern of features, among which were the hero's virgin birth, dual parenthood, and abandonment after birth. Subsequent study by other investigators have confirmed and extended Rank's basic findings (Jung 1956; Kerenyi 1959; Slater 1968). In one of the most systematic examinations of the hero myth, Raglan (1956) identified some twenty-two elements which clustered around the three universal rites of passage: birth, initiation, and death.

Our interest is limited here to the cluster of features surrounding the birth of the hero. A re-examination of the mythological sources indicates that, in actuality, genealogical and family information about the hero falls into two basic patterns. One of these, like the 'begat' sections of the Bible, is clearly intended as a means for affirming the hero's divine origins and establishing rights to the inheritance of privilege and power. The second pattern furnishes details of the family, even to such specificity at times as the age spacing of siblings. The universal features of the hero's birth, which fall for the most part into the first pattern, may be interpreted as a symbol appropriate to the hero's divine fate. At the human level, this corresponds to the sense of destiny evoked by the fated accident of birth.

If the universal features of the hero myth have to do with the hero's divine inspiration and his call to destiny, the variable details of setting and family serve mainly to define the hero's task and his fitness to accomplish it. With this we are in a position to suggest that the hero of myth and the heroic leader coalesce in a common psychological reality. That is to say, the ancient legend of Moses and the contemporary legend of Mahatma Gandhi, show each as a liberator of his oppressed people. In this sense, Moses and Gandhi are identical psychological types. If we pursue this example for a moment, many obvious parallels spring to mind. *Homo religiosus* is applicable to both; but beyond that, their lives exhibit a mysteriously successful blend of religion and politics for which Erikson (1969) has coined the apt phrase 'religious actualism'. It would be easy to multiply parallels and a more thorough analysis of common elements in the lives of Moses and Gandhi would be an illuminating study. But for the moment I shall limit myself to mentioning one additional element of similarity, the one most pertinent to this research, that is, sibling position. Each is a last-born and has a next older brother and an older sister.

This little excursion into mythology in search of the cultural significance of sibling position has now brought us close to our thesis. It also serves to remind us of the elemental dilemma of human existence, suspended as we are between two realms of being, the mythological vision and the everyday world. This reminder prepares us for thinking about findings I shall present in the next chapter which urgently suggest that the careers of such world-renowned leaders as Lincoln, Roosevelt, and Churchill, to mention a few, would be but footnotes to the pages of history were it not for a fateful concatenation of events in which a matching of sibling position and the political *Zeitgeist* are essential elements. A critical factor is the individual's sense of mission which, coupled with a complementary response from others, leads to success. In effect, we shall be considering the question that Erikson has explored so deeply in *Gandhi's Truth*:

> Why certain men of genius can do no less than take upon themselves an evolutionary and existential curse shared by all, and why other men will be only too eager to ascribe to such a man a god-given greatness surpassing that of all others?
>
> (Erikson 1969: 129)

THE POLITICS OF BIRTH ORDER

Now for a closer look at the everyday world of the family where the roots of political leadership are to be found for a Gandhi as surely as for the leader of lesser stature. Family life through its major functions of cultural transmission and the nurturance of children ensures that every child is equipped with a microcosmic vision of society while at the same time being provided with a relatively-sheltered arena for the testing of life's practical skills. Parents are the prime agents of all this and, as we well know from personal experience and the findings of depth psychology, their character and personality, the values they cherish, and the quality of their personal relationship carry critical significance for a child's development.

Parental influences alone are not sufficient to account for the impact that sibling position in the family may have on development. Underlying and intermingling with these parental influences at all levels of the child's conscious and unconscious experience lies the filtering envelope of sibling position. This is an on-going system of reinforcement which is built into the very structure of the family itself, and which resides in the simple fact of age differences between siblings. From this basic element of the family, a whole host of consequences may be seen to flow.

First among such consequences are the purely existential priorities which are so indelibly imprinted on our memory by the ritual observance of birthdays. Far greater in importance, though, are the cumulative effects of the daily ebb and flow of family life which faces children time after time after time with the often painful awareness of just where it is they stand with their siblings in the hierarchies, for example, of size and strength, of mobility, of privilege, and of knowledge and experience which exist simply because of age differences and, in turn, by virtue of the order of their birth. Need we look further? The deep-flowing currents of emotion implicit in these sibling relationships are surely what make sibling-position-related experiences so binding and so freighted with far-reaching consequences.

Just listen to this recital by 10-year-olds of the tactics they employ to get a sibling to do what they want: 'I beat him up, hit him, boss him, spook him, belt him, exclude him', or 'I get mad, shout and yell, cry, pout, sulk, ask other kids for help, threaten to tell Mom and Dad' (see Sutton-Smith and Rosenberg 1970). So elemental and universal are these responses that no one need be told that the participants are older and younger brothers and sisters, nor need anyone be in doubt that the high-power tactics are those of the older siblings. This is the litany of sibling rivalry. We may deplore, moralize, excuse, and point to other kinds of behaviour, but it is impossible to deny that this is often how it is with brothers and sisters. If we now permit ourselves the vagrant thought that Mahatma Gandhi was once just such a brother among brothers and sisters, we come abruptly face to face with the near impossibility of comprehending the transformation that takes place from childhood to sainthood.

But to return to our litany of sibling rivalry, are not these the raw materials of power politics? It requires no great leap of imagination to perceive in adult political leaders the same kinds of behaviour: Lyndon Johnson, a first-born son, in the Capitol cloakroom 'twisting arms'; Richard Nixon, a second-born son, angry, pouting, crying on television; John Foster Dulles, a first-born son, exploiting atomic brinkmanship; or Dwight Eisenhower, a third-born son, holding Nixon at arm's length. Is this not the true state of political affairs?

POLITICAL LEADERSHIP AND THE SIBLING COMPLEX

With this background we are now in a position to discuss more specific hypotheses. Briefly stated, my major thesis is that sibling position provides the basis for a psychological typology comprising four principal types and a number of minor variants. The basic types correspond to the four sibling situations: the only, first-born, intermediate born, and last-born child. Each has an absolutely unique bit of experience. The only child never knows what it is like to have siblings; the first-born begins life as an only child and then experiences the birth of a sibling; the intermediate-born begins life as a last-born and then experiences the birth of a sibling; and the last-born is always last and never experiences the birth of a sibling. These types have many variations which are a function of family size, sex of siblings, age spacing, and other personal and family factors. Age spacing may be of particular importance in determining one's essential typology based on experiences during the child's formative years. Each psychological type arises in a particular family constellation. For example, there is a first-born male type with sisters only and a first-born male type with brothers only, and so on. It is obvious that the number of possible combinations of ordinal position, sex of sibling, and family size is large but finite.

No two children in a family have quite the same experience. Each, from his or her own individual sibling perspective, interiorizes – to use Laing's concept – a particular 'family' experience. Birth order is one of the structural elements of such interiorized 'families'.[2] Moreover, it is an *a priori* position in the individual's ontogeny that places sibling position at the centre of the process of identity formation.

With respect now specifically to leadership, the burden of the argument is that within the family each sibling position promotes a unique view of society and provides a unique experience in dealing with power and authority. This view of society and the acquired leadership skills are normally refined in the peer play group, and then become the repertoire of adult political behaviour. From this perspective, the family's role in the development of political expectations and behaviour is as a microcosm of society:

> The primary group (what one might call the political system of the family) influences the expectations of the individual with regard to authority in the larger political system. Within the primary group, the individual receives training for roles that he will play within the society. This training consists in both the teaching of certain standards of behaviour that can be applied to later situations, and, perhaps more significantly, the playing of roles in the family and other primary groups that are similar to roles later to be played in the political or economic system.
>
> (Verba 1961: 31)

To summarize so far, there should be four basic styles of leadership corresponding to the four sibling experiences – the only, first-born, intermediate, and last-born child. Moreover, 'successful leadership . . . rests on a latent congruence between the psychic needs of the leader and social needs of the followers' (Rustow 1970: 23), and as a result, there should of necessity be four major situations of the body politic which cry out for the leader of appropriate sibling position. These situations are respectively: (1) the breakdown of social institutions, for example, the 1930s Depression; (2) expansion and/or confrontation, for example, early years of the United States; (3) retrenchment and realignment of domestic and foreign commitments, for example, the 1950s; and (4) rebellion and revolt, for example, the Civil War.

The exercise of fitting this empirically-derived matching of leadership styles and social crises to birth order hypotheses is obviously complex. For its suggestive value, I offer the following example of the pathway my speculations have followed. Let us begin with the notion that leadership styles and social crises may be mirror images, so to speak, of childhood sibling experiences. Take, for example, the only child. If we assume that from the child's eye view of the family the parents represent past society and the children represent present society, it follows that of all the birth order positions the only child, being the sole heir of past society and the sole member of present society, would on both counts be the best able to identify with society as a totality. Thus in a crisis involving the collapse of vital social functions where the essential task of leadership is to unite all the people in a genuinely co-operative effort of regeneration, it would presumably be the only child who is most likely to succeed.

Pursuing this line of thought with the other sibling experiences I arrive at the following for the first-born. As first heir of past society and first citizen of an expanding society all the members of which are of lower rank than himself or herself, the first-born would be uniquely in touch with the demands of an expanding society while also inheriting responsibility for weaker members. This experience prepares him or her presumably for effective leadership in times of territorial expansion and confrontation.[3] The intermediate-born shares with the first-born the experience of an expanding society, although in other respects his or her situation is quite different. For example, intermediate-borns find themselves in the midst of a society with higher-ranking classes on one side and lower-ranking classes on the other, a position which appears to maximize opportunities for diverse relationships while at the same time demanding adeptness at mediation and accommodation. This experience, it would seem, would incline the intermediate-born to leadership skills that involve arbitration and the realignment of power. Finally, with the last-born, society has completed its growth and all classes are obviously of higher rank than the lowly last-born. Just so, we may imagine, is created the natural champion of the oppressed and the leader of choice in times of rebellion and revolt. (It should be noted that intermediate-born children were once last-borns. As we shall see, they may under particular circumstances, become the leaders in rebellion or revolt.)

METHODOLOGY AND REVIEW OF THE LITERATURE

With respect to the kind of exploratory research presented here and in the following chapters, it is essential to keep constantly in mind the limitations placed upon the generalization of results by any failure to meet various requirements of methodology. I have made every effort to obtain the complete basic family constellation whenever possible. This has been achieved in all but a few instances for our primary subjects, USA presidents and English prime ministers. It will also become obvious as the results are discussed that some of the implications of this research cannot be pursued with the data at hand. I have at times identified family constellations which appear to stimulate characteristic types of psychological development only to find myself unable to do more than speculate because of the limitations of the data. Because of these limitations, whenever results are presented I have tried to make clear the frame of reference, what the data are, and how complete they are, so that others may be enabled to draw their own conclusions.

Completely satisfactory data for this kind of research is difficult to obtain. Ellis, while preparing his *A Study of British Genius* (1926), was probably the first to encounter the frustrations imposed by incomplete, unsystematic, and ambiguous biographical facts. Not one to suffer in silence, Ellis for many years used his not inconsiderable influence to convince editors of the value of accurate facts about the origins and family life of eminent individuals. He eventually achieved limited success with the British *Dictionary of National Biography* (Stephen and Lee 1885–1900) (perhaps also indirectly with the *Dictionary of American Biography*), which began to supply with increasing regularity both sibling position of children, and sibling position of sons or daughters (for example, second-born child, only son). This, of course, is only a beginning and is far short of what would be desired, namely, ordinal positions, sex of siblings, birth dates, and dates of death with indications of early death for at least two generations.

Still, all is not lost. Though the frustration level remains high, there are just enough usable facts provided with a reasonable degree of accuracy to make the use of basic biographical source books worthwhile, particularly for preliminary explorations. Fortunately, these general source books can often be supplemented by individual biographies. With biographies it is a pleasure to report the situation is definitely improved and improving. There is clear evidence of the impact of depth psychology. Early childhood experiences which fifty years ago were relegated to a few pages or even paragraphs now command respectable attention, and a genuine effort is made by many biographers to integrate the events of childhood with later life.

Nevertheless, the accumulation of any sizeable sample of accurate and relatively complete family constellation data on public and historical figures remains time-consuming. As may be expected, the present study suffers to some extent from the vagaries of the biographical sources just described, particularly the dearth of information about age-spacing between siblings. This will be made clear whenever it is felt these deficiencies may seriously affect the results.

The primary sources of the biographical data used in these studies were J. N. Kane's (1959) *Facts About the Presidents* (FATP), the *Dictionary of American Biography* (DAB), the British *Dictionary of National Biography* (DNB), the journal *Current Biography* (CB), and some hundred or more individual biographies. In an effort to ensure accuracy in the family data, one or more individual biographies were consulted whenever possible for each of the presidents and prime ministers. This procedure was also followed with the other political leaders referred to in the research. In cases where biographies were not available, and in the few instances where biographies were in disagreement, the DNB, DAB or CB were relied upon.

In these studies, the sibling position of the political leader is determined primarily by the family constellation of the children who survived birth and who lived with one another for any significant portion of their early childhood. I have settled more or less arbitrarily on the period from birth to at least five years of age by which time many researchers suggest the nucleus of character formation has been established. It will occasionally occur that there is some discrepancy between the sibling positions reported here and those found in biographical source books which, as mentioned, often include stillbirths and deaths in infancy. In addition to the death of a sibling, further complications involve age-spacing, as well as half-siblings and other issues related to the extended family.

Methodology

Before proceeding further, some questions of nomenclature and methodology need to be clarified. For example, there are at least three basic definitions of sibling position (see Jones 1933). One is pregnancy order. For research in which pregnancy order is appropriate data, it is often not imperative that full-term infants be born. A second definition is based upon the actual births occurring but may include stillbirths and deaths early in infancy. (This is the ordinal position frequently reported in general biographical sources.) In the third definition interest centres primarily upon the children who survive birth and who live with one another for a significant portion of their formative years. The last of these definitions is what I will use.

One way to come to grips with complications of the family constellation is to make use of a traditional genealogical diagram. In Figure 3.1, the sons and daughters in a family are listed in the bottom row in the order of their birth from left to right. A more complete diagram would include birth dates beneath each child, to indicate the essential element of age-spacing between siblings. In the row just above the sons and daughters are their parents. The parents are likewise represented in order of birth among their siblings. And above the parents are their parents (the grandparents of those at the bottom). Generations could be added *ad infinitum*, all the way back to the original progenitors.

In its totality, this genealogical chart would constitute the most comprehensive definition of the term 'family constellation'. For most research purposes I would be more than delighted if it were possible to obtain data for three generations of a family, that is, the bottom three rows of the diagram.[4] In actual fact, and certainly with respect to historical and public figures, the data from general biographical sources is often limited to the bottom row, the basic elements of which are ordinal position, sex of siblings and, in the best of circumstances, the relative ages of siblings.

Although we have spent more time than may seem warranted in this discussion of relatively simple, even self-evident facts, it is precisely over such issues that much research in this area has come to grief. These basic methodological requirements were formulated by Jones (1933) many years ago, but they have been more honoured in the breach than in the observance. A major reason for this neglect of such elementary considerations is the complexity they introduce. As one disillusioned investigator (Schooler 1972: 174) frankly admits, 'if, in order to be

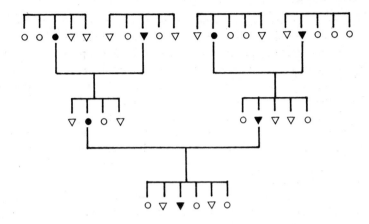

Figure 3.1 Traditional genealogical diagram
Note: Circles stand for females, triangles for males. The blacked-in figures represent the individual in question (bottom row), his parents (middle row), and grandparents (top row).

fruitful, the study of birth order necessitates dealing with the complexities of such variables as sex of siblings and family density, or of collecting data on hard-to-define control groups, it loses much of its appeal'. Although Schooler's reassertion of methodological strictures is welcome, the very selective nature of the review and the apparent lack of acquaintance with a significant body of earlier literature makes the other conclusions less tenable.

Review of the literature

For many years the psychology of sibling position in the family constellation – commonly referred to as birth order – has been a very perplexed subject. This is partly because on the surface the variable seems so simple and straightforward. One need only compare a number of only children with first-born children on any characteristic one may choose and obtain a result, positive or negative. And this is what innumerable researchers did in the 1920s (Sutton-Smith and Rosenberg 1970: 152). The characteristic that many of them focused on was the presumed handicap under which the only child was supposed to operate. Their expectation was that only children would be found to suffer from more psychological symptoms than other children. The results were anything but conclusive, and when these contradictory studies began to accumulate at an amazing rate the academic establishment stepped in and declared the subject a nonentity, a waste of time. These pronouncements had their desired effect, at least temporarily, and the quantity of birth order studies declined markedly. A few committed researchers, however, pursued the subject with diligence and with a broader perspective.

These findings are reviewed in the thorough and well-informed analysis of the total body of birth order research up to 1968 to be found in the *The Sibling* (Sutton-Smith and Rosenberg 1970). One of the significant contributions made in this work is the demonstration of consistent findings by a persistent group of investigators – Koch (1958), Lasko (1954), Levy (1937), Sears (1951), to mention a few – who were not deterred by the difficulties and complexities of the subject matter. I have adopted, and adapted, for use here the system of signs proposed by Sutton-Smith and Rosenberg (1970: 17) for simplifying reference to family constellations.[5]

In the post-Second World War years birth order research experienced a renaissance that fostered a prolonged pursuit of the will o' the wisp notion that first-borns are more likely than others to scale the heights of eminence. The criterion of achievement used in most of these studies was college attendance, and the results seemed overwhelmingly to support the hypothesis. In the end though, these studies served mainly to show that psychologists are as vulnerable to the myth of the birth of the hero as anyone else.

The origin of this hypothesis goes back at least as far as the nineteenth century when Sir Francis Galton published a study which purported to prove that the first-born sons of the British upper class achieved higher positions in government and society than did their younger siblings (1869). Despite the obvious defects of Galton's study which took no account of the prevailing patriarchal privileges of inheritance, this idea spawned a rash of other studies seeking to substantiate his findings. Another Englishman, Havelock Ellis (better known for his pioneering studies in human sexuality), conducted a study of what he called *British Genius* (1926). Ellis chose a thousand subjects from the *Dictionary of National Biography*. Using a number of criteria to establish their superior level of achievement, he compared his subjects on several variables including family origin and birth order. His results with regard to birth order again seemed to support the then prevailing view that first-borns outstripped other children in achievement.

A re-examination of Ellis's and other early studies (Stewart 1961) revealed that they do not prove what they contend. Some are riddled with errors, others do not control for such factors as family size, use biased samples, and so on. Although there may be some association between birth order and vocation (for example, in such hierarchical professions as the military and the church, younger sons tend to shine, whereas in the law, first-born and only sons are slightly more likely to attain eminence), all professions considered, there is little, if any evidence to support a belief in the greater frequency of eminence or achievement in first-borns. Harris (1964) reaches similar conclusions on slightly different grounds. A subsequent study (Smelser and Stewart 1968), using a sample of subjects drawn from the longitudinal research of the Institute of Human Development, University of California at Berkeley, gave no support to the hypothesis that first-borns achieve more education than others. However, the issue refuses to go away. A recent study of 113,000 people reported in *Science* by Dr Judith Blake (1989), showed once again that the order of birth made no difference in how far the subjects went in school or how intelligent they were. 'What matters', said Dr Blake,

> is how large a family one comes from. What had seemed to be birth-order effects were artifacts. The real effects were due to parents' characteristics – the lower social class and the less educated the parents, the bigger the family.
>
> (Blake, in Goleman 1990: 9)

A study by Cecile Ernst and Jules Angst (1983) appears to have reached conclusions similar to Dr Blake's. Ernst and Angst attempted to review all of the extant research on birth order between 1946 and 1980. They also conducted a study in 1971 of 'a representative sample of 6,315 19-year-old [Swiss] males and [a slightly less representative sample of] 1,381 20-year-old [Swiss] females' (p. 246). In both their survey of the world literature and their own study, the authors found largely negative results with respect to the effects of sibling position on personality and behaviour. Their final conclusions were that:

> Birth order and sibship size do not have a strong impact on personality. The present investigation points instead to a broken home, an unfriendly educational style, and a premature disruption of relations with parents as concomitants of neuroticism, and to higher

income and social class (with all assets implied) and an undisturbed home as concomitants of higher achievement. Beside these influences, details of socialization seem to shrink to insignificance.

(Ernst and Angst 1983: 284)

Posing the question in the way they have, Ernst and Angst have proved once again that sibling position does not predict either psychopathology or high achievement. The authors also seem to suffer from a misconception about the expectations for research on the sibling position. They state in their preface: 'Everybody agrees that birth order differences must arise from differential socialization by the parents' (ibid.: x). But everyone does not agree that birth order differences are rooted in different treatment by the parents. Ernst and Angst seem to ignore the fact that siblings interact with and have an effect upon each other.

With regard to political leadership, Ernst and Angst neglected important studies, and interpreted findings in arbitrary ways. For example, an early study which I reported in 1970 to the annual meeting of the American Psychological Association was cited, but only a single and minor aspect of the study was mentioned. Their evaluation of the study did not address the central argument that birth order is related to the likelihood of an individual being elected president under certain specified social-political conditions. My more extensive report on this subject, published a few years later as a chapter in *A Psychological Examination of Political Leaders* (1977b), was not included in their survey. Only one other study is reported on the subject of sibling position and political leadership: Wagner and Schubert (1977) reviewed the birth order of the USA presidents but no hypotheses were examined that concerned the relationship of sibling position and style of leadership, or the like.

On the basis of a careful reading of their review of the literature and their own study of Swiss subjects, I must conclude that Ernst and Angst have done both a service and a disservice to our understanding of the family constellation and its influences on the destiny of the individual. The positive aspect of their study is their overall finding that there is no evidence for the assumption that birth order is directly related to either high achievement or psychopathology. The issues of achievement and pathology have plagued the study of birth order from the very beginning. The conclusions of Ernst and Angst, as well as those of Blake, may help to set these issues to rest. The negative aspect of their study is the failure to understand the effects of the family constellation and sibling position *per se* on style of life and world-view. Their own study does not attempt to assess such factors. Thus in a way, they have tried to throw out the baby with the bath water.

As far as I can determine, the study I am presenting in this book is the only one of its kind. Another study, however, which appears to have some bearing on my work, was reported to the American Academy for the Advancement of Science in February 1990. The author of the paper, Dr Frank Sulloway, is a historian of science, a visiting scholar at the Massachusetts Institute of Technology. His study has been under way for the past nineteen years. It includes his analysis of 2,784 participants in twenty-eight of the major scientific controversies over the last 400 years. The author's conclusions are that a disproportionately high percentage of later-born scientists supported most of the theories that challenged accepted beliefs. Daniel Goleman describes Sulloway's research in the science section of *The New York Times*:

> Of the 28 scientific revolutions, 23 were led by later borns. And in those with a firstborn as the leader – Einstein and Newton for example – their prominent allies were for the most part later borns.
>
> (Goleman 1990: 9)

Sulloway is reported to be finding similar results in a new study of the same birth order effect among 'social reformers in historical movements like the abolition of slavery, civil rights, union organizing and women's rights' (ibid.). Sulloway's rationale for his findings is that: 'As the eldest, firstborns identify more closely with parents and through them, with other authorities . . . And they play the role of parental surrogate to later children. They end up more conforming, conscientious and conventional than later siblings' (ibid). On the other hand, he said 'later siblings tend to rebel against the first-born's authority' (ibid.). In support of his study, Sulloway points to one of the few positive findings of the Ernst and Angst study: that is, first-borns are more accepting of parental authority and identify more with parental values than do those born later.

> Laterborns generally favor scientific innovation, whereas firstborns, who identify more closely with parents and authority, typically oppose them. In microcosm, then, the childhood family constellation fosters the same divisive psychological forces that later determine, in adulthood, the battlelines of revolutionary thought.
>
> (Sulloway n.d.: 22)

Sulloway's findings agree with my own with respect to the fact that all new advances in any field whatsoever are likely to be initiated by a younger son or daughter (Stewart 1961, 1962, 1970, 1976, 1977b, 1988). But in my view, Sulloway may be somewhat mislead by his method of inquiry. He apparently mixes supporters of a theory with innovators, and hence obscures the world cycle of creative change which I intend to show corresponds with Kuhn's cycle of scientific discovery. Sulloway does not seem to recognize the need to separate the original innovators from others, nor does he separate only children and only sons/daughters from other first-borns with siblings of the same sex. For example, in Sulloway's study, Einstein and Newton are first-borns; whereas Einstein is an only son with a younger sister, and Newton is essentially an only child.[6] Thus he appears to miss the synthetic role of the only child and only son/daughter, as well as the mediating role that the intermediate-born plays in bringing innovative ideas to fruition.

In concluding this survey of the literature I should like to compare briefly the early contributions of Adler and Jung. Both were interested in the family constellation but from different perspectives. Jung (1909) showed that children often tend to be identified with the family atmosphere created by their parents.[7] Adler focused on the child's sibling position, to show characteristic differences in personality between children in the same family (Adler 1956: 376–83). Between them, they covered the two fundamental dimensions of the family, that is, family atmosphere (Jung) and sibling position (Adler). As we shall see, the differences between Jung and Adler in their interest in, and interpretation of the family, can perhaps in part be traced to their own sibling positions and sibling complexes. Jung was an only child (**M1F**) for nine years and then a sister was born, while Adler was the second child, second son (**MM2F[m]FMM**).

From this survey of the literature it can be concluded that psychopathology, except for genetic and catastrophic influences, is a consequence of the atmosphere of the family determined by the unlived life of the parents and their ancestral complexes. The character, behaviour, values and other qualities of the parents appear to be critical factors. The literature is less definitive on the significance of the child's sibling position in the family. Some of the early studies, reviewed by Sutton-Smith and Rosenberg in *The Sibling*, established the importance of the subject. Sulloway's study is a welcome contribution. But on the whole, little research has attended to the subject with sufficient care and with adequate hypotheses to specify the parameters of each sibling position and its implications for the individual, family and society. These lacunae I seek to address.

NOTES

1 Following Cassirer, Jung, and others, myth is a meaningful product of our symbol-producing psyche. Its universal features symbolize stages in the psychological development of humans. The myriad variations of myth reflect social, philosophical, artistic, and religious aspects of the culture within which it originates.

2 Although the concept of the interiorized 'family' was developed through studies of schizophrenic families, it provides a useful way of thinking about the internalization dynamics of any family. Laing's definition follows (single inverted commas are used to make clear that it is the internalized family that is in question):

> The family here discussed is the family of origin transformed by internalization, partitioning, and other operations, into the 'family' and mapped back onto the family and elsewhere.
>
> (Laing 1972: 3)

3 Much of what has been said here regarding the first-born child is applicable to first-born sons – first male heirs in a male-dominated society. However, as larger samples of all of the critical family constellations become available, we should be able to differentiate more clearly the specific aspects of leadership which distinguish first-born children from first-born sons (with older sisters) and first-born daughters (with older brothers).

4 We know very little yet about the effects of parents' expectations as a function of their own sibling position on the development of children. There are many suggestive examples of the apparent preference for, or rejection of, a particular child which may be related to birth order, for example, the elder and younger Pitts who were both second sons; the singular education of John Stuart Mill by his father James, both of whom were first-borns; younger son Neville Chamberlain's rejection by his first-born father; and first-born Joseph Kennedy's high hopes for his first-born, Joseph, Jr.

5 M refers to brother; F, to sister. The order of sequence from left to right is the order of siblings in the family from oldest to youngest. The individual under consideration is printed in bold type and with a number after M or F. That number represents that person's sibling position in the family. Significant variations based on age-spacing, or gender (for example, only son, only daughter) will be described in the text. When age-spacing is unusually wide, it may also be indicated with square brackets around the number of years between siblings, for example, (**M1**[14]MF). When the death of a sibling is taken up in the text, it may be indicated with square brackets around [m] or [f].

6 Newton had three younger half siblings, but he is essentially an only child. He never knew is father. His mother left him soon after birth; he was raised as an only child by his grandmother. When he was 11 years old, he went to live with his mother and got to know his half siblings.

7 Jung used Wundt's word association methods in his study of the family constellation.

Chapter 4

The American presidents and the British prime ministers

In this chapter I present findings from my study of American presidents and British prime ministers covering a period of nearly 200 years. We shall discuss first the American presidents, starting with the election of George Washington in 1789. We shall then look at the British prime ministers, starting with William Pitt the Younger in 1783. The two groups of leaders serve, of course, as cross-validation for each. In the narrative of the chapter the cycles of sibling position are shown over time. From this data we gain a useful vantage point for our purposes.

THE AMERICAN PRESIDENTS

Table 4.1 shows the American presidents in the order of their election (1789–1988). Each election is considered separately. For example, George Washington was elected for two terms, while John Adams was elected for only one term, and so on. What we are interested in here is the cyclical alternation in the sibling positions of the presidents, and whether or not this is correlated with meaningful variations in the political *Zeitgeist*.

Sibling position and political *Zeitgeist*

This leads to the central research question, the relationships between sibling position and political *Zeitgeist*. A chronological look at the sibling positions of the presidents in Table 4.1 shows that the distribution is not random with respect to election periods. Presidents of the same or similar sibling positions follow each other in close succession for varying periods of time. In order to get a closer view of a segment of Table 4.1, we shall look at the first twenty elections, divided into two parts of ten elections each, which is reflected in the sibling position of the leaders and the types of political situations covered. Between the elections of 1789 and 1824 (thirty-five years) there were five presidents who were first-born sons and one president who was a younger son; whereas between the elections of 1828 and 1864 (thirty-six years) there were five presidents who were younger sons, two first-born sons and one only son.

The next question is whether or not this cyclical alternation in the sibling positions of the presidents is correlated with meaningful variations in the political *Zeitgeist*. A comparison of the two eras 1789–1824 and 1828–64 suggests that this is so. In the 1789–1824 era the newly-established government of the United States was primarily engaged in expanding and consolidating its boundaries and asserting its sovereignty. Here are some of the outstanding political events and issues of those days (Langer 1948): 1791–4, Indian wars leading to expansion westward; 1794, Jay's treaty leading to evacuation of border posts by the English; 1795, Pinckney's treaty negotiated with Spain to establish southern boundaries and rights to navigation on the Mississippi; 1791–9, the XYZ affair and near war with France; 1801, Marines sent to Tripoli to prevent pirating; 1802, Ohio becomes the seventeenth state; 1803, Louisiana Purchase; 1804–6, the Lewis and Clark expedition; 1806–7, the Chesapeake Affair with American shipping threatened by England; 1810, rise of the War Party and growing demand for war with England and conquest of Canada; 1812–14, war with England; 1815, Jackson wins battle of New Orleans; 1817–18, Seminole War with Jackson invading Florida and the consequent treaty with Spain and acquisition of Florida; 1819–24, Supreme Court decisions supporting centralization of power in the Federal government; 1820, the Missouri Compromise and admission to statehood of Louisiana, Indiana, Mississippi, Illinois and Alabama; 1823, the Monroe Doctrine.

In sharp contrast, the period following the election of Andrew Jackson in 1828 was, with three notable exceptions, a time primarily devoted to domestic accommodations. The issues of the day were in large part monetary and political, with the dispute over slavery gaining in ascendance (Langer 1948): by 1829, white male suffrage established in all the states; 1829, the Working Man's Party organized; 1830, the Mormon Church founded; 1831, William Lloyd Garrison established the *Liberator*, a newspaper advocating unconditional abolition of slavery; 1830–4, Jackson's policy of relocating Indians west of the Mississippi; 1832, the USA Bank controversy; 1838, the Underground Railroad; 1838–9, Congress adopts gag resolutions against anti-slavery

Table 4.1 Sibling position of USA presidents* (1789–1988)

Election years	Last-born son	Middle son	First-born son	Only son	Only child	Elected presidents
1789			○			G. WASHINGTON
1793			○			G. WASHINGTON
1796			○			J. ADAMS
1800			○			T. JEFFERSON
1804			○			T. JEFFERSON
1808			○			J. MADISON
1812			○			J. MADISON
1816			○			J. MONROE
1820			○			J. MONROE
1824			○			J. Q. ADAMS
1828	○					A. JACKSON
1832	○					A. JACKSON
1836		○				M. VAN BUREN
1840	○					W. H. HARRISON
1844			○			J. KNOX POLK
1848		○				Z. TAYLOR
1852		○				F. PIERCE
1856		○				J. BUCHANAN
1860				○		A. LINCOLN
1864				○		A. LINCOLN
1868		○				U. S. GRANT
1872			○			U. S. GRANT
1876	○					R. B. HAYES
1880	○					J. A. GARFIELD
1884		○				G. CLEVELAND
1888		○				B. HARRISON
1892		○				G. CLEVELAND
1896		○				W. MCKINLEY
1900		○				W. MCKINLEY
1904			○			T. ROOSEVELT
1908		○				W. H. TAFT
1912			○			W. WILSON
1916			○			W. WILSON
1920			○			W. G. HARDING
1924				○		C. COOLIDGE
1928	○					H. HOOVER
1932					○	F. D. ROOSEVELT
1936					○	F. D. ROOSEVELT
1940					○	F. D. ROOSEVELT

Table 4.1 Continued

Election years	Last-born son	Middle son	First-born son	Only son	Only child	Elected presidents
1944					○	F. D. ROOSEVELT
1948			○			H. TRUMAN
1952		○				D. EISENHOWER
1956		○				D. EISENHOWER
1960		○				J. F. KENNEDY
1964			○			L. B. JOHNSON
1968		○				R. NIXON
1972		○				R. NIXON
1976			○			J. CARTER
1980	○					R. REAGAN
1984	○					R. REAGAN
1988		○				G. BUSH

*See Note 1 on p. 79.

petitions; 1850, the Compromise of 1850 making California a free state but leaving other territories undecided; 1850, Clayton-Bulwer Treaty with respect to British encroachments in Latin America; 1853, the Gadsden Purchase; 1853, railroad between New York and Chicago; 1854, Kansas-Nebraska Act repealing the Missouri Compromise allowing homesteaders to decide for or against slavery; 1854, trade treaty with Japan; 1854, Ostend Manifesto, warning Spain of USA interest in Cuba; 1854, the Know-Nothing and Republican parties appear.

The preceding brief summary of the era from 1828–54 does not include President Polk's term of office from 1844–8. It is clear that this period stands out in bold relief from the preceding period. To turn now to the election of Polk in 1844, the single overriding issue of the election was the outcry for annexation of Texas and Oregon; '54-40 or Fight' became a popular campaign slogan of the Democratic Party. Polk, as it turned out, was the first 'dark horse' candidate to be nominated by a major political party, his nomination hinging on support of an expansionist position in the annexation controversy. Immediately following his election he set out with a will to acquire, in addition to Texas, both New Mexico and California. In this he was successful, although not without provoking a war with Mexico. Also during his term in office, Polk negotiated with England for the acquisition of Oregon, offered to buy Cuba from Spain, and obtained a

Latin American treaty that gave the USA rights of passage across the isthmus of Panama for a future railroad or canal. At the end of his four-year term he claimed, not immodestly, that

> the acquisition of California and New Mexico, the settlement of the Oregon boundary and the annexation of Texas, extending to the Rio Grande, are results which, combined, are of greater consequence and will add more to the strength and wealth of the nation than any which have preceded them since the adoption of the constitution.
>
> (Polk, in Whitney 1967:105)

From this brief, although fairly representative review, it is evident that periods of territorial expansion and/or confrontation, leading at times to war, occurred far more frequently, in fact almost exclusively, when the presidents in office were first-born in their families, or first-born sons, that is John Adams (**M1**MM), Thomas Jefferson (FF**M3**FFFFM), James Madison (**M1**MMFMFFMMM), James Monroe (**M1**MMMF), and James Knox Polk (**M1**FFMMMMFFMM); whereas, during times when attention focused more on internal affairs and mediation involving treaties, and the like, the presidents were younger sons, that is, Andrew Jackson (MM**M3**), Martin Van Buren (MFMFF**M6**MM), William Henry Harrison (FFMFMF**M7**), Zachary Taylor (MM**M3**MFMMFF),[1] and Franklin Pierce (FMFMFM**M7**FM).

To summarize at this point, we can see in the above data evidence for a relationship between the political *Zeitgeist* and the sibling position of the presidents. An understanding of this relationship is as yet confined to a distinction between periods of expansive nationalism often leading to war, and other periods devoted more to internal readjustments of a political-social nature, the former having first-born and only sons as presidents, the latter having younger sons as presidents. Further on we shall identify other aspects of this correlation between *Zeitgeist* and sibling position. For the moment, however, let us consider some of the implications of these findings with respect to the political process. The critical questions are where and when such selections are made and by whom?

In attempting to answer these questions, I noted that similar sibling positions were found in samples of both elected and defeated presidential candidates. This result suggests that the selection process takes place at the national conventions or even earlier. To learn more about the selection process, sibling position data were obtained for a sample of nominees for the presidency at national conventions during the period from 1832 to 1920. This sample represents nearly all of

Table 4.2 Birth order (as son) of presidential nominees (1832–1920)

Birth order (as son)	All nominees		Presidential candidates	
	Number	Percentage	Number	Percentage
Only son	21	15	5	11
First-born son	44	32	16	35
Younger son	74	53	25	54
Total	139	100	46	100

the leading contenders in each election. Those for whom biographical data were not available fall mainly into the category of 'favourite sons' who were nominated for honorary reasons. As may be seen from Table 4.2, there is very little difference between the sibling position of all the leading contenders (that is, all nominees) versus the sibling position of those who were finally selected (that is, presidential candidates).

This sample suggests that in many elections, in fact more often than not, the voter has very little choice at all regarding sibling position since both candidates tend to be matched. For example, in a comparison of the elections from 1828 (when the public first began to have a direct impact on the elections) to 1956, I found nineteen elections in which the major candidates were of matched sibling position in contrast to thirteen elections in which the major candidates were not matched. In the period 1960 to 1988, I found seven elections in which the major candidates were of matched sibling position in contrast to one election in which the major candidates were not matched. But more significant than the predominance of matched sibling positions among presidential candidates is the hypothesis that the sibling position of the president and the political *Zeitgeist* vary concordantly. There would inevitably be some elections in which the president-elect is of a different sibling position than the incumbent. A good example of this state of affairs is the election of 1828 when Andrew Jackson, a third-born son (MMM3) (with whose election it has appropriately been remarked the flood gates of democracy were opened) defeated John Quincy Adams, a first-born son (FM2FMM). As we have seen, Jackson's election marked the end of an unbroken succession of first-born sons covering a span of

twenty-eight years and inaugurated a period of similar length domi-
nated by second-and third-born sons. Another example of an unmistakable shift in both the sibling position of a president and the *Zeitgeist* was
the election of first-born Polk in 1844. A more recent shift occured in
1980 when last-born Reagan won the election over first-born Carter
who was the incumbent.

The matching of candidates may also be considered in terms of other
aspects of the family constellations such as family size, ratio of brothers
and sisters, and the ordinal position and sex of siblings just surrounding
the subject. All these ways of matching show a considerable degree of
concordance.

From the foregoing it is apparent that we have plunged into the truly
difficult question of how and where in the electoral process the
correlation between political *Zeitgeist* and the president's sibling position is achieved. Sometimes that decision is made by the voters; more
often than not, however, it is made somewhere else prior to election
day. Some further understanding of this issue may be provided by a
closer look at what actually occurs in critical election periods. Let us
begin with one of the most memorable conventions in this country's
history, the Republican convention of 1860. Roseboom, in his *A History
of Presidential Elections* has captured a not uncommon reaction to that
convention:

> To the believers in the hand of Providence in American history, the
> Chicago nomination must afford an amazing example of its myster-
> ious way. Midnight conferences of liquor-stimulated politicians,
> deals for jobs, local leaders pulling wires to save their state tickets,
> petty malice, and personal jealousies – a strange compound and the
> man of destiny emerges.
>
> (Roseboom 1957: 180)

Before proceeding, let us return briefly to our historical survey of the
period from 1828 to 1860 to refresh our memory as to the political
climate. What is of highest interest, of course, are the signs of a
continual escalation of the dispute over slavery. A signal event was the
establishment in 1831, by William Lloyd Garrison, of the *Liberator*, with
its editorial policy advocating the unconditional abolition of slavery. In
short order followed the Underground Railroad of 1838, the rules of
Congress against anti-slavery petitions in 1838–9, the 1850 Compromise, the Kansas-Nebraska Act of 1854, the Dred Scott decision of
1857[2], and in 1859 John Brown's famous raid on Harper's Ferry[3]. This

then was the political climate in which the Republican delegates convened in Chicago in 1860.

When the convention opened, Seward was the leading contender, with Abraham Lincoln a close second. Earlier in the year Seward had been far and away the favourite, but in the months just before the convention Lincoln's star had risen rapidly, largely as a consequence of his famous Cooper Union speech. In the final analysis, however, most observers agree (Roseboom 1957; King 1960) that the whirlwind campaign conducted at the convention by Lincoln's manager, William Winter David, must be given a fair share of the credit for toppling Seward and swinging the convention to Lincoln. For our purposes it should be noted that, of all the leading nominees at the convention, Lincoln alone was an only son (**FM2**); Seward was a third son, with the other potential candidates likewise being younger sons.

Another factor to be considered in Lincoln's selection by the Republican delegates is the fact that he had originally gained national fame in his debates with Stephen Douglas which Lincoln was generally conceded to have won (although he subsequently lost the Illinois Senatorial race). Moreover, Douglas, who had long been actively seeking the Democratic Party nomination, seemed assured of success in 1860. Such, of course, turned out to be the case, although not without some slight hitches. When the Democratic Party convened in the south, the delegates became deadlocked in the selection of a candidate and split into two factions, one of which met in Baltimore and nominated Douglas, while the other remained in the South and nominated John Cabell Breckenridge. Like Lincoln, (**FM2**), both Douglas (**FM2**) and Breckenridge (**M1FFF**) were only sons; as we see, Douglas was of exactly the same sibling position as Lincoln, both having a single older sister. Thus, in that decisive election year in which the nation anxiously faced the threat of secession, the slate of presidential candidates presented to the electorate made certain that, no matter what party won the election, the presidency would be held by a man who was an only son.

From the above we might draw the conclusion that there is an increased proportion of candidates of the appropriate sibling position in critical elections. Such a trend is clearly evident in the data of Table 4.3, where the percentage of first-born and only-son candidates is compared with the percentage of younger-son candidates for the five elections preceding and including the Civil War (1852–68) and the First World War (1904–20), and for a similar number of elections just prior to these crisis periods, namely, 1832–48 and 1884–1900. These data

Table 4.3 Birth order (as son) of presidential nominees during periods of confrontation and accommodation

Birth order (as son)	Periods of confrontation				Periods of accommodation			
	1852–68		1904–20		1832–48		1884–00	
	N	%	N	%	N	%	N	%
Only or first-born son	26	55	29	66	7	22	14	36
Younger son	21	45	15	34	25	78	25	64
Total.	47	100	44	100	32	100	39	100

suggest that the selection of a candidate of a sibling position concordant with the temper of the time is statistically more probable ($X^2 = 7.43$, $p <$ .01 for comparison of the Civil War crisis and less critical periods; $X^2 =$ 6.30, $p < .05$ for comparison of the First World War crisis and less critical periods) just on the basis of the greater availability of appropriate candidates.

It could be argued that there must occur at some stage in the political process a mutual responsiveness between candidates of the appropriate sibling position and some segment of the population to account for the results which we find. Hence, one would expect to encounter in critical elections candidates of the appropriate sibling position in contention for some period of time before the election. Such was the case in 1860. Lincoln and Douglas, as we know, had been rivals. In 1850, they contested for the USA Senate in Illinois. Their widely-publicized debates propelled them both to national attention. John Cabell Breckenridge had also attained national exposure in 1856 as the vice-presidential running mate of Buchanan.

In concluding this discussion of the election of 1860, it should be noted that in the Civil War an example of a third type of political *Zeitgeist* and leadership style has been identified. This type of political situation involves a threatened breakdown in major functions of society due either to unresolved tensions among divergent factions as in the Civil War or, as we shall see later on, through a failure to meet fundamental social needs. Among USA presidents the correlated sibling position for this political situation appears to be the only son or only child.[4]

Discussion

So far we have identified three types of political *Zeitgeist*, each implying a particular type of leadership. The first type is characterized by expansive territorial aims and/or confrontations which frequently lead to military conflict; the second may also lead to military conflict, but it has tended to be more domestically oriented,[5] preoccupied with adjustments of power among different factions such as business, labour, political parties; and the third involves a threatened breakdown of major functions of a society due either to unresolved tensions among divergent factions or through a failure to meet fundamental social needs. As we have seen, the leaders are in the first case first-borns, in the second case younger sons, and in the third case only sons or only children.

There is one type of political situation which may be clearly distinguished from the three already identified. I refer, of course, to revolution. It is obvious why this study has so far failed to turn up revolutionary leaders, since it has been confined to governments which have been able to maintain national unity. The situation in the data so far which approached revolution was the American Civil War. In the original analysis I approached that struggle from the standpoint of the federal government. If we now turn our attention to the Confederacy we find a different type of leadership. The president chosen by the rebellious southern states was Jefferson Davis, a long-time advocate in the USA Senate of the rights of the individual states to resolve for themselves such domestic issues as slavery. Davis was a last-born son, the youngest of ten children (MMMFMFFFFM10). Is this a characteristic sibling position for revolutionary leaders? A survey shows that in many cases they are last-born children, e.g. Sun Yat-Sen (MMM3), Gandhi (MFMM4), Bolivar (FFMM4). Others such as Lenin (FMM3FFM), Castro (FMM3MF), Garibaldi (MM2MMF), Ho Chi Minh (FMM3M), Aquino (MFFF4MF) and Joan of Arc (MMFF4M) although not last-borns, are younger sons or younger daughters.

It is difficult to determine whether the American and French revolutions fit this pattern. One reason is that in neither of these cases did one person emerge early on as the single undisputed leader. However, in America it was certainly Samuel Adams (a younger son) in the New England colonies who organized the Sons of Liberty, who inspired the initial acts of rebellion, and who was instrumental in organizing the Continental Congress, and who presided at its meetings. And of course George Washington (MMFM4FMMF) became the commanding general of the army. In the southern colonies, it was Patrick Henry (**MM2FFFFFF**) who first gave clear expression to the cry for liberty.[6] In France, the original revolutionary impulse was eventually co-opted in a military coup led by Napoleon (**MM2MFMFFM**), the most famous general of the revolution. As we see, each of these leaders was a younger son.

The identification of this fourth type of political *Zeitgeist* poses some interesting questions. With respect to sibling position, the leadership type in revolution often seems to be the same as in the domestically-oriented political situation. Can these be the same men and women? At first that seems unlikely, since a major distinguishing feature of revolution is aggression and usually armed conflict, whereas a hallmark of the domestically-oriented era seems to be the absence of confrontation and military engagements. But perhaps we are overlooking more important characteristics of revolutionary periods. First, it may not be true that revolution implies military engagement. Gandhi, for one, has demonstrated the possibility that a resolute, one-sided refusal to resort to arms may have revolutionary effects. Also we should note that Jefferson Davis, the pre-revolutionary leader, was merely one among many advocates of change. If we examine the lives of revolutionary leaders before their emergence as prime movers in a revolution, we note that they have engaged for many years in advocacy of the causes they support. It is primarily the nature of the government under which such revolutionary leaders live which determines the extent to which they are free to hold office and to seek change through the establishment. Thus, up until the time at which it is no longer possible for a dialogue to continue between divergent factions, there is probably no marked distinction between advocates and potential revolutionaries (cf Gipson 1962).

Issues like the foregoing, which we have barely touched upon, make us aware of the many perplexing questions raised by these findings. For example, while we have cleared away some of the underbrush, we have still left largely untouched such basic problems as just how the selective matching of sibling position and *Zeitgeist* may occur at various levels of the electoral process, quite without any awareness on the part of the participants of the facts we have investigated here. Before pushing further into these difficult questions, I compared these findings to a similar investigation of the British political system. It should be evident to the reader by now that in our discussion of the American data, we recapitulated history at times. This procedure seemed desirable in order to revive acquaintance with some of the events of political history, particularly with the transitions from one period to another. The analysis of British prime ministers will include less of a guided tour of British history. However, in view of the unique characteristics of the British mode of government, such an analysis illuminates the interactions among political leaders during periods of transition.

THE BRITISH PRIME MINISTERS

The choice of the British political system as a source of validating data was natural on several counts. The British prime minister is a close analogue to the USA president. He or she is the leader of his/her political party; he or she is the head of government and, like the American president, is given the responsibility for forming a cabinet. Second, although the British and American electoral processes differ in important details, they both require popular election of their heads of government. The prime minister is not, as is the president, elected directly by all the people. However, in a general election, the prime minister is known throughout the country and is the spokesperson for his/her party's platform. In earlier years the choice of prime minister depended upon a number of factors. At one time the monarch had the power to actively intervene in the selection, as did the House of Lords. But, nowadays, although the monarch nominally requests the prime minister to form a government, there is no question but that the leader of a political party will ordinarily become prime minister when that party has a majority in the House of Commons. The House of Lords no longer has a say in the matter nor can a member of the House of Lords become prime minister (cf Mathiot 1967).

A comparison of the relative powers and responsibilities of the British prime minister and the American president shows that they are very similar. Historically, the office of president and the office of prime minister have gradually acquired greater and greater powers. If there is anything that students of government agree about, it is the increasing concentration of power in the hands of the USA president and the British prime minister (see, for example, Berkeley 1968).

Most students of British government also agree that the first true prime minister was Robert Walpole. As Berkeley puts it: 'Walpole virtually created the office of prime minister and made possible the evolution of the modern system of ministerial responsibility' (1968: 21). However, following Walpole's thirty-year tenure as prime minister, there was a period of some thirty-two years in which no further progress was made in the development of the office of prime minister, primarily because of internal party division and the fact that George III had no intention of allowing authority to pass into the hands of his ministers. According to Berkeley, not until William Pitt the Younger became prime minister in 1783 was there any further substantial development in the powers of the office. In view of this, as well as the less accurate data available in the earlier years, the principal emphasis in this chapter will be the time between 1783 and 1963 or, in other words, from Prime Minister William Pitt the Younger to Prime Minister Macmillan. Table 4.4, however, covers the years up to 1991.

Results

The comparisons over time presented in Table 4.4 show that like American presidents, prime ministers of the same or closely-related sibling positions (that is, first-born sons and only sons as contrasted with younger sons) follow each other into office for certain periods of time. Naturally, due to the nature of the British political system, ministers are replaced more frequently than are USA presidents. Basically, the shifts from one prime minister to another follow the same patterns as for the American presidents. For example the third-born son Walpole's reign of 'peace, ease and freedom' (Bingham 1920) led on through a succession of second-born sons to end finally with a first-born son during the stormy period of the American revolution. A similar sequence of ministers is seen during the period of the French Revolution and the subsequent wars with Napoleon and First and Second World Wars.

With respect to the correlation between sibling positions of British prime ministers and the political *Zeitgeist*, periods of British history have been classified in terms of the four types of political *Zeitgeist* previously identified, using as criteria the presence or absence of war or peace for types one and two respectively, severe economic depression and threatened breakdown of important social functions for type three, and open, prolonged civil conflict for type four. The worst international crises faced by the British between 1783 and 1963 were the Napoleonic Wars (particularly 1806–15) and the First and Second World Wars. Other less serious conflicts were the War of 1812, the Crimean War of 1854, the Indian Mutiny of 1857, the Afghan and Zulu Wars of 1874–80, and the Boer War of 1899–1902. The less critical periods which were devoted extensively to internal affairs were 1784–1801, 1828–52, 1868–74, 1880–95, 1905–14, and 1945–63. These constitute types one and two. Type three is represented by the period

1924–37 which included the long period of labour unrestculminating in the General Strike of 1925 and the severe economic stress of the world-wide depression. The struggle for Indian independence led by Gandhi (MFMM4) may be considered representative of type four.

The prime ministers in the crisis periods were Liverpool (M1[14 years]MF),[7] Palmerston (M1FMF)*, Disraeli (FM2MM), Salisbury (MFFM4M), Lloyd George (FM2M) and Churchill (M1M). Among these six prime ministers there were five first-born sons of whom three were also first-born children. During the periods of disengagement and mediation, we find Pitt (FMFM4M), Wellington (MMFM4MM), Melbourne (MM2MMF), Grey (M1MMMMF), Peel (FFM3MMFFMMMF), Russell (MMM3MMMMMMMFFF), Gladstone (MMMFM5F), Salisbury (MFFM4M), Rosebery (FFM3M), Campbell-Bannerman (FMFM4), Asquith (MM2FF), Attlee (MMFFFMM7M), Churchill (M1M), Eden (FMMM4M), and Macmillan (MMM3). Eleven of these fifteen prime ministers were younger sons. Using a Fisher exact probability test, a comparison of first-born sons with younger sons in crisis and less critical periods is statistically significant at the .05 level, confirming the similar finding in the sample of USA presidents. Type three prime ministers or those leading the country through periods of severe economic depression were only children, Baldwin (M1) and MacDonald (M1). Type four, the revolutionary leader is represented by Gandhi (MFMM4) who is not, of course, a prime minister. (We could also refer back to the Civil War of 1642 when King Charles I was deposed and an early attempt at parliamentary government was instituted. The leader of that revolution was Oliver Cromwell, a younger son.)

As I suggested earlier, the workings of the British political system provide an opportunity to observe more directly the forces at work which determine shifts in political power from one sibling position to another. In this regard, Lord Beaverbrook's *Politicians and the War* (1926) furnishes us with an insider's account of Herbert Henry Asquith's early First World War ministry and its transformation to a coalition ministry under David Lloyd George. Asquith, as Campbell-Bannerman's first lieutenant, inherited the ministry at Campbell-Bannerman's death in 1908. In 1914 war broke out, and a year later, Asquith was forced to reconstruct the ministry on a coalition basis. But this did not relieve the growing tensions over the conduct of the war, either in the Cabinet or in the House of Commons. These tensions became focused around two Cabinet members, first Winston Churchill (M1M) and then Lloyd George (FM2M). The problem that Asquith (MM2FF) found with each

Table 4.4 Sibling position (as son or daughter) of British prime ministers (1783–1991)

Time line	Last-born	Middle	First-born	Only	Only ch.	Years in office & sibling position
1783		O				1783–1801, W. PITT (FMFM**4M**)
1785		O				
		O				
		O				
		O				
		O				
1795		O				
		O				
		O	O			1801–4, ADDINGTON (**M1** & younger brothers)
		O	O			1804–6, W. PITT (FMFM**4M**)
		O				1806–7, GRENVILLE (MMM**3FFFFF**)
1805	O		O			1807–9, PORTLAND (**M1**FFM)
	O				O	1809–12, PERCEVAL (MMMFFMM**7FFFFF**)
	O				O	1812–27, LIVERPOOL (**M1**[14 YEARS]MF)
					O	
1815					O	
					O	
					O	
					O	
					O	
1825					O	
	O	O		O	O	1827, CANNING (only son); GODERICH (last son)
	O	O	O			1828–30, WELLINGTON (MMFM**4MM**)
		O	O			1830–34, GREY (**M1MMMMF**)*

1834, MELBOURNE; PEEL

1835–41, MELBOURNE (MM2MMF)

1841–46, PEEL (FFM3MMFFMMMF)

1846–52, RUSSELL (MMM3MMMMMMMFFF)*

DERBY (M1MMFFFF); 1852–5, Aberdeen (M1MMMMF)*

1855–58, PALMERSTON (M1FMF)*

1858, DISRAELI (FM2MM)

1859–65, PALMERSTON (M1FMF)*

1865, RUSSELL (MMM3MMMMMMMFFF)*

1866–68, DERBY (M1MMFFFF)*

1868, DISRAELI; 1868–74, GLADSTONE (MMMFM5F)

1874–80, DISRAELI (FM2MM)

1880–85, GLADSTONE (MMMFM5F)

1885, SALISBURY (MFFM4M)

1886, GLADSTONE 1886–92, SALISBURY

1835

1845

1855

1865

1875

1885

Table 4.4 Continued

Time line	Last-born	Middle	First-born	Only	Only ch.	Years in office & sibling position
		O				1892–94, GLADSTONE (MMMF**M**5F)
		O	O			1894, ROSEBERY (FF**M**3M)
1896		O				1895–1902, SALISBURY (MFF**M**4M)
		O	O			1902–05, BALFOUR (FF**M**3MFMMM)
		O	O			
1905	O		O			1905–08, CAMPBELL-BANNERMAN (FMF**M**4)
	O					1908–16, ASQUITH (M**M**2FF)
	O					
	O					
1915	O		O			1916–22, LLOYD GEORGE (F**M**2M)
			O			
			O			
	O		O			1922, LAW (MMM**M**4F)
					O	1923–24, BALDWIN (**M**1)
1925					OO	1924, MACDONALD; 1924–29, BALDWIN
					O	
					O	1929–35, MACDONALD (**M**1)
					O	
					O	
1935					O	1935–37, BALDWIN (**M**1)
	O				O	1937–40, CHAMBERLAIN (FM**M**3FFF)
	O		O			1940–45, CHURCHILL (**M**1M)

1945

1945–51, ATTLEE (MMFFFMM**7**M)

1951–55, CHURCHILL (**M1**M)

1955

1955–57, EDEN (FMMM**4**M)
1957–63, MACMILLAN (MMM**3**)

1963–64, HOME (**M1**FMFM)
1965   1964–70, WILSON (**FM2**)

1970–74, HEATH (**M1**M)

1974–76, WILSON (**FM2**)
1975   1976–79, CALLAGHAN (**FM2**)

1979–90, THATCHER (**FF2**)

1985

1989–90   1990– MAJOR (**MFM3**)*
1991

time line	Last-born	Middle	First-born	Only	Only ch.

* An asterisk indicates that the order of brothers (M) and sisters (F) is in question.

of these men was the same; they were aggressive, impatient, ambitious for power, and interested in pressing the war effort more vigorously. Asquith managed to thrust the young Churchill out of the Cabinet, but Lloyd George soon gained ascendancy and in 1916 became prime minister. Here is Beaverbrook's account of how that occurred:

> People have sometimes talked and written as though his [Asquith's] downfall in December 1916 was a sudden, inexplicable catastrophe – or only to be explained as the result of a secret intrigue hastily engineered by unscrupulous rivals. Nothing could be further from the truth. Ever since the spring of 1915 the Premier had been engaged in knocking the props out from under him[self], or in watching them fall without replacing them . . . Why did not Asquith simply take up Lloyd George and make him his executive arm while retaining the titular authority? In this summer, the answer to the question is a simple one. Asquith would not promote Lloyd George for the same reason that he had come to distrust Churchill, even to the point of permitting his dismissal the year before. Asquith was the *man of peace in the war* – these ministers of nervous action fretted his very soul. He did not want them about him – always bustling and hurrying and driving. This tendency of his seems to have increased as the war went on.
>
> (Beaverbrook 1926: 23)

In this graphic description we can see portrayed at the personal level the struggle between second-born son Asquith (**MM2FF**) and first-born sons Churchill (**M1M**) and Lloyd George (**FM2M**) over the very issue which our hypothesis would predict, the conduct of a war. Obviously, Churchill's time came later in the Second World War when the British government once again backed into war under the leadership of a second-born son, Neville Chamberlain (**FMM3FFF**), only to switch almost immediately to Churchill's leadership as hostilities broke out and England itself was threatened.

Churchill's history is also illustrative of the issue we raised much earlier concerning the role the individual plays in effectuating his own destiny. Were it not for the Second World War, Churchill would most probably be remembered today as a politician of great promise who never quite realized his potential.[8] More than likely, political pundits would be explaining his failure as due in part, to the difficult traits in his personality such as overbearing ambition, egocentricity, and aggressiveness. Such criticisms would not be wide of the mark. However, once Churchill's star had risen, it would be these very same traits which would stand him in good stead. Then he was praised for his indomitable will, his bulldog courage, and his fierce vengeance.

Churchill's mercurial political career actually spanned some sixty years, many of which were spent in and out of the government, switching back and forth between political parties, often at odds with the leadership. For the ten-year period just prior to the Second World War he was deliberately kept out of the Cabinet, isolated, often ignored, a one-man political party unto himself. Throughout this period of his splendid isolation, Churchill was viewed as a Jeremiah, thundering his dire prophecies of death and destruction, lamenting England's lack of preparedness. Of course, as the war clouds gathered between 1936 and 1939, his prophecies began to be heard, and, almost miraculously, when war struck he became, at the age of 65 the only choice to lead England through the years of her greatest crisis (cf Taylor 1952).

NOTES

1 Both Zachary Taylor and William Henry Harrison died in office and were succeeded by vice-presidents Tyler and Fillmore. Our data do not include Tyler and Fillmore nor the other two vice-presidents, Andrew Johnson and Chester A. Arthur, who succeeded to office on the death of a president but who were not subsequently elected president themselves. In more recent years, Gerald Ford was appointed to the presidency but was not subsequently elected.

2 Dred Scott was a slave who sued for his freedom on the grounds that he had at one time lived in a free state. Although a lower court supported his petition, it was reversed by a higher court; in 1857 the Supreme Court took the position that as a slave, he was not a citizen and therefore did not have the right to sue. A major effect of the Dred Scott decision was that slaves who escaped to the north had no legal protection against slave catchers.

3 John Brown was a passionate abolitionist who did everything he could to help fugitive slaves escape to the north. In 1859 he captured the US arsenal at Harper's Ferry, but in the battle that followed he was taken prisoner, convicted of treason and was hanged. He inspired a glorious legend. Even today, people sing: 'John Brown's body lies a mouldering in the grave, but his soul goes marching on.'

4 The election of Franklin Delano Roosevelt (**M1**) during the Depression in 1932 is the other example of this category. Although there have been a number of only sons, (ex. Lincoln) Roosevelt was the first and, up to 1990, the sole only child to be elected president.

5 Although intermediate-born presidents have generally been engaged with the mediation of domestic factions, there is ever-increasing need for mediation and accommodation on an international level. Domestic issues are now completely interwoven with such wider concerns as arbitration of

differences among nations as well as the building of various partnerships and coalitions. With the United Nations, the development toward a United Europe, and an emerging vision of the world as a 'global village', concerns that used to be limited to the domestic realm now seem to include the larger 'family of nations'. An example of this is suggested by reports of George Bush's frequent use of the telephone to keep in touch with various world leaders.

6 George Washington (MMFM4FMMF) probably belongs here also, although his revolutionary role was always overshadowed by his unquestioned position as commanding general of the army.

7 Liverpool was fourteen years older than his younger brother which implies that he was as much an only child as a first-born child. But this fact only increased his fitness for leadership at this time, since as a consequence of the long-drawn-out crisis of the Napoleonic Wars, England faced near paralysis of its civil functions.

8 Two other leaders mentioned earlier in this regard were Abraham Lincoln and Franklin D. Roosevelt. Both were relative failures until their great opportunity arrived. Lincoln for the better part of his career was a relatively obscure lawyer and politician. Defeated for the US Senate in 1858, he was unexpectedly elected president two years later, just as the Civil War erupted. Roosevelt as a vice-presidential candidate in 1924 suffered a disastrous defeat. Not long afterwards he contracted polio and his political career seemed over. However, only a few years later, during the depths of the Depression, he was elected president.

Chapter 5

The world cycle of creative change

At this point we cross a threshold. It is essential that we now engage the study of political leadership at a new level of discourse. So far it has been shown that individual, family and society are entwined in ways which find expression in the sibling positions of political leaders. Through more than 200 years of history in two nations, the USA and Great Britain, a consistent pattern has been traced which shows a congruence between leaders who are of particular sibling positions and corresponding shifts in the social-political *Zeitgeist*. This process has gone on, and goes on at this very time. It seems to occur without any awareness on the part of the participants, and, of course, without any notion of the significance of the sibling position in the determination of leadership qualities. At the time I concluded my original study of leaders, this in itself seemed to me to be extraordinary. It still does. At the same time, however, I became aware of a niggling question: is this round of presidents and prime ministers just that, a great merry-go-round that revolves eternally through the same old problems of the socio-political situation, and the vagaries of the *Zeitgeist*? After some period of not knowing I realized that the answer to this question lay in the deeper and far more complex question of change itself, creative change. What appears at first to be a merry-go-round, is from this new perspective, a spiral. I shall now take up what I have come to speak of as the 'world cycle of creative change'.

A FOURFOLD CREATIVE CYCLE

By the world cycle of creative change I mean a fourfold creative process through which any and every great innovation in any field of endeavour appears to proceed. This fourfold creative process is initiated by a younger son or daughter, frequently a last-born son or daughter. The idea proposed by the younger son or daughter is then taken up, explored and its dimensions taken, by one or more first-born sons or daughters. Following, and often overlapping with the foregoing stage, is that of the work of intermediate-borns, who usually produce a further development from the original idea which tends toward a mediation of the original idea and a first-born's extension of that idea, or another development based upon the work of a first-born. The last stage is that of the only child, or only son or daughter, who produces a final synthesis of the original idea, with the first-born's extension of the idea. This final synthesis also incorporates the contribution of the intermediate-born.

Dynamically the cycle begins with an individual who breaks with tradition; the current view of things is in error; the emperor wears no clothes. Basically it is a cry of freedom from constraint, a new world view is acclaimed, be it political-social, religious, philosophic-scientific, or aesthetic. The measure of this new world is then taken by one or two experts in the field, who affirm and extend the idea. Soon controversy arises and the mediators and accommodaters wrestle with the issues and reach some kind of temporary accommodation. In the process divergent views are clarified. Then an individual appears who has a grasp of the whole situation and who creates a synthesis of the essential elements – the new world is now a reality. This does not lead to immediate acceptance. For some time the synthesis is tested and criticized, but sooner or later it becomes acknowledged as the accepted world-view for that time. In the course of my exploration it soon became apparent that this cycle of creativity takes place in every field of endeavour.

Before proceeding further, I wish to make it unmistakably clear that this is not an attempt to explain creativity *per se*. Creativity involves a mysterious interweaving of conscious and unconscious factors. Its ultimate source is at present beyond human comprehension, and perhaps will always remain so. As Jung puts it in describing his own experience, creativity seizes upon an individual like a daemon, and has its way with the individual's life.

I have had much trouble getting along with my ideas. There was a daemon in me, and in the end its presence proved decisive. It overpowered me . . . I was in the grip of the daemon. I could never stop at anything once attained. I had to hasten on, to catch up with my vision.

(Jung 1961: 356)

What we are discussing at the moment, then, is the *form* that creativity takes in an individual, and, the relationship of the individual's contribution to the cycle of creative change in the world at large.

THE AMERICAN REVOLUTION

Take, for example, the founding of the American republic. A surprisingly large number of outstanding individuals emerged in the early revolutionary phase – Samuel Adams (second-born son), John Adams (**M1MM**), Thomas Jefferson (**FFM3FFFFM**), George Washington (**MMFM4FMMF**), Benjamin Franklin (**FMFMFMMFMFMMM13FF**), Tom Paine (**M1**) – to mention the most pre-eminent. This group of leaders very closely represents individuals of each of the basic sibling positions. Is this just coincidence? I think not. In what follows I hope to show that this is to be expected in any and every field of endeavour.

The unfolding of creative change in all its manifold aspects appears to require the contributions of individuals of genius who embody the viewpoints inherent in the four basic sibling positions. The underlying causality, I have suggested, must lie in the unique world-views that are inherent in each of the sibling positions: The last born is the rebel, the doubter, the iconoclast, finely tuned to the winds of change; the intermediate-born is also frequently a rebel but because of the vantage point between older and younger, a master of accommodation and mediation; the first-born is the preserver, the extender and developer, the carrier of tradition; and the only child is the synthesizer, the carrier of the opposites being both first and last. (The only son or daughter share in the characteristics of the only child, more so as the age-spacing between siblings increases.)

But this confluence of ideas does not *alone* account for creative change. There is another fundamental ordering factor inherent in the cycle of creativity. This other factor only becomes apparent when we take the long view of history. Turning again to the early revolutionary period in America with this historical perspective in mind, we find that it was younger son, Samuel Adams, who set the revolution in motion. Gradually he drew others into the process; his cousin John Adams early on, and others soon joined him. Over a period of years of constant planning, of goading reluctant participants, and unflagging persistence, Samuel Adams forged a spirited group of rebels, The Sons of Liberty; he inspired the initial acts of rebellion; pressed for the first Continental Congress and so on. In the southern colonies his counterpart was Patrick Henry (**MM2FFFFFF**) who fired the revolt with his passionate cry for freedom: 'Give me liberty or give me death!'

As in this case of the American revolution, it will become clear as we proceed that the cycle of creative change appears invariably to be given its original impetus by an individual who is a younger child, most frequently a second son or daughter, often a last-born. These are the original 'change-makers' who set the cycle in motion. In Greek mythology they are such as Hermes (FM**M2**) stealing cattle from his elder brother Apollo, and bartering with his new invention the lyre when caught; and the young Zeus (FFFMM**M6**)[1] killing his father and releasing his siblings; and younger son Dionysus, introducing revolutionary religious ideas; and the titan Prometheus (**MM2**M) who stole fire from the gods and gave it to humans. One and all these gods and heroes are rebels.

It is startling to realize that amongst humans these original 'change-makers' may set in motion a cycle of development that requires hundreds of years for its realization.[2] Moreover, this cycle ordinarily comes to fruition through the cumulative innovations of different types of 'change-makers', those who represent the other three basic sibling positions: the first-born, intermediate-born and the only child, or only son/daughter. The Copernican revolution is an extraordinary case in point.

THE COPERNICAN CYCLE

In a seminal article published in *Science*, Thomas S. Kuhn (1962) outlined a theory of the structure of scientific revolutions. He has subsequently revised and enlarged the scope of his original ideas in a number of publications. The essence of his argument is that the progress of scientific theory is in practice far different from the way it is often presented after the fact. Central to his argument is the concept of paradigm or exemplar, which represents the more-or-less agreed-upon view of any specific scientific problem at any particular time. Kuhn's prime example is the Copernican revolution that overthrew the previous Ptolemaic paradigm of the cosmos and set in motion a succession of developments by Kepler, Galileo, Huygens, Descartes, Borelli, and others. The culmination of the Copernican revolution was a new synthesis worked out by Newton,[3] which subsequently became the new paradigm, the accepted view of physics, until it was challenged by new developments in relativity and in quantum mechanics by Einstein, Planck and others.

The setting for such a revolution is, according to Kuhn, a state of growing crisis which may be seen as a loss of faith in the adequacy of the currently-accepted paradigmatic theory. This is precisely the state of affairs with respect to the Ptolemaic theory when Copernicus was moved to publish his new theory.

> An honest appraisal of contemporary astronomy, says Copernicus, shows that the earth-centered approach to the problem of the planets is hopeless. The traditional techniques of Ptolemaic astronomy have not and will not solve that problem; instead they have produced a Monster; there must, he concludes, be a fundamental error in the basic concepts of traditional planetary astronomy. For the first time a technically competent astronomer had rejected the time-honored scientific tradition for reasons internal to his science, and this professional awareness of technical fallacy inaugurated the Copernican Revolution.
>
> (Kuhn 1957: 139)

Copernicus had discovered for himself that the Ptolemaic system was riddled with errors of prediction and was incapable of determining the length of the seasonal year. He further discovered that by his calculations these difficulties could be overcome although the resulting cosmology would result in a surprising alteration in our conception of the place and movement of the planet earth. This was the revolutionary notion contained in his proposals which he well understood and which prompted him to alert his readers particularly the Pope in the very first sentence of the prefatory letter that he prefixed to the *De Revolutionibus*.

> I may well presume, most Holy Father, that certain people, as soon as they hear that . . . I ascribe movement to the earthly globe, will cry out that, holding such views, I should at once be hissed off the stage.
>
> (Copernicus, in Kuhn 1957: 137)

Copernicus was a cautious man who put off publication of his book; it appeared when he was on his death-bed. When his ideas did become available, there was neither widespread acceptance nor rapid change. Instead, a process of development and controversy ensued. The stages of this process are thoroughly documented in the works of Kuhn (1957), Koyre (1965) and others. What emerges from these historical studies is a view of scientific change which is at odds with the textbook model that knowledge is accumulated through an orderly acceptance of the better solution. In Kuhn's terms it is more like a revolution that leads to the development of opposing camps which fight for their views and in the process produce the elements of an emerging solution which is finally accomplished through a major synthesis such as Newton's. The synthesis does not achieve immediate acceptance, but in turn is submitted to testing and questioning until finally it becomes the new, 'accepted view'.

Without a doubt Kuhn's view of the cyclical process of the Copernican revolution is very like the cycle of creative change that I have discussed above. It remains to be seen, however, if the sibling positions of the key figures fit the cycle. The cycle began with last-born Copernicus (**MFFM4**) and his revolutionary assertion that the earth moves around the sun. It was followed by first-born Kepler (**M1MFM**) and his discoveries of the laws of movement of the planets in their orbits, and by first-born Galileo (**M1MMFFF**) with his telescope and his look at the moon, as well as his further studies of the laws of motion. The concepts were developed further by others, notably intermediate-born Huygens (**MM2MMF**) with his understanding of the interlocked identity of centrifugal-centripetal force. These ideas were disputed by last-born Descartes (**MFM3**) and his followers, but finally all of these efforts were brought together in only child Newton's (**M1**) great synthesis which laid the groundwork for all of the developments of physics for many years. (I should note here that Kuhn, of course, was not aware of the implications of sibling position for the cycle of creative change.)

TOWARD 'FREEDOM AND JUSTICE FOR ALL'

What conclusions can we draw from this discussion of the Copernican revolution? It seems to confirm our expectations, but science and politics are worlds apart. Should we expect to find a similar cycle of creative change in the study of political leaders? What are the criteria against which change is measured? Science is an endeavour that seems to have an objective and definable cycle of creativity. It is motivated by the ideal of the *true*, and its criteria are defined as the correspondence of theory with reality. Leaving aside for the moment philosophical quarrels about the definition of reality; in science, theory must correspond with observation and measurement.

In contrast to science, what are the criteria against which change in the socio-political world can be evaluated? What are the goals of society as reflected by political leaders? Progress in the socio-political sphere is presumably motivated by the ideal of the *good*, the Utopian community, measured as an increase in the rights of the individual fostered by a government that attempts to maximize the equilibration of freedom and co-operation. The free and responsible citizen is an ideal toward which enlightened and forward-looking members of society strive.

Looking back now over the history of the United States with these thoughts in mind, we see that the road toward a society which can govern itself in accord with the principles of freedom and justice for all appears to be a long and rocky one. The United States came into being through a revolution which espoused high principles and which sought to embody those principles in a new form of constitutional government. The Constitution and the Bill of Rights are documents of unusual quality which immensely improved the situation of the ordinary citizen, even though unresolved issues still remained. The subsequent two hundred and some years have witnessed the struggle of fallible humans as they have sought to realize the high principles embodied in those documents. The question then is whether we can discern a cycle of creative change or not?

The findings of the political leadership study (see Chapters 3 and 4) offer a clue in the alternating cycles of leaders. For example, in the early years of the new republic there was a period of some forty years (1789–1828), beginning with the election of George Washington, during which the great majority of the presidents were first-born sons. This sequence was followed by a period of near equal length (1828–64), inaugurated by the election of Andrew Jackson, in which the presidents were primarily a mixture of intermediate-born or last-born sons. The climax of this period was the election of only son Abraham Lincoln, and the outbreak of Civil War in 1860 (see Table 4.1). This total progression covers seventy-two years. What was going on during these two periods?

The first period between 1789 and 1828 reflects efforts to consolidate the results of the revolution and to deal with a growing sense of nationalism. The presidents elected in this period were, in order of election: George Washington (MMFM4FMMF), John Adams (**M1MM**), Thomas Jefferson (FFM3FFFFM), James Madison (**M1MM FMFFMMM**), James Monroe (**M1MMMF**) and John Quincy Adams (**FM2FMM**). Three of these presidents were first-borns in their families; Thomas Jefferson and John Quincy Adams are both first-born sons.

The election of last-born Andrew Jackson (**MMM3**) in 1828 brought a dramatic change of a near revolutionary nature. With his election it was aptly observed that the floodgates of democracy were flung open. The interests of the people and the leadership swung to internal affairs, to monetary issues, and expansion westward. The presidents during the years 1828–56 were predominantly intermediate-born and last-born: Jackson (MMM3), Van Buren (MFMFFM6MM), Harrison (FFMF MFM7), Taylor (MMM3MFMMFF) and Pierce (FMFMFMM7FM). There was one exception to this trend when the expansion to the west led to demands for the annexation of Texas and Oregon. To accomplish this mission first-born Polk (M1FFMMMMFFMM) was elected in 1844.

During this period the issue of slavery became an all absorbing source of contention in Congress and throughout society. The election of Abraham Lincoln (FM2) in 1860 and the outbreak of the Civil War faced the republic with its greatest conflict since the revolution. Would the country hold together as 'one union', or would it split into two separate nations? Lincoln's strong, compassionate leadership, and his unshaken conviction that the 'union' must survive, were major factors in the outcome of that struggle. The slaves were freed and slavery was abolished. It would appear that only son Lincoln's role in holding the union together represents the stage of synthesis. Let us look at another development before we discuss further that question.

Take, for example, the depression of the late 1920s and the 1930s. That great convulsion in the American society brought only child Franklin Delano Roosevelt (M1) to the presidency and led to fundamental changes in the relationship between the federal government and the people. The social security legislation is perhaps the symbol of what those changes represented, namely a shift towards a new sense of responsibility for the welfare of the people by the Congress and the president. But the depression was not the deeper cause of that change; it was only the catalyst that put into action ideas that had been stirring for some time. We might look back to the administration of Andrew Jackson (MMM3) for one of the earlier signs of the need for change in monetary policy and attention to the economic needs of the struggling individual. This country is right now on the verge of another of those convulsions as the plight of the poor and the homeless becomes increasingly apparent. The solutions have not yet been found to the problems that were only partially dealt with during the 1930s.

Does the foregoing very brief review of the sequence of historical events correspond with the cycle of leaders of the expected sibling positions? I believe the answer is, yes.

To recapitulate: The revolution was set in motion through the

Copernican-like revolt inspired above all by younger son Samuel Adams (second-born son), and by Patrick Henry (**MM2FFFFFF**). These original 'change-makers' were followed by the Keplerian-Galilean confirmation and extension of first-born sons: John Adams (**M1MM**), Thomas Jefferson (**FFM3FFFFM**), James Madison (**M1MMFMFFMMM**) and James Monroe (**M1MMMF**), who consolidated and extended the principles and the boundaries of the new republic. Then came a period of Huygenian-Descartean mediation and dissent of intermediate-borns and last-borns: Andrew Jackson (**MMM3**), Martin Van Buren (**MFMFFM6MM**), William Henry Harrison (**FFMFMFM7**), Zachary Taylor (**MMM3MFMMFF**) and Franklin Pierce (**FMFMFMM7FM**), who struggled with many internal social issues, but who could not resolve the conflict over slavery – the Achilles heel of the original revolution. The southern states rebelled and attempted to secede from the union under the leadership of Jefferson Davis (**MMMFMFFFFM10**). Only son Lincoln (**FM2**), president during this divisive crisis can be seen to have created the Newtonian synthesis which held the union together.

Subsequent history reveals similar trends. The USA gradually became a world power under first-born sons Theodore Roosevelt (**FM2MF**) and Woodrow Wilson (**FFFM3M**), and sought to influence world policy. Neglected, however, was the domestic situation. The Russian revolution of 1917 brought Lenin to power and militant communism began to worry Europe, particularly when it became apparent that the economies of all the major powers of Europe as well as the USA were seriously eroding. In the USA, the First World War was followed by a series of what might be called caretaker presidents: Harding (**M1FFFMFMF**), Coolidge (**M1F**), and, as the world economic situation worsened, Hoover (**MM2F**), who was elected president, largely on the basis of his success in aiding the battle-torn countries of Europe after the First World War. However, Hoover's conservative policies only worsened conditions in the USA. By the end of his period in office the country was in the throes of the worst depression it had ever experienced. Roosevelt (**M1**) was elected in 1932 and remained in office until his death in 1944. His vigorous attack on the domestic problems, his openness to new solutions, and his experimental approach began slowly to turn around the widespread despair throughout the country. It was no doubt Roosevelt's ebullient personality and his reaching out to the whole country through use of the radio that bolstered confidence as much as any of the changes he sought to make. In this regard there can be little doubt that his expression of such confidence in the face of his own sad loss of the use of his legs through poliomyelitis was also an inspiration. In any case he managed to maintain a balance between the opposing elements of the political spectrum and to achieve a considerable degree of synthesis of the divergent points of view which set the course for the country until very recently. The social security legislation can be seen as a hallmark of his presidency.

From this brief retrospective view of crucial elements of the history of the United States it seems that there is evidence of a spiral movement of events which has gradually improved the laws that support the rights and the welfare of the individual citizen. This is equally true in Britain and some other countries as well. The recent collapse of communist dictatorship in the Soviet Union and the turn toward democracy of the satellite countries of Poland, East Germany, Czechoslovakia, Hungary and Romania is further evidence of a world-wide struggle for freedom of thought and the protection of human rights. In other countries such as Iran, Iraq, Syria and others, much less has been accomplished. Yet in South Africa an extraordinary effort is being made to dismantle apartheid and create a democratic society. The deep-lying spiritual principle which motivates this cycle of change is the ideal of the good, of a Utopian community rooted in a common morality. It is also evident, however, that the future of this high ideal is problematical.

We can conclude that the central dynamic of the cycle of creative change as it is manifest in political leadership is the underlying struggle for human rights in the face of oppression. The free and responsible citizen is an ideal toward which enlightened and forward-looking members of society strive. Opposed to this striving is contempt for the alien, and contempt for alien gods. As far back as Homer's *Iliad*, war has been cast as a struggle between opposing gods. No doubt, the affect contempt will continue to fuel divisiveness and warfare until the human race can come together as one world-wide community. Whether this goal can be reached before we destroy ourselves with our atomic arsenal, remains to be seen. The thunderbolts of Zeus are now in human hands.

Although we are discussing a creative cycle of development, I am not suggesting that progress is inevitable, particularly in the alternation of political crises. There is no certainty that the good will of enough individuals will prevail at any moment in history. On the whole, history is a discouraging story of small successes and large failures. Nevertheless, it is possible to discern that the human spirit remains wedded to the ideal of a Utopian community with freedom and justice for all. The spirit works its way with individuals who are seized by that ideal. Equally true is the fact that others are called to an opposing view which is based in contempt for the 'alien', and 'alien' views, and which stresses hierarchical principles of the superiority of one nation or people, and hence privileges and rights determined by dictatorial leadership.

NOTES

1 Zeus, the last-born, was spirited away by his mother to protect him from his father Chronos who had swallowed all the other children. Zeus eventually killed Chronos and his siblings were de-gorged, or rather reborn. Zeus now became the first-born, followed by his siblings in the reverse order of their original birth (**M1MMFFF**). This is the patriarchal first-born Zeus that we meet in Homer.
2 This may not be any different from the cycle of change at the mythical level. After all a clear evolution is apparent in the Greek pantheon toward the ascendency of only son Apollo.
3 Newton had three younger half-siblings, but he is essentially an only child. He never knew his father. His mother left him soon after birth; he was raised as an only child by his grandmother. When he was 11 years old, he went to live with his mother and got to know his half-siblings.

Chapter 6

The innate affects and the complex family emotions

In the preceding chapters, I have shown how the world cycle of creative change advances new ideas through individuals of great talent who are of the basic sibling positions. Yet to be explored are the motivating forces that underlie the individual's commitment to such efforts. This requires an understanding of the emotions and an understanding of the archetypal imagination. The task is to show how the child's heritage of innate instincts and emotions is transformed in the crucible of family relationships into an amazingly complex and sensitive matrix of feeling-toned complexes and the subtleties of the human family emotions.

It could be said that sibling rivalry is part of what makes the cycle of creativity go. Not rivalry between the siblings of one family but the projection of that rivalry on to the plane of society. Copernicus put himself in rivalry with those who supported Ptolemy's theory when he declared that the present state of astronomy had created a monster. Did Kepler then put himself in rivalry with Copernicus? It would seem so since Kepler seeks to give an adequate explanation to ideas that Copernicus had only roughly sketched out. And Galileo too? Presumably. A recent book on the discovery of DNA portrays the rivalry of Watson and Crick with others, all hot on the trail of the elusive DNA (Watson 1968). We see a similar rivalry in the history of the search for the fundamental particles of matter (Riordan 1987). Without doubt there is rivalry amongst scientists. In depth psychology the same situation holds true. The question then is: What gives sibling rivalry its energy? The answer is to be found in the emotions.

THE NATURE OF THE EMOTIONS

Of first importance is the natural division in the human emotions between the universal, inherited affects of the collective unconscious, and the 'complex family emotions' (Stewart 1988) of the personal unconscious which are also universally known, yet are not innate. Jealousy and envy are prime examples of the complex family emotions. Jealousy and envy assume such importance in the family because they are the shadow aspects of the two polar dynamics of the family; the desire for love and the wish for power. As Jung puts it:

> Now it is, as a matter of fact, true that apart from the personal striving for power, or *superbia*, love, in the sense of *concupiscentia*, is the dynamism that most infallibly brings the unconscious to light. . . But what can love mean to a man with a hunger for power! That is why we always find two main causes of psychic catastrophes: on the one hand a disappointment in love and on the other hand a thwarting of the striving for power.
>
> (Jung 1963: 86)

In his book *The Expression of the Emotions in Man and Animals*, Darwin (1872) was the first to make a distinction between the *innate* emotions and the *complex* emotions. Although he uses many synonyms and other terms that describe wide ranges of emotional intensity and a variety of expressive actions, as well as other subtle variations, Darwin's study is primarily focused on the fundamental emotions: joy, grief, anger, fear, disgust, shame, surprise, which are innate and inherited and shared in large part with our mammalian predecessors. Each has a prototypical form of expressive behaviour. For example, the facial expression and bodily action of a grieving person is immediately recognized by humans everywhere.

In addition to these innate emotions, Darwin identified a number of other emotions that are well known to people all over the world, but lack a consistent or prototypical form of expression. In contrast to the fundamental, innate emotions, he called these 'complex emotions'. Complex emotions cannot be 'read' by facial expression or bodily action alone, rather we are guided by our general or intuitive knowledge of the situation, the presence of other persons or tell-tale objects. Darwin's list of complex emotions includes jealousy, envy, avarice, revenge, suspicion, deceit, slyness, guilt, vanity, conceit, ambition, pride, humility, and so on. 'It is doubtful', he says, 'whether the greater number of the above complex states of mind are revealed by any fixed expression, sufficiently distinct to be described or delineated' (Darwin 1872: 261).

After Darwin, the contribution of Silvan Tomkins has had the greatest influence on contemporary studies of the individual emotions. A comprehensive, thoroughly researched work by Tomkins, entitled *Affect Imagery Consciousness* (1962, 1963) played a pivotal role in the current renewal of affect studies. Since then, a series of cross-cultural and developmental studies by Ekman, Izard, Trotter, Eibl-Eibesfeldt and others have confirmed Darwin's early observations. There has been but one major addition: In 1962, Silvan Tomkins identified the single innate emotion that Darwin had overlooked, that is, interest, with its range of intensity from interest to excitement. As has been reported from personal observations, and has recently been confirmed by studies of the physiological changes during the birth experience, the infant normally comes out of the birth canal wide-eyed and alert, already showing interest in its environment (Lagercrantz and Slotkin 1986).

In his G. Stanley Hall lecture at the 1988 conference of the American Psychological Association in Atlanta, Caroll Izard presented an overview of research to date on the structure and function of emotions in human development. His review confirms and reaffirms the existence of the following innate affects. These are: joy, interest, surprise, sadness (grief), fear, anger, contempt (disgust), and shame (shyness) (Izard in Denton 1988:16). From a Jungian perspective these are the innate affects of the collective unconscious.

It may be helpful to keep in mind that every innate affect is described by many different words that express a continuum of intensity. For example, the lower intensities of fear are uncertainty, uneasiness, apprehension, anxiety. The higher or extreme intensities of fear are panic, terror. Grief ranges from mild distress through sadness, to the extreme of anguish. Shame ranges from shyness and embarrassment to the extreme of humiliation. Contempt ranges from mild antipathy, to disdain, to dislike, to the extreme of disgust. Both shame and contempt are stimulated by rejection; together they comprise a bi-polar affect (Lynd 1958). Whether we experience shame or contempt is determined by the direction of the rejection toward oneself (shame) or toward the other (contempt). It is likely that contempt and shame have evolved out of the primal affective reflex disgust, which is present in mammals from birth.

One of my contributions to this field has been to recognize that these inherited affects are the foundation of the primal Self and the libido, and that the complex family emotions, as well as feelings, and other functions of the psyche develop out of the innate affects, or have evolved from them. The fourfold affects of existential crisis (grief, fear, anger, contempt/shame) are structured around a fifth innate affect, startle, that has a centring function. These affects comprise a *mandala* at the base of the primordial Self. They appear to have evolved as a kind of self-protective system. In addition to survival, these affects sensitize the psyche to the fundamental existential and spiritual crises of life, namely: *loss of a loved one* (grief); *the unknown* (fear); *threat to autonomy* (anger); *rejection* (contempt/shame); and *the unexpected* (startle).

The remaining two affects, joy and interest, are a pair of opposites that flow into every aspect of life as the twin streams of the libido. These affects may be recognized as the root of the dynamics that Jung speaks of as mythical consciousness, personified in alchemy as Luna, and, logos consciousness, personified as Sol. The innate affects joy and interest, energize respectively the dynamisms play/imagination and curiosity/exploration, and ultimately are culturally evolved as the syzygy, anima and animus: Eros and Logos. When the affects of the libido (joy and interest) erupt in their extreme intensity as ecstasy and excitement, they may potentiate the archetypal imagination in the cultural form of a vocation in its original meaning as a 'calling'. As a co-ordinated totality and in their relations with each other, the innate affects are the foundation of the collective unconscious (Stewart 1985, 1987b). Jung has referred to them as the 'inborn archetype which is universally human' (Jung 1975: 537).

In Table 6.1 I show the seven innate affects, each with its own range of intensity. I also include the stimulus, that is, the typical life situation that stirs a particular emotion. To recapitulate: the fundamental emotions joy, interest, surprise, grief, fear, anger, disgust (contempt/ shame), are innate sources of energy and patterns of expressive behaviour that originate in the depths of the primordial unconscious. By contrast, the complex emotions such as love, hate, jealousy, envy, greed, admiration, generosity and the like, are constellated simply, and solely, because there is a family. It is only through the relationships between children and parents, and siblings with each other that the complex emotions come into being. At bottom, of course, they derive from the innate affects. They ordinarily acquire their unique qualities through mixtures and modulations of the innate affects through relationships with mother, father and siblings.

THE COMPLEX FAMILY EMOTIONS

This leads to the critical question: How are the innate affects transformed into the sensitive network of feelings and complex family

Table 6.1 The innate affects

Affect	Range of intensity	Life stimulus
Joy	(Enjoyment – Joy – Ecstasy)	*Relationship to the familiar*
Interest	(Attention – Interest – Excitement)	*Novelty*
Grief	(Distress – Sadness – Anguish)	*Loss*
Fear	(Apprehension – Fright – Terror)	*The unknown*
Anger	(Irritation – Frustration – Rage)	*Restriction of autonomy*
Contempt/	(Disdain – Dislike – Disgust)	*Rejection* (toward other)
Shame	(Shyness – Embarrassment – Humiliation)	*Rejection* (toward self)
Startle	(Surprise – Astonishment – Startle)	*The unexpected*

emotions? The first year of life sees the constellation of all of the innate affects in the infant's daily experience, no matter how attentive and nurturing the mother and father may be. But it is the empathic responsiveness of the 'good enough' parent that provides the modulating effects which make the eruptions of the innate affects bearable and containable. Through the infant's own play and curiosity, mirrored by the parent's responsive playfulness and attentive interest, the innate affects are continually modulated and transformed. These transformed affects make up the 'archetypal complexes' of the collective unconscious. It must be remembered that during this first year of life when these earliest transformations are taking place, the infant is living in a world of relative unconsciousness. Its consciousness progresses from the Uroboric stage (Neumann 1973, 1990: 3) just following birth, to a recognition of the parent as marked by the first clear-eyed smile, followed by a laughing recognition of Self (through the sheer exhilaration of self-initiated movement), and then to the more evolved stages of the recognition of the other as existing in absence, that is to say, the peek-a-boo stage, and finally, just beyond the first birthday, the consciousness of 'pretend' and the development of imagination and the symbol. This means that for that first year of development, the structures of the unconscious complexes are in archaic forms, not easily accessible to later ego consciousness.

The foregoing is a capsule view of how the innate affects are modulated and transformed through family interactions. Their development is also shaped through the family structure. By family structure I refer here primarily to the family constellation and the sibling configuration which determine certain relationships that inevitably lead to each child developing, quite unconsciously, an individual world-view and tendencies to specific emotional complexes. For example, the response of a first-born to the birth of a sibling is often, in varying degrees, one of disorientation and tentative or strong rejection. Jealousy is our word for the resultant complex family emotion that develops. Basically what the child experiences is the startling presence of an unwanted intruder, and a realization of the mother's perceived betrayal of love. Now what of the second child who is born into a world which already includes an older sibling? From the beginning, as I have said, most younger children are received by the older sibling with disapproval of varying degrees of intensity. At its worst this takes the form of physical attacks on the younger child. But if the atmosphere of the family is accepting, empathic and understanding, the relationship between the siblings may become relatively peaceful, and love and admiration may prevail. In any case, the younger sibling soon recognizes the discrepancy in power and privilege between him or herself and the older sibling, and attempts to benefit through imitation, or accelerated efforts to gain power and privilege for himself or herself, or by trying to wrest them from the older sibling often through guile and theft. The complex family emotion that results is envy. If we now consider the situation of the older and younger sibling as time passes, it is evident that each no doubt is internalized as the shadow for the other.

In a sense, jealousy and envy express two perspectives on the central dynamic of family life, namely the tension which inevitably arises between desires for love and power. Everyone knows from personal experience what jealousy and envy are like. Primal jealousy is about love and suspected betrayal, it is the resultant of a three-party relationship. It is constellated when we feel displaced in the affections of another: We are enraged when someone takes what, in our eyes, belongs to us, as witness Cain and Abel. In this eternal tale of two brothers, Yahweh preferred the offering of Abel. In a jealous rage, Cain killed his younger brother. But Cain's emotion was not simply rage. When jealous, we are also aware of the fact that we have loved the one who now betrays our love. Classic situations in the family which can lead to a jealousy complex are the birth of a sibling, and the rivalry of a boy with the father over the mother, or the girl's rivalry with the mother over the father, the famous Oedipus and Electra complexes.

But what about envy? In a sense envy is the mirror image of jealousy; it is the emotion we experience when we desire what someone else has. It is a two-party relationship and it has to do with power. The polarity of envy and jealousy is brilliantly portrayed in Shakespeare's play Othello through the entwined roles of Iago and Othello. Iago is envious of Othello's prestige and power, and he sets about unseating Othello by arousing Othello's jealousy. Envy is about power denied; jealousy is about love betrayed. The classic family situation which can lead to an envy complex is the relationship of a younger sibling to an older one, as in the famous tales of Hermes and Apollo, of Jacob and Esau, or the relationship of the son or daughter to the father or the mother.

Children born into a family that already contains older siblings are most susceptible to envy. Alfred Adler was one of those, and in his theory he puts feelings of inferiority in a prime aetiological position. Melanie Klein was another, the youngest of four children. As we know, she was consumed with envy and determined not to let herself be overlooked:

> I was very keen to get some attention and to be more important than the older ones.
>
> (Klein, in Grosskurth 1987: 13)

Klein's biographer points out that in letters to mother and sister, Melanie was clearly ill disposed to her eldest sister Emilie. The author sums up:

> Why did Melanie adopt such an intransigently judgmental attitude toward her sister, unless she envied Emilie for seeming to have the fulfilled emotional life that she herself craved, as well as – in the face of all her troubles – a certain serenity? More fundamentally, she still retained the envy of a powerless baby sister. Melanie Klein was an embodiment of her own later theories: the world is not an objective reality, but a phantasmagoria peopled with our own fears and desires.
>
> (Grosskurth 1987: 62)

It can hardly be an accident that the theories of later-borns Adler and Klein are rooted in inferiority and envy, whereas first-born Freud's theory is one of jealousy.

How serious a matter envy or jealousy is for an individual is determined by many factors. It is important to acknowledge that all the complex family emotions are 'normal' experiences. Everyone is envious and jealous to some extent. Emotions become deep-seated complexes only when, as Jung puts it in terms of his own experience, the individual is strongly influenced by unanswered questions of the ancestors passed on through the family atmosphere.

There are, of course, a myriad of other family emotions as human experience and the pages of a thesaurus show. The many terms express finer and finer differentiations of the basic inherited emotions. The complexity and subtlety of the human emotional capacity is extra-ordinary. The number of distinct emotions that are traceable to the dynamic relationships of family life, however, is also limited. This limited number may have many fine degrees of expression. Most of the emotions we experience are in fact varying degrees of intensity of the innate affects, as well as their many co-minglings.

THE ARCHETYPAL IMAGINATION

Building on Jung's view that the affects are the primal source of energy, value, imagery and new consciousness, I have developed a hypothesis that contributes to a comprehensive theory of the structure of the psyche (Stewart 1985, 1986, 1987a, 1987b, 1987c). It involves specific innate affects as the primal source of specific higher functions.

When the innate affects of existential crisis (grief, fear, anger, contempt/shame) erupt, they potentiate the archetypal imagination. Each affect is the primal source of a particular imaginative form. For example, when awakened by an unexpected sound in the middle of the night, we ordinarily startle, and then may begin to fluctuate between fear and interest, as we strain to hear more. The image-producing function of the psyche (that is, the imagination) attempts to create meaning through spontaneous fantasies. Here we see the ongoing, intrinsic relationship of affect and image. The images that play through the mind offer infinite possibilities as to the origin of the sound that awoke us. Is it friend or foe? Our fantasies may play back and forth between spouse, child, pet, dishwasher; to wild animal, burglar, intruder, alien.

If the source of the sound remains unknown, the fear grows. Bodily innervations (dry mouth, heart pounding, and so on), expressive physical actions (trembling, gasping, and so on), and escalating fantasies can lead to panic. Whether raised in a formal religious tradition, or not, at such a moment we're likely to quiver and quake as all attention is drawn to a desperate encounter with the dreaded unknown.

The archetypal imagination is an innate function that shapes the development of the affects from their source (the primal self) toward their goal (the realized self). With respect to the primal self, the affects of existential crisis manifest as experiences of the images of pre-creation: the *abyss* of fear, the *void* of sadness, the *chaos* of rage, the *alienation* of contempt/shame, and the total *disorientation* and *darkness* of startle. With respect to the realized self, these affects evoke compensatory images that express the highest aspirations of the human spirit: the sacred, the beautiful, the true, the good and wholeness. Here we see images that plumb the heights and depths of human experience.

Out of the *abyss of fear*, the archetypal imagination produces images that ultimately draw us into the rituals of prayer and worship. This development has evolved through daemonic dread toward a sense of awe and the holy. Out of the *void of grief*, the archetypal imagination produces visions of the lost loved one(s); the emptiness of the void evokes memories of the beloved in life – images of the beauty and bounty of nature. The Aids quilt (made to commemorate Aids victims) shows this process so clearly; it is at once an expression of universal grief – and a memorial of terrible beauty. Out of the muddled, tumultuous *chaos of anger*, the archetypal imagination produces compensatory images of the cosmos, the ordering principle of reason. From the *alienation of contempt/shame*, the archetypal imagination produces compensatory images of relationship, ultimately 'Utopian communitas'. Finally, from the *dark unconsciousness and disorientation of startle*, the archetypal imagination produces the centring process, orientation, self-reflective consciousness and the image of wholeness. Here we see how the *mandala* of the archetypal imagination evolves out of the primal Self toward the expressive cultural attitudes: the religious, the aesthetic, the philosophic, the social, and the penultimate: self-reflective consciousness of wholeness.

This discussion of the highly-evolved forms of the archetypal imagination leads to the next chapter: 'The spirit chooses'.

Chapter 7

The spirit chooses

In Chapter 5 I discussed the world cycle of creative change through which new ideas are advanced in a dialectical process involving individuals of the four basic sibling positions of the family. In Chapter 6 we explored the emotions that are the energic source of the cycle, and distinguished between the innate emotions of the collective unconscious and the 'complex family emotions' of which the 'sibling complexes' are examples. This chapter is focused on the innate emotions which are the energic source of choice by the spirit. The 'choice' of an individual to carry forward an idea, or a task, such as that of political leadership (or, of course, in any field of endeavour, art, religion, science or society), depends in part on a concatenation of the *individual's sibling position* in the family and *the specifics of the social-political situation*. But more is required for the 'choice' of a *particular* leader in a *specific* political situation than just the match of sibling position and political *Zeitgeist*. The question is then: What is that 'more?'

MOSES

From time immemorial the answer to that question has been referred to the 'spirit'. The heroic man or woman who takes on a task is said to have been 'called'. As we know, Moses (FMM3) was called by Yahweh from the burning bush. In that confrontation Yahweh distinguished between Moses and his elder brother Aaron. For when Moses sought to decline the invitation because he was not eloquent of speech, Yahweh proposed that Aaron could speak for him. Why did not Yahweh simply 'call' Aaron rather than Moses, since Aaron apparently could speak eloquently? The reason is to be found presumably in Yahweh's discernment of 'spirit'. That is to say, Yahweh recognized in Moses a 'natural' revolutionary leader, and the 'soon to become' spiritual leader of the Israelites, Yahweh's 'chosen' people. In our terms that would mean recognition, first, that Moses' sibling position was that of a last-born, and second, that he would make himself accessible to the ruthless demands of the 'spirit'.

Now we are left with the question: how does a *particular* leader of the appropriate sibling position come to dedicate him or herself to preparation for the role for which a 'call' will come? Not every last-born would aspire to the task that Moses took on, and not every last-born would be up to the task. At first Moses did not feel that he was up to the task, but he rallied and did assume the role assigned to him. Why was this? Obviously he had little choice. He could not deny Yahweh. But what does that mean psychologically? Moses must have come to recognize his own fitness for the task, just as we find is true in the lives of contemporary leaders in similar situations as, for example, Churchill, Gandhi and Walesa. Moses knew that he had a strong commitment to freedom – he had been banned from Egypt because he killed a slave-owner who was abusing his slave. Moreover, at birth he had been saved by his mother and elder sister from the Pharaoh's command to kill all male babies born to the Jews. He had been adopted by the Pharaoh's daughter, and raised in the Pharaoh's palace. He had, then, a dual identity, and knew from the inside the ways in which the Pharaoh dealt with power. He was prepared to contend with the Pharaoh, with the help, of course, of Yahweh.

JOAN OF ARC

Perhaps the most extraordinary example of being chosen by the spirit is the history of Joan of Arc (MMFF4M). A young peasant girl from the provinces of France, she knew at the age of 13 that France could be saved from her enemies only through the crowning of the dauphin as King. By 17 to 18 years of age she had accomplished that. At 19 she had been burned at the stake for heresy. It is no wonder that the historian Dunham speaks in hyperbole when he approaches this subject:

> The new world which, five centuries later, we still live in and have not yet built arrived with more flame and mystery than would attend a collision of comets or sudden perturbations among the stars. For the whole new world, the modern world, existed in concept, in the mind of an illiterate, teen-age peasant girl, who, in the year 1429, knew, though no one else knew, what was necessary to be known.
>
> (Dunham 1963: 240)

And we too may marvel. Imagine, as if we could, how thunderstruck the brothers and sisters of Joan must have been when she revealed to them the commands of her voices: Saints Michael, Catherine and Margaret. For the western world, Joan is unquestionably a historical paradigm of the coalescence of the heroine of myth and the heroic leader. Joan's inspiration came to her through the voices of her saints, who called her the Maid of Orleans, daughter of God. Any lurking doubts we may have that a sense of destiny erupting in the right person at the right time can move mountains and sweep masses of people along in its wake are quickly dispelled as we contemplate the towering figure of Joan of Arc.

SPIRIT AND INSPIRATION

And here we ask again: What is that extra something that comes from the gods? Can it be anything other than an indefinable element of the 'spirit' which has its way with the individual through what we may call inspiration – a special degree of insight, daring, passion, courage and the like? Later on I shall discuss this further in relation to the innate existential affects of the collective unconscious which are the ultimate source of the dynamics and energy and transmission of the 'spirit'.

Following Jung now, we may say that it is a special attunement to the spirit of the ancestors and the spirit of the times which accounts for the leader who is 'prepared' at the particular moment which calls for his or her abilities. And this, as Jung says, is a special access to the energy of the life source, through the archetypes of the collective unconscious.

> The energy underlying conscious psychic life is pre-existent to it and therefore at first unconscious. As it approaches consciousness it first appears projected in figures like mana,[1] gods, daemons, etc., whose numen seems to be the vital source of energy, and in point of fact is so as long as these supernatural figures are accepted. But as these fade and lose their force, the ego – that is, the empirical man – seems to come into possession of this source of energy, and does so in the fullest meaning of this ambiguous statement: on the one hand he seeks to seize this energy, to possess it, and even imagines that he does possess it; and on the other hand he is possessed by it.
>
> (Jung 1961: 346–7)

Speaking further of the nature of possession, Jung clarifies that 'no conscious will can ever replace the life instinct'. 'This instinct', he says, 'comes to us from within, as a compulsion or will or command'. It has from 'time immemorial' been given the name of a 'personal daemon' and this, Jung says, aptly expresses 'the psychological situation'. He concludes that 'if, by employing the concept of the archetype, we attempt to define a little more closely the point at which the daemon grips us, we have not abolished anything, only approached closer to the source of life' (Jung 1961: 349).

JUNG ON THE MEANING OF THE SPIRIT

In several essays Jung explored the various meanings given to the term spirit and sought to relate these meanings to his conception of the unconscious. In his view the spirit moves us from the unconscious; it is a phenomenon of unconscious contents of a collective nature which become dominant forces in the life of an individual. Jung also speaks of the phenomenology of the spirit, that is, the image/ideas through which it becomes available to consciousness. These are the archetypes of the collective unconscious which impress themselves upon the soul and thus become the guiding principles of an individual life. But that life is not an expression of that individual, but rather an expression of the spirit which dominates the individual.

As we follow Jung's developing thought it becomes apparent that the central concepts of his analytical psychology all coalesce around the concept of spirit: the archetypes, the affects, the self, active imagination, the *coniunctio*. And always the spirit is paired with its opposite, matter. In one of his early papers on the subject of 'spirit', Jung (1926) posed the question: Do we really know the meaning of 'spirit' and 'life'? He was quick to admit that he knew 'as little what "spirit" may be in itself as . . . what "life" is' (1926: 320). This did not, of course, hinder his efforts to find a 'real basis for spirit – and not at the expense of life' (ibid.). He first satisfied himself that he knew life only through its quintessence the 'living body'. Then he concluded that 'spirit' is 'the quintessence of the life of the mind' (ibid.: 326). From this perspective he saw that

> 'Spirit' exists in the same transliminal realm as 'living being,' that is, in the same misty state of indistinguishableness. The doubt as to whether mind and body may not ultimately prove to be the same thing also applies to the apparent contrast between 'spirit' and 'living being.' They too are probably the same thing.

(Jung 1926: 326–7)

Jung then compares the concepts of 'God' and 'spirit'.

> Spirit, like God, denotes an object of psychic experience which cannot be proved to exist in the external world and cannot be understood rationally. This is the meaning of the word 'spirit' if we use it in its best sense.

(Jung 1926: 329)

Exploring the etymology and common usage of the term 'spirit', he points to the close connection with the affects:

> Psychologically we would say: every affect tends to become an autonomous complex, to break away from the hierarchy of consciousness and, if possible, to drag the ego after it. No wonder, then, that the primitive mind sees in this the activity of a strange invisible being, a spirit. Spirit in this case is the reflection of an autonomous affect, which is why the ancients, very appropriately, called the spirits imagines, 'images.'

(Jung 1926: 330)

The spirit is also experienced as a kind of attitude, or frame of mind:

> Most attitudes are based, consciously or unconsciously, on some kind of *maxim*, which often has the character of a proverb. . . Those sayings or ideals that store up the richest experience of life and the deepest reflection constitute what we call 'spirit' in the best sense of the word. When a ruling principle of this kind attains absolute mastery we speak of the life under its guidance as 'ruled by the spirit,' or as a 'spiritual life.' The more absolute and compelling the ruling idea, the more it has the nature of an autonomous complex that confronts the ego-consciousness as an unshakable fact.

(Jung 1926: 331–2)

All of Jung's examples include the emotions:

> Only under the stress of an emotion can the idea, or whatever the ruling principle may be, become an autonomous complex; without this the idea remains a concept subservient to the arbitrary opinions of the conscious mind, a mere intellectual counter with no compelling power behind it.

(Jung 1926: 332

He notes further that 'you cannot, so to speak, *will* to be spiritual. . . It is far more a matter of fate what principle will rule our attitude' (ibid.: 332).

Jung concludes from this that 'because the problem we are concerned with here, namely the life-ruling power of the spirit, is connected with processes outside ego-consciousness' (ibid.: 334), then it is necessary to entertain the idea of a higher consciousness. Jung is quick to admit, however, that it may not necessarily be 'higher' consciousness: Perhaps, he says, 'wider' is a better way to describe it. Consciousness is not 'necessarily higher in the intellectual or moral sense. There are many spirits, both light and dark. Spirit is not absolute . . . it needs completing and perfecting through life' (ibid.: 336). Summing up, Jung states that

> Only a life lived in a certain spirit is worth living. . . Life is a touchstone for the truth of the spirit. Spirit that drags a man away from life, seeking fulfilment only in itself, is a False spirit – though the man too is to blame, since he can choose whether he will give himself up to this spirit or not. Life and spirit are two powers or necessities between which man is placed. Spirit gives meaning to his life, and the possibility of its greatest development. But life is essential to spirit, since its truth is nothing if it cannot live.
>
> (Jung 1926: 337)

We can see prefigured in these early formulations some of the basic issues which preoccupied Jung throughout the latter half of his life, namely, the relationship of archetypal image to the 'archetype', the relationship of archetype to 'instinct', and a precise definition of archetype. In one of his last formulations (1947), late in life, he considers the same issues in terms of the spectrum of light. By this time Jung had come to understand the archetypes as an expression of the spirit. Jung creates a visual image to help us imagine the different qualities of 'instinct', 'instinctual image', and the 'archetype' itself. He visualizes the dynamism of instinct as being suited to the 'infra-red part' of the spectrum of colour. The instinctual *image*, however, belongs 'in the ultra-violet part'. This is because the colour violet is appropriate for the archetype in view of its 'mystic' or 'paradoxical quality'. Jung then explains further that the nature of an archetype is irrepresentable, although it may be known by certain manifestations.

> The archetype as such is a psychoid factor that belongs, as it were, to the invisible, ultra-violet end of the psychic spectrum. It does not appear, in itself, to be capable of reaching consciousness. We must

constantly bear in mind that what we mean by an 'archetype' is in itself irrepresentable, but has effects which make visualizations of it possible, namely, the archetypal images and ideas.

(Jung 1947: 213)

Jung compares his understanding of the archetype to the situation in physics where the smallest particles are also irrepresentable, but just like the archetypes, 'have effects from the nature of which' a model can be built. Moreover, Jung considers that 'it is not only possible but fairly probable, even, that psyche and matter are two different aspects of one and the same thing'. Continuing in this vein Jung suggests that

> Just as the 'psychic infra-red,' the biological instinctual psyche, gradually passes over into the physiology of the organism and thus merges with its chemical and physical conditions, so the 'psychic ultra-violet,' the archetype, describes a field which exhibits none of the peculiarities of the physiological and yet, in the last analysis, can no longer be regarded as psychic, although it manifests itself psychically. But physiological processes behave in the same way, without on that account being declared psychic. . . We must apply this argument logically to the archetypes as well. Since their essential being is unconscious to us, and still they are experienced as spontaneous agencies, there is probably no alternative now but to describe their nature, in accordance with their chiefest effect, as 'spirit,' in the sense which I attempted to make plain in my paper 'The Phenomenology of the Spirit in Fairytales.' If so, the position of the archetype would be located beyond the psychic sphere, analogous to the position of physiological instinct, which is immediately rooted in the stuff of the organism and, with its psychoid nature, forms the bridge to matter in general.
>
> (Jung 1947: 215–16)

To summarize: It is clear from the beginning that Jung thought of spirit and matter as opposites which nevertheless represent two aspects of a common factor. As his thinking about the unconscious, particularly the archetypes, developed he came to see the spirit as the symbolic expression of instinct, and that was precisely the meaning he gave to the archetypal image/idea. However, the emotions were from the beginning understood as the energic factor which determined the 'charge' and the 'numinous effects' of the archetype. This implied then that the emotions give expression to the archetypal image/symbol – spirit. In addition, when he spoke of the phenomenology of the image/

symbols that represent the spirit, he turned to the concept of the central organizing archetype of the collective unconscious, the self, represented in dreams and fairy-tales as the figure of the Wise Old Man/Woman.

SPIRIT AND NATURE: JUNG'S SEIZURE

Jung early on said to anyone who asked that he wanted to be a philologist like his father, but he really meant to be an archaeologist. Archaeological studies would have cost a great deal of money and would have required his going away to a distant university. As it was, his father had to get a scholarship for him to attend the University of Basel. His decision to study medicine was a compromise. He says it occurred to him that his paternal grandfather had been a doctor, and he knew he could make a good living as a doctor. All the time, though, he was plagued by thoughts of the psyche and of spiritualism and séances and all those stories he had heard as a boy. His choice of psychiatry came about quite by chance it would seem.

Jung found university life immensely stimulating and he participated with enthusiasm in student discussions covering a wide spectrum of topics; medical, philosophical and theological. But he quickly discovered that although 'science opened the door to enormous quantities of knowledge, it provided genuine insights very sparingly, and these in the main were of a specialized nature' (1961: 98). His philosophical reading had convinced him that the psyche was the immediate cause of this dilemma. 'Without the psyche there would be neither knowledge nor insight. Yet nothing was ever said about the psyche' (ibid.). Jung's puzzlement over the role of the psyche was given a new emphasis during his second semester at the university. He discovered a book on 'spiritualistic phenomena'. In these writings he found confirmation of the authenticity of the stories he had heard as a boy:

> The material, without a doubt, was authentic. But the great question of whether these stories were physically true was not answered to my satisfaction. Nevertheless, it could be established that at all times and all over the world the same stories had been reported again and again. There must be some reason for this, and it could not possibly have been the predominance of the same religious conceptions everywhere, for that was obviously not the case. Rather it must be connected with the objective behaviour of the human psyche. But with regard to this cardinal question – the objective

nature of the psyche – I could find out absolutely nothing, except what the philosophers said.

(Jung 1961: 99)

In his typical fashion Jung immersed himself in the literature of spiritualism. He notes that his 'mother's No. 2 [personality] sympathized whole-heartedly . . . but everyone else I knew was distinctly discouraging'. It was as if, he says . . . 'I had pushed to the brink of the world; what was of burning interest to me was null and void for others, and even a cause for dread' (Jung 1961: 100).

It is but a small step from this enthusiasm, which was shared by his mother, to Jung's interest in the 'spiritual' séances being held by a female cousin, to which his mother had directed him, and from which came the material for his graduation thesis. Yet all during this time he was torn by the feelings engendered in him of being different. This, as he says '. . . eventually brought back all the old doubts, inferiority feelings, and depressions – a vicious circle I was resolved to break at all costs. No longer would I stand outside the world, enjoying the dubious reputation of a freak' (ibid). With this resolve Jung devoted himself to his course of study in medicine.

During his medical training Jung was introduced to psychiatry but found it of little interest:

Though I had attended psychiatric lectures and clinics, the current instructor in psychiatry was not exactly stimulating, and when I recalled the effects which the experience of asylums had had on my father, this was not calculated to prepossess me in favour of psychiatry. In preparing myself for the state examination, therefore, the textbook on psychiatry was the last I attacked. I expected nothing of it, and I still remember that as I opened the book by Krafft-Ebing the thought came to me 'Well, now let's see what a psychiatrist has to say for himself.' The lectures and clinical demonstrations had not made the slightest impression on me. I could not remember a single one of the cases I had seen in the clinic, but only my boredom and disgust.

I began with the preface, intending to find out how a psychiatrist introduced his subject or, indeed, justified his reason for existing at all. By way of excuse for this high and mighty attitude I must make it clear that in the medical world at that time psychiatry was quite generally held in contempt. No one really knew anything about it, and there was no psychology which regarded man as a whole and included his pathological variations in the total picture. The director was locked up in the same institution with his patients, and the institution was equally cut off, isolated on the outskirts of the city like an ancient lazaret with its lepers. No one liked looking in that direction. The doctors knew almost as little as the layman and therefore shared his feelings. Mental disease was a hopeless and fatal affair which cast its shadow over psychiatry as well. The psychiatrist was a strange figure in those days, as I was soon to learn from personal experience.

(Jung 1961: 108)

As he continued to read, Jung suddenly saw the possibility of a resolution of his own inner conflict. He came across the statement by Krafft-Ebing that the psychoses were 'diseases of the personality'. At that moment, in a state of exaltation, his vocation was revealed to him:

My excitement was intense, for it had become clear to me, in a flash of illumination, that for me the only possible goal was psychiatry. Here alone the two currents of my interest could flow together and in a united stream dig their own bed. Here was the empirical field common to biological and spiritual facts, which I had everywhere sought and nowhere found. Here at last was the place where the collision of nature and spirit became a reality.

(Jung 1961: 108–9)

Jung's excitement erupted at the moment when he read that the 'psychoses are diseases of personality', that is to say, they have some psychological meaning. Was he thinking of his father at this moment? Or was he also thinking of himself and his experience since he was a boy of having two personalities that he had named 'Number One' and 'Number Two'? Until this moment, his interests had drawn him in different directions: 'Science met to a very large extent, the needs of No. 1 personality, whereas the humane or historical studies provided beneficial instruction for No. 2' (Jung 1961: 72).

We all know what the experience of excitement is like. But what is its role in the psyche? Interest-Excitement is an archetypal affect of the libido. It signals a discovery, something novel has been recognized which has connected with an archetypal symbol in the collective unconscious. The story of Archimedes running into the street shouting 'Eureka!' comes to mind. What would the archetypal symbol of excitement be? The brilliant light of insight, illumination: In this instance nature and spirit united in the study of psychiatry:

Here was the empirical field common to biological and spiritual facts. . . Here at last was the place where the collision of nature and spirit became a reality. My violent reaction set in when Krafft-Ebing spoke of the 'subjective character' of psychiatric textbooks. So, I thought, the textbook is in part the subjective confession of the author. With his specific prejudice, with the totality of his being, he stands behind the objectivity of his experiences and responds to the 'disease of the personality' with the whole of his own personality. . . I saw that once again I had obviously got myself into a side alley where no one could or would follow me. But I knew – and nothing and nobody could have deflected me from my purpose – that my decision stood, and that it was fate. It was as though two rivers had united and in one grand torrent were bearing me inexorably toward distant goals. This confident feeling that I was a 'united double nature' carried me as if on a magical wave through the examination, in which I came out at the top.

(Jung 1961: 109)

The intensity of Jung's emotional reaction can only be understood as a seizure by an archetypal image/idea. But what is that image/idea? The things he notes as specifically important are: the subjective nature of psychiatry; the confluence of his two interests – the biological and spiritual, in the empirical field of psychiatry – the place of the collision of nature and spirit; and finally that he was now a 'united double nature'. Clearly the images depict a synthesis of the biological and spiritual through the study of the empirical field of psychiatry, and this synthesis gives Jung a sense of uniting his two personalties, No. 1 (who was grounded in the facts of the world the way it is) and No. 2 (who existed outside of time in a mythic, imaginative realm).

As I have said elsewhere, the pull toward synthesis is characteristic of the only child. The content of Jung's synthesis can be seen in part as a confluence of the ancestral heritage of his two grandfathers, the maternal was spiritual, the paternal was biological. Jung's maternal grandfather, Samuel Preiswerk, was a clergyman who lived much of his life surrounded by spirits; he scheduled time each week in his study for a conversation with the spirit of his deceased first wife. As a girl Jung's mother Emilie used to sit behind her father's chair when he wrote his sermons so that he would not be disturbed by spirits. Jung's paternal grandfather studied medicine and became a protégé of the great naturalist Humboldt. He joined the medical faculty of the University of Basel, enlarged it, and eventually became rector. Late in his life he devoted much time to a home for retarded children. The constellating factor of Jung's seizure may well have been his father's dilemma as a clergyman who suffered from a loss of faith. The result for psychiatry is that in Jung the genius was found who would articulate the purpose and goal of this newly-emerging field of psychology – the problem of modern men and women in search of their own souls.

Jung spent the better part of his professional life seeking answers to these questions. He encourages us to see his entire childhood and his student years as preparation for his life and the development of his theory of Analytical Psychology. This is clear in what he says late in his life referring to the occasion in the winter of 1955–6 when at the age of 80 he chiselled the names of his paternal ancestors on stone tablets and ensconced them in the courtyard of the Tower at Bollingen:

> When I was working on the stone tablets, I became aware of the fateful links between me and my ancestors. I feel very strongly that I am under the influence of things or questions which were left incomplete and unanswered by my parents and grandparents and more distant ancestors. It often seems as if there were an impersonal karma within a family, which is passed on from parents to children. It has always seemed to me that I had to answer questions which fate had posed to my forefathers, and which had not yet been answered, or as if I had to complete, or perhaps continue, things which previous ages had left unfinished. It is difficult to determine whether these questions are more of a personal or more of a general (collective) nature. It seems to me that the latter is the case. A collective problem, if not recognized as such, always appears as a personal problem, and in individual cases may give the impression that something is out of order in the realm of the personal psyche. The personal sphere is indeed disturbed, but such disturbances need not be primary; they may well be secondary, the consequence of an insupportable change in the social atmosphere. The cause of disturbance is, therefore, not to be sought in the personal surround-ings, but rather in the collective situation.
>
> (Jung 1961: 233–4)

The form that Jung's ancestral heritage took in his early life was in part an identification with Goethe's Faust, an identification which was facilitated by the family myth that Jung's paternal grandfather had been an illegitimate son of Goethe's. So deeply did Jung experience this identification that in his youth he vowed to atone for Faust's murder of the wise, loving couple Philemon and Baucis. Attesting to his vow is an inscription Jung placed over the gate to the Tower: '*Philemonis Sacrum – Fausti Poenitentia*' (Shrine of Philemon – Repentance of Faust) (Jung 1961: 235).

'*Faust* struck a chord in me', Jung says, 'and pierced me through in a way that I could not but regard as personal. Most of all, it awakened in me the problem of opposites, of good and evil, of mind and matter, of light and darkness' (ibid.). Jung saw his own 'inner contradictions . . . in dramatized form'. In Goethe's Faust, 'the inept, purblind philosopher' encounters 'his sinister shadow, Mephistopheles'. 'I was directly struck', Jung says, 'and recognized that this was my fate. Hence, all the crises of the drama affected me personally; at one point I had passionately to agree, at another to oppose.' Later on Jung came to see that his own work was 'consciously linked . . . to what Faust had passed over: respect for the eternal rights of man, recognition of "the ancient," and the continuity of culture and intellectual history' (Jung 1961: 235).

Looking back on his life Jung came to see just how much his childhood experiences had, as he says,

anticipated future events, and paved the way for modes of adaptation to my father's religious collapse as well as the shattering revelation of the world as we see it today – a revelation which had not taken shape from one day to the the next, but had cast its shadows long in advance.

(ibid.: 91).

Jung reached the conclusion that though we have a personal life we are nevertheless at the same time 'the victims and promoters of a collective spirit whose years are counted in centuries'. Thus he concludes that

We can well think all our lives long that we are following our own noses, and may never discover that we are, for the most part, supernumeraries on the stage of the world theatre. These are factors which, although we do not know them, nevertheless influence our lives, the more so if they are unconscious. Thus at least a part of our being lives in the centuries – that part which, for my private use, I have designated 'No. 2.' That it is not an individual curiosity is proved by the religion of the West, which expressly applies itself to this inner man and for two thousand years has earnestly tried to bring him to the knowledge of our surface consciousness with its personalistic preoccupations: '*Non foras ire, in interiore homine habitat veritas*' (Go not outside; truth dwells in the inner man).

(Jung 1961: 91)

NOTE

1 'Mana' is a Melanesian word for extraordinarily powerful psychic energy that is projected on to (and emanates from) all kinds of things, natural and supernatural.

Chapter 8

Depth psychology and the world cycle of creative change

In this chapter I seek to show that the history of depth psychology is an example of the cycle of creativity. That depth psychology is having an effect on society far beyond any expectations held in the period prior to the First World War is obvious. It is worth recalling that at the same time that the world was slipping into the horrors of the First World War, depth psychology *per se* was just coming into being. There can be little doubt that depth psychology represents one of the great changes taking place in the world today. When the blows to the human ego are listed they begin with Copernicus and his statement that the earth is not the centre of the cosmos. Then comes Darwin and his statement that humans have evolved from animals. Freud is given credit for the third blow, namely, that the conscious ego is not in charge of its own house.

At this juncture, then, I shall try to show how the world cycle of change which led to depth psychology found expression in the theories of the pioneers Freud, Adler, Rank and Jung. In clarification of this cycle it will be helpful to review the underlying meaning of change itself, in whatever field of endeavour it may occur. This will lead to an explanation which draws on Jung's synthesis of the divergent theories of Freud and Adler, as well as his theory of the individuation process that fosters the development of wholeness in the individual. In this we shall be directed to the ongoing, innate dialectical relationship of the emotions of joy and interest, with their dynamisms play/imagination and curiosity/exploration, and their evolution toward relatedness and discrimination, and ultimately the principles of Eros and Logos. In addition we shall examine the forms of the fourfold archetypal imagination of the Self as it evolves out of the primordial depths toward the ultimate values of human culture: the sacred, the beautiful, the true and the good/moral. In the most fundamental sense, these are the four forms of the spirit. The evolution and development of each is energized by a crisis affect; as the affect interweaves with imagination and curiosity, the experience is expressed and transformed through a symbolic cultural attitude. Chodorow shows how this is an inevitable part of normal development:

> All children, if given the slightest opportunity, will express their fantasies through dance and song and paintings and drawings and clay and dramatic play (aesthetic imagination). Similarly, all children have fantasies about the Unknown, the world of angels, ghosts, spirits and things-that-go-bump-in-the-night – even infants have sleep rituals, wordless, self-comforting, repetitive actions, so similar to prayers, to ease the transition from the day world to sleep (religious imagination). Every child asks endless questions and wonders about and imagines possible answers, as he or she seeks a rational explanation of the order of the universe (philosophic imagination). And every child has to grapple with feelings about being included or excluded, and has fantasies about how to get along with others (social, ethical, moral imagination). A child's potential to develop all of the cultural forms is innate. The rest of the story has to do with genetic variations and the question of whether the child's environment will foster or inhibit cultural development in general and/or the development of a particular form. But the powerful emotions that are the source of artistic expression, religious ritual, philosophic/scientific inquiry and social relationships are innate.
>
> (Chodorow 1991: 86)

As a developing theory of the human psyche in its destructive and healing potentials, depth psychology is understandably going through an evolution similar to that of other fields of endeavour. Its development demonstrates the same transformative cycle of creativity as does physics, or any other field. However, depth psychology itself is about the very processes which underlie this evolution. The basic tenet of depth psychology, 'know thy Self', directs attention to the individual. To know thy self, however, one must become conscious of both the inner and the outer manifestations of the self, and, of the relationship between them. This implies a need to know our heritage, through the spirit of the ancestors, the *Zeitgeist*, and the present environment of family and society.

Both Jung and Neumann have observed that it is the sensitive, creative, often troubled individuals who are attuned to the developing spirit of the times long before it is known to society as a whole. As Neumann puts it:

> The future of the collective lives in the present of the individual, hard pressed as he is by his problems – which can, in fact, be regarded as the organs of this collective. The sensitive, psychically disturbed and creative people are always the forerunners. Their enhanced permeability by the contents of the collective unconscious, the deep layer which determines the history of happenings in the group, makes them receptive to emerging new contents of which the collective is not yet aware. But these are also the people for whom problems become insistent in their personal lives a hundred years or more before the collective has woken up to their existence.
>
> (Neumann 1969: 30)

Freud, Adler, Rank and Jung, the most creative of the pioneers of depth psychology, were just such individuals. Their own works reveal this, as do the articles and biographies that have been written about them. The source of their creativity and their woundedness, can, in retrospect, be discerned in their early childhood experiences. This is most clearly documented in the case of Jung. In *Memories, Dreams, Reflections* we see that from mid-life on Jung was engaged in coming to terms with the experiences of his childhood and later life, and in transforming them into the substance of his theory and practice of analytical psychology.

> It has taken me virtually forty-five years to distill within the vessel of my scientific work the things I experienced and wrote down at that time. As a young man my goal had been to accomplish something in my science. But then, I hit upon this stream of lava, and the heat of its fires reshaped my life. That was the primal stuff which compelled me to work upon it, and my works are a more or less successful endeavor to incorporate this incandescent matter into the contemporary picture of the world. The years when I was pursuing my inner images were the most important in my life – in them everything essential was decided. It all began then; the later details are only supplements and clarifications of the material that burst forth from the unconscious, and at first swamped me. It was the *prima materia* for a lifetime's work.
>
> (Jung 1961: 199)

Jung is speaking of the fateful period in his life that had its beginnings in the disruption of his relationship with Freud when he was 37 years of age. The break with Freud left him in a disturbing state of disorientation. Nothing he could do – interpreting his dreams, reviewing his early memories – relieved his distress. As a last resort he submitted to the unconscious and waited for what might arise. What came up was a memory of himself when he was 10 or 11 years of age 'playing passionately with building blocks'. He recalled how he built 'little houses and castles using bottles to form the sides of gates and vaults'. To Jung's astonishment this memory carried a great deal of emotion. 'The small boy is still around', he says, 'and possesses a creative life which I lack. But how can I make my way to it?' It seemed impossible that as a grown man he could bridge the distance to his childhood. Yet he realized that to re-establish contact with that period he would have to 'take up once more that child's life with his childish games':

> This moment was a turning point in my fate, but I gave in only after endless resistances and with a sense of resignation. For it was a painfully humiliating experience to realize that there was nothing to be done except play childish games.
>
> (Jung 1961: 173–4)

Jung took up playing again as a child on the shore of Lake Zurich. This playing led him down the path of memory to the recovery of the most frightening and significant dream of his early childhood. This dream which had haunted his childhood, had for long been forgotten. Recovering this dream put him on the course to the development of his method of active imagination and his theory of analytical psychology. I shall take this up again further on in the discussion of Jung's synthesis (Chapter 9). For now it suffices to note that Jung developed his method out of his own need to cope with the affects and images that almost engulfed him. This can be seen to be true of Freud, Adler and Rank as well.

In the practice of depth psychology much has been made of the theme of the 'wounded healer'. The theme appears to have its origins in the ancient tales of Asclepius, the early Greek god of medicine. Asclepius learned about healing from his teacher, the centaur, Chiron. Part human, part animal instinct, Chiron suffers from an incurable wound. Thus the teacher of the archetypal physician is at once wounded and preoccupied with questions about healing (Kerenyi 1947: 83). The healer is found in all societies, from the most ancient tribal groups to the most modern nations. In the earliest societies the healer (as shaman or medicine man/woman), dealt with both physical and psychological illness, and this continued to be the role of the medical doctor for many centuries. Psychotherapy *per se* is a very recent development. Jung suggests the beginnings of psychotherapy lie in the Reformation, when the priest no longer mediated between God and suffering humans, and confession was no longer offered as surcease for the troubled soul.

It is the failure of relationship to oneself and to others that is at the core of all need for psychotherapy. This is the basic reason why psychotherapists have been found necessary for psychological healing. Freud and Jung both came to realize that a depth psychologist should undergo analysis. They themselves had a need for a psychotherapist. Freud was the first to experience this when he found in his friend Fliess a confidant with whom he could conduct his own self-analysis. Freud was Jung's first therapist, and they analysed each other's dreams. During Jung's further self-analysis after his break with Freud, he appears to have had Toni Wolff as companion and no doubt, muse. We do not know if Adler had someone who served as therapist for him. He certainly studied Freud very thoroughly. However, Adler's theory has little to say about the unconscious; perhaps this is a consequence of his not having had someone with whom to explore the transference experience. It is possible that Rank was analysed by Freud.

We turn now to a brief review of depth psychology. The history of depth psychology provides an unusual opportunity to understand better the fourfold cycle of creative change. First, we find that the theories of the pioneers of depth psychology reflect the personalities of their authors. Second, we find that the sequence of development of the general theory of depth psychology passes through stages representing the unique contributions of each of the pioneers. Third, this sequence follows the pattern of the fourfold cycle of creativity I discussed in Chapter 5. The cycle is initiated by a younger son or daughter (Mesmer, consolidated in the school of Charcot); tested and extended by a first-born son or daughter (Freud); and modified and adapted by intermediate-born sons or daughters (Adler). It may be disputed by last-borns or younger sons or daughters (Rank) – and perhaps others as well, before it is finally brought to a synthesis by an only child, or only son/daughter (Jung).

In overview it is apparent that the works of the great pioneers of depth psychology reveal a complexly interwoven fabric of conceptions in which the unique genius of each is revealed through the psychological viewpoints inherent in the four basic sibling positions: first-born son, Sigmund Freud (**M1**[m]FFFFFM); second son, Alfred Adler (MM2F[m]FMM); last son, Otto Rank (M[f]**M2**); and only son, Carl Gustav Jung (**M1F**). Of course depth psychology had early precursors, as Jung points out in the following brief accounting of the stages of development that the idea of the unconscious passed through:

> Freud is borne along by a particular current of thought which can be traced back to the Reformation. Gradually it freed itself from innumerable veils and disguises, and it is now turning into the kind of psychology which Nietzsche foresaw with prophetic insight – the discovery of the psyche as a new fact. Some day we shall be able to see by what tortuous paths modern psychology has made its way from the dingy laboratories of the alchemists, via mesmerism and magnetism (Kerner, Ennemoser, Eschimayer, Baader, Pasavant, and others), to the philosophical anticipations of Schopenhauer, Carus, and von Hartmann; and how, from the native soil of everyday experience in Liebeault and, still earlier, in Quimby (the spiritual father of Christian Science), it finally reached Freud through the teachings of the French hypnotists. This current of ideas flowed together from many obscure sources, gaining rapidly in strength in the nineteenth century and winning many adherents, amongst whom Freud is not an isolated figure.
>
> (Jung 1930: 324–5)

Depth psychology *per se* appears to have emerged with younger son Mesmer, and his concept of animal magnetism. Gradually it was transformed in the ways Jung mentions above until it was taken up by the French hypnotists, Charcot and Janet in particular, and the theory of abreaction developed. Hypnosis and abreaction demonstrated that the ego was not fully in control of its own house. Breuer's famous case of Anna O. seemed to confirm the theory of abreaction. Freud, who had originally been impressed by Charcot's off-the-cuff remarks on the role of sexuality in the etiology of neurosis was now seized by the findings of Breuer (**M1M**) with his famous patient Anna O. In no time at all Freud developed the 'psychic telescope'. His direct exploration of the unconscious through the interpretation of dreams, the technique of free association and the revival of personal history in the transference carried as great a shock value then, as had Galileo's exploration of the moon with the newly-invented telescope some two centuries earlier. Just as many sceptics at first refused to look at Freud's (**M1[m]FFFFFM**) moonscape of the unconscious as refused to look through Galileo's (**M1MMFFF**)[1] telescope at the moon in the heavens.

Adler rebelled at what he saw as the limitations of Freud's views; his own experience was different. And when Freud refused to accept his contributions, and forced him to leave the Vienna group, Adler formed his own society and developed a coherent theory of individual psychology. On the whole he seemed to profit from his removal from the Freudian circle. Rank was a typical last-born rebel who eventually disputed and disavowed the theories of Freud, Adler and Jung. His contribution to the non-directive psychological movement and to the development of the art psychotherapies may be seen as his Copernican step.

In the early years Jung, too, was a disciple. He was trained and analysed by the master, had incorporated much of Freud's thought and based his early practice of psychotherapy on Freud's concepts. To be sure, he was also critical of some aspects of Freud's theory, particularly his concept of libido as the sex drive. For several years he saw no need to push these differences; he did not yet have a theory of his own. But when he and Freud abruptly ended their collaboration, Jung found himself disoriented and without any firm footing. It took him a number of years to work his way through his own self-analysis to a solid theoretical and practical basis for his work. Gradually his theory evolved into a synthesis and transformation, built on the work of both Freud and Adler. He cited Rank's early writings and may have followed his developing thought. The full impact of the synthesis of depth psychology achieved by Jung with the affects as the foundation of the psyche, his concept of the archetype and his understanding of the process of individuation is yet to be realized.

The foregoing is a very brief sketch of stages in the evolution of depth psychology from younger son Mesmer to only son Jung. In the following section I shall give substance to this summary by seeking to show how Freud, Adler, Rank and Jung approached depth psychology from the unique viewpoints they acquired in their families and from the culture around them.

THE EARLY MEMORIES OF FREUD, ADLER, RANK AND JUNG

The first approach to the uniqueness of each of these pioneers is through their own early memories. Early memories are those mysterious bits of a past life which float up from the vast abyss of time in brief vignettes which are like icons. We immediately recognize ourselves even though we may not be able to penetrate back to any other memory of that time, which for some exceptional individuals may have been as early as the first year of life. These vignettes usually do not bring with them a cluster of other memories. They are vivid but isolated recollections of a time that we have little personal knowledge of at all. Yet they are convincingly real. The focus here is on 'what is remembered' by an individual, and this specificity is significant. For Hillman, the specificity is due to their archetypal nature:

> The *memorability* of specific images – the little neighbor girl in a yellow sunsuit digging to China on the July beach, the lost bloodied tooth in the party cake – that precisely these images, and these images precisely, have been selected, retrieved, recounted tells that their vital stuff is archetypally memorable. Memory infuses images with memorability, making the images more 'real' to us by adding to them the sense of the time past, giving them historical reality. But the historical reality is only a cover for soul significance, only a way of adapting the archetypal sense of mystery and importance to a consciousness engrossed in historical facts. If the image doesn't come as history, we might not take it for real.
>
> (Hillman 1983: 41)

It is difficult to know what Hillman is trying to convey by his willingness to make memory sound like the guardian of our sense of reality. Nothing could be more true, a loss of memory is a loss of identity. Thus it is that every individual with a sense of identity will have specific memories of what may be called an 'archetypal' nature. The very early memories of childhood particularly carry the numinous quality of archetypal significance. It was just for this reason that Jung, in the throes of the unshakeable malaise which overtook him following the bitter break with Freud, reviewed all the details of his childhood memories, twice, in search of any clues that might suggest he was having a mental breakdown (Jung 1961: 173).

Early memories represent critical events in what might be called the child's myth. Early memories also reveal details of the developing sibling complex. Each child enters the family at a specific point in the family's cycle; for each child there is a 'basic' family which is its starting point in life. Let us begin with Sigmund Freud, whose family constellation was a complicated one, and who has left a series of early memories which were of great significance to him. When Freud was born his mother, Amalia, was in her early twenties. His father, Jakob, was in his forties. Young Sigmund was his mother's first child. Jakob had two sons from an earlier marriage: Emanuel was in his mid-20s; Philipp was a year or two younger, perhaps 22 or 23. Emanuel was married and had two children, a son (John) about a year older than Freud, and a daughter about his age. Emanuel and his family lived three or four blocks away. Philipp, who was not married, lived across the street (Vitz 1988).

Sigmund Freud

First-born children are likely to be sensitized to jealousy when they are 'dethroned', to use Adler's apt term, by the birth of a sibling. Many of the 'famous' child cases reported in the depth psychology literature have been first-born children: Little Hans (Freud 1909), Jung's daughter Agathle (Jung 1910), Dibs (Axline 1964), the Piggle (Winnicott 1977), and so on. Freud was his mother's first-born child. His earliest memory is in response to his younger brother Julius who was born when Freud was 1 year and 5 months of age, and who died when Freud was not quite 2:

> I welcomed my . . . younger brother (who died within a few months) with ill wishes and real infantile jealousy . . . his death left the germ of guilt in me.
>
> (Freud 1954: 219)

Of course, for Freud's jealousy complex to have become so important an element of his psychology it is necessary to assume that the family atmosphere fostered it. For most of the first three years of his life, perhaps from as early as one month, it is very likely that a 'nanny', a Czech woman, called Resi (Theresa) took care of him (Vitz 1988: 12–16). During those early years of his life Freud had to cope with a complicated family situation. As we see, he experienced jealous rage, loss and humiliation at being replaced by another baby, and then, in addition, his own remorse and his mother's mourning when the infant died. His mother was almost immediately pregnant with his sister Anna. Julius died in April 1858; Anna was born the last day of that year, 31 December, 1858. Amalia suffered another major loss during this same period. Her younger brother Julius (after whom her baby had been named), died on 15 March, 1858, just one month before the baby died.

It appears that perhaps as early as a month to a few months after his birth Freud's nanny became a substitute mother to whom he became closely attached. Even so closely as to suggest to himself when reflecting on his own life, and to others who have studied the details of his early life, that she was in essence his primary mother (Vitz 1988: 3–30). When he was about 3, she was accused of stealing, was peremptorily dismissed, reported to the police and imprisoned. The loss Freud experienced when she was dismissed was as great or greater than the original sense of abandonment by his mother when she gave birth to Julius, as witness the following. In a letter to Fliess, Freud wrote:

My 'primary originator' (of neurosis) was an ugly, elderly but clever woman who told me a great deal about God and hell, and gave me a high opinion of my own capacities. . . If . . . I succeed in resolving my hysteria I shall have to thank the memory of the old woman who provided me at such an early age with the means of living and surviving.

(Vitz 1988: 8)

A short time later Freud wrote to Fliess again on the same theme.

I asked my mother whether she remembered my nurse. 'Of course,' she said, 'an elderly woman, very shrewd indeed. She was always taking you to church [in alle Kirche – in all the churches; Freiberg, though small, had at least three Catholic churches.] When you came home you used to preach, and tell us all about how God [der liebe Gott – the loving God] conducted His affairs.' At the time I was in bed when Anna was being born she turned out to be a thief, and all the shiny Kreutzers and Zehners and toys that had been given to you were found among her things. Your brother Philipp went himself to fetch the policeman, and she got ten months. [German from the original letter]

(Vitz 1988: 14)

Related to the threat of abandonment that Freud must have felt is the following memory and reflections on it, reported by Freud:

If the woman disappeared so suddenly . . . some impression of the event must have been left inside me. Where is it now? Then a scene occurred to me which for the last twenty-nine years had been turning up from time to time in my conscious memory without my understanding it. I was crying my heart out, because my mother was nowhere to be found. My brother Philipp . . . opened a cupboard for me, and when I found my mother was not there either I cried still more, until she came around the door, looking slim and beautiful. What can that mean? Why should my brother open the cupboard for me when he knew that my mother was not inside it and that opening it therefore could not quiet me? Now I suddenly understand. I must have begged him to open the cupboard. When I could not find my mother, I feared she must have vanished, like my nurse not long

before. I must have heard that the old woman had been locked, or
rather 'boxed' up.

(Vitz 1988: 22)

Vitz and others have drawn attention to the interest Freud showed in
the theme of the two mothers, as witness his articles on Leonardo and
Moses, and, of course his interest in the Oedipus drama. Freud was
suspiciously observant of his mother from early on as the memory
reveals. His next most moving and disturbing childhood memory
occurred around the same time at the age of 3. While on a train journey
with his mother from his original home to a new home in another city
he reports having seen his mother in the nude. This experience carried
such a numinous and forbidding charge that when he wrote of it as an
adult, when he was some 40 years of age, he could name it only in a
dead language, Latin.

To add another twist to the complications of Freud's first three years
of life, it has been suggested that Freud's mother Amalia and his adult
half-brother Philipp were sexually involved around the time that the
nanny was discharged. Although the evidence is circumstantial, it is
highly suggestive, and has been accepted as probable by some (Vitz
1988: 39–45). Whether literally true or whether in the air, this would
have added to the early sexualization of Freud's fantasy life. Freud's
associations to the memory of Philipp and the cupboard led him to
suspect that his mother had been pregnant again and had delivered
another baby, for she appeared in the dream slim and youthful in
appearance. He also felt that Philipp was implicated in this in some
way, as he had been in the disappearance of Freud's Catholic nanny just
a short while before. This time in Freud's life corresponded with the
birth of his sister Anna, whom he is said never to have liked.

In these memories of Freud's early years, there can be little question
but that the seeds of a sibling jealousy complex were planted as early as
17 months of age when his brother Julius was born, and, moreover, that
this complex was fostered and complicated by the subsequent death of
his brother Julius, and the birth a few months later of another sibling.
The seeds of another complex of loss were planted during this same
period as a consequence of the complications of his 'two mothers',
Amalia and Resi. He first experienced loss with Amalia when she
turned him over to Resi, and then perhaps an even more disturbing loss
when Resi, who by then had become his 'primary' mother, suddenly
disappeared when he was about 3 years of age. The normal
developmental stage of the Oedipus complex was also complicated by

the puzzling question of just who his father was, Philipp, or his biological father who in age could have been his grandfather. And perhaps Philipp was actually involved with Amalia in a sexual relationship. With all this possible stimulus to fantasy, and with babies appearing regularly, eight in all over a period of ten years, and Freud's numinous experience of seeing his mother naked on the train trip to Leipzig, it is safe to say that sex was in the air. In this light, Freud's later preoccupation with sex and the primal scene in his theory of psychoanalysis seems a not improbable outcome.

To add to this conclusion is the recent evidence that Jakob Freud sexually molested his children. Certain portions of letters that were long kept a secret, speak directly to the issue. In a letter to Wilhelm Fliess dated 21 September 1897, Sigmund Freud reviews some of the symptoms of hysteria, and notes that his own father was responsible for the hysteria of his brothers and sisters. As we know, in the early stages of psychoanalysis Freud traced the origins of hysteria to the sexual seduction and abuse of children.

> Unfortunately, my own father was one of these perverts and is responsible for the hysteria of my brother (all of whose symptoms are identifications) and those of several younger sisters.
>
> (Freud 1985: 230–1)

In another letter to Fliess, Freud points again to his father's perversion.

> Then the surprise that in all cases, the *father*, not excluding my own, had to be accused of being perverse.
>
> (Freud 1985: 264)

Vitz (1988) does not accept the implication that Jakob molested young Sigmund. 'Freud's comments about his father primarily implicate Jakob with respect to Freud's siblings, not himself' (Vitz 1988: 132). Drawing from numerous sources, Vitz turns his attention instead to the nanny as a possible source of Freud's childhood sexual 'seduction'. Vitz quotes from a letter Freud wrote to Fliess as follows: 'She was my instructress in sexual matters, and chided me for being clumsy' (ibid.). Vitz goes on to say that the 'she' in this letter has been assumed to be Freud's nanny, but he also suggests that it might have been a servant girl. In the end, after reviewing all the evidence, Vitz says:

> I conclude . . . that Freud as a child was eroticized by his nanny or by some other female servant, and that his half-nephew John also probably contributed to this; the seductions set up a kind of

compulsive masturbation combined with sexual fantasies. The childhood erotic behavior was also severely challenged by a strong castration threat, reinforced by the nanny but ultimately traceable to Freud's father.

(Vitz 1988: 141)

Here we see the personal origins of Freud's theory of sexuality, in which libido and incest are intricately intertwined. Freud originally understood incest in the conventional sense as sexual relationships between members of the immediate family. When his women patients told him that their fathers or older brothers had taken sexual liberties with them as children and adolescents, Freud reasoned that this was the traumatic source of their neurotic symptoms. Later, as we know, he was persuaded by indignant fathers who denied such behaviour, that it was a mistake to believe these stories. Freud then recanted and proposed instead that his patients were telling him their childhood fantasies. Thus, the Oedipus complex became the cornerstone of his theory of neurosis.

This decision turns out to have been a double-edged sword. On the one hand there was an apparent psychological gain in this shift from trauma as literal experience to trauma as a function of fantasy; it focused attention on the role of fantasy in the psychic life of the individual. But there was an unfortunate legacy from this way of thinking. It haunts us still today in the tortured lives of children who are sexually abused by family members, but whose stories are often not believed and are dismissed as the fantasies of the child's 'normal' libidinous and seductive nature (Russell 1986). It would appear that much of the psychological trauma suffered by children and young adults results from this incestuous rupture of the family *temenos* and the intense humiliation it engenders. As Masson (1984) has shown, Freud was right in the first place to believe what his patients told him. Incest in families was common in Freud's time as it is today. Then as now, it tends to remain a shameful secret, publicly unacknowledged.

Alfred Adler

For a later-born it is often the emotional impact of the older sibling or siblings who live in the home that is reflected in early memories. Adler's earliest memory was of:

sitting on a bench bandaged up on account of rickets, with my healthy elder brother sitting opposite me. He could run, jump, and move about quite effortlessly, while for me movement of any sort was a strain and an effort. Everyone went to great pains to help me, and my mother and father did all that was in their power to do. At the time of this recollection I must have been about two years old.

(Adler, in Bottome 1957: 30–1)

The core of this memory is the sense of inferiority engendered by his illness. One can recognize in this memory the seed of his later preoccupation with 'organ inferiority'. Later memories and comments refer to the two- or three-year-older brother as the successful, competent one and to himself as the envious one suffering from sickliness and feelings of inferiority.

Another memory when he was 3 years of age impressed him with the idea that he 'must in the future judge mankind not by their spoken words and sentiments, but by their actions'. The memory was of a time when he and his older brother were left alone for a few days in the care of a governess. When his parents came back he met them as he was singing a street song:

The song was about a woman who explained that she couldn't eat chicken because she was so hurt by the killing of her little hen. At this, the singer asks how she can have such a soft heart when she thinks nothing of throwing a flower pot at her husband's head. My father at once decided to dismiss the governess, concluding quite rightly that she had taken me to musical shows in the evenings. In spite of the fact that he was pleased at my singing, he looked at what lay behind it; looked deeper, something I also learned to do. But I, too, was deeper, in that I realized that I must in the future judge mankind not by their spoken words and sentiments, but by their actions. Once the song had put this into my head, the idea remained forever and grew stronger and stronger.

(Adler, in Bottome 1957: 11)

A younger brother was born when Adler was 4 years of age and he suffered the usual feelings at losing the full attention and care he had received because of his sickliness.

I was nearly four years old. My younger brother had been born. I remember him only very slightly, but his death remains firmly fixed in my mind. Before he was born, there can be no doubt that I was reared and watched with the greatest solicitude on account of my sickliness. I am sure that I must have been forced to put up with a great deal less of the attention when my younger brother was born. I have a vague idea that I took this apparent loss of attention on the part of my mother very much to heart. But it did not affect me in regard to my father, who was out all day working and to whom I became deeply attached. As I found out later, I wronged my mother in feeling that she deprived me of her affection. Throughout her life she loved all her children with the same degree of warmth and affection.

(Adler, in Bottome 1957: 9–10)

One thing to be noted about this memory is that it sounds as if the brother who died was the next-born child, but this was not the case. A sister was born when Adler was 1 year and 8 months of age. He reports no memory related to her birth or her impact on his life. The birth of a sister probably carried less sense of displacement in a patriarchal family. It is of interest to note that Adler, like Freud, experienced the death of a younger brother in early childhood. At the time of the death of his younger brother, Freud was 1 year and 7 months of age. Adler was slightly over 4 years of age when his brother died.

Death was an early and prominent experience for Adler, not only on account of the death of his younger brother, but in his own experience. Referring to this fact when he wrote his memories down as an adult, Adler speaks of his reaction in rather distant terms:

My early realization of the fact of death – a fact which I grasped sensibly and wholesomely, not morbidly; not regarding death as an insurmountable menace for a child – was increased when I had pneumonia at the age of five, and the doctor, who had suddenly been called in, told my father that there was no point in going to the trouble of looking after me, as there was no hope of my living. At once a frightful terror came over me, and a few days later, when I was well, I decided definitely to become a doctor so that I should have a better defense against the danger of death and weapons to combat it superior to my doctor's . . . After that the determination to become a doctor never left me. I never could picture myself taking up any other profession. Even the fascinating lure of art, despite the fact that I had considerable abilities in various forms of music, was not enough to turn me from my chosen path, and I persisted although many complex difficulties lay between me and my goal.

(Adler, in Bottome 1957: 11–12)

Despite the easy way in which Adler appears to have dealt with his fear of death it carried more lasting significance as he reveals in the following discussion:

> In the joy over my recovery, there was talk for a long time about the mortal danger in which I was supposed to have been. From that time on I recall always thinking of myself in the future as a physician. This means that I had set a goal from which I could expect an end to my childlike distress, my fear of death. Clearly, I expected more from the occupation of my choice than it could accomplish: The overcoming of death and of the fear of death is something I should not have expected from human, but only from divine accomplishments. Reality, however, demands action, and so I was forced to modify my goal by changing the conscious form of the guiding fiction until it appeared to satisfy reality. So I came to choose the occupation of physician in order to overcome death and the fear of death.
>
> (Adler 1956: 199)

But the fear of death did not disappear so easily. In another memory Adler describes his daily fear of passing over a cemetery on the way to school when he was 5. The pivotal moment though, is when he becomes aware of his perceived inferiority and decides to do something about it. The idea of being less courageous than the others is at once problem and solution.

> I remember that the path to the school led over a cemetery. I was frightened every time and was exceedingly put out at beholding the other children pass the cemetery without paying the least attention to it, while every step I took was accompanied by a feeling of fear and horror. Apart from the extreme discomfort occasioned by this fear I was also annoyed at the idea of being less courageous than the others. One day I made up my mind to put an end to this fear of death. Again, I decided upon a treatment of hardening. I stayed at some distance behind the others, placed my schoolbag on the ground near the wall of the cemetery and ran across it a dozen times, until I felt that I had mastered the fear.
>
> (Adler 1959: 179–80)

Curiously enough, at the age of 35 Adler was told by a childhood school chum that there had never been a cemetery on the way to their school. Memory, or remembered fantasy, it was real enough for the boy to remember into his adult life. And even as a physician Adler found it difficult to tolerate death:

Adler gave up his general medical practice after the death of several of his diabetic patients. Powerless to forestall these patients' deaths in the days before the discovery of insulin, Adler was overwhelmed by his old enemy.

(Monte 1977: 313)

There are obvious differences in the early memories of Freud and Adler. Adler is born into a family where another child had recently been born. His earliest memory is a comparison of himself and his elder brother. Feelings of inferiority – shame – and envy are evoked. These are cornerstone emotions of Adler's theory of individual psychology. The other significant emotion is fear, no doubt terror, at the age of 5, when the insensitive doctor proclaimed his imminent and inevitable death. One can see that Adler's childhood decision to become a doctor reflects another tenet of his theory of individual psychology, namely, what he called the 'style of life' which was determined by conscious decisions to achieve goals made with an 'as if' state of mind. His conscious decision to master his fear of the cemetery (rather than be less courageous than others) is an earlier example of this.

Otto Rank

Rank also constructed a theory of depth psychology, although later than the others. For various reasons it hasn't received as widespread attention as the theories of Freud, Adler and Jung. Throughout the time of his association with Freud, Rank was highly creative and productive. After Freud excluded Adler and Jung, Rank became his most intimate confidant, and was considered by Freud to be his heir apparent. Rank's *The Myth of the Birth of the Hero* (1909) undoubtedly had an influence on Jung who cites it in 'Symbols of transformation' (1956). In a letter to Freud, Jung responds with praise for Rank's initial work which Freud had sent him (Freud and Jung 1974: 32). In subsequent letters Jung remarks positively on Rank's other contributions. Rank's most wide'y known publication is *Art and Artist* which he revised several times over the years. A very early version of this book was Rank's entrée to Freud's circle.

Unfortunately biographical information about Rank's early childhood is very scant. It comes almost entirely from a journal he kept for a few years as a young adult. Rank was the youngest of three children. He had an exemplary elder brother and a sister who died when she was a few weeks old. From early on he was a sickly child suffering from rheumatism. His father was an alcoholic and a tyrant who seems to have had no interest in his children except to traumatize them. But most of the time, the father left the boys to themselves. The mother attended to seeing that they were fed and clothed; then she too left them to their own activities. From time to time the elder brother stood up to the father in what Rank describes as horrendous shouting matches. On these occasions Rank and his mother regularly fled the scene. Finally the two brothers and the mother stopped speaking to the father and things became more tranquil although not improving in any other way.

The elder brother, by virtue of his patriarchal privilege, was sent to the university. Otto was sent to middle school, and then to a technical school where he was trained in an occupation which he hated. His older brother introduced him to the theatre and opera when he was a teenager and that opened wide the door to his own self-education in art, music, philosophy and literature, through intensive reading. He began a journal which reveals his extraordinary insight into literature in general and philosophy in particular. He quickly absorbed the writings of Nietzsche, Schopenhauer and others. During this period of his splendid isolation, he seems not to have had any friends, and to have held very juvenile, contemptuous attitudes toward humanity in general. He was suicidal at times and once purchased a gun for that purpose. Gradually, however, as his self-education continued, his depression began to lift. Then one day his journal contained a new kind of entry. It referred to a man named Freud and to *The Interpretation of Dreams* (Freud 1900). Before long Rank had read all of Freud's works and, what is more, he understood them thoroughly, almost matter of factly, as if this was what had been at the back of his own mind for some time. He began to believe in himself as a creative writer, and made a number of attempts at writing plays and novels, only fragments of which have survived. However, he became very serious about one project which he entitled *Art and Artist*. It was a psychological treatise on the creative artist, and it drew heavily on Freud's ideas. When it was completed he somehow managed to bring it to Freud's attention. Freud was enthusiastic about the book and the creative intellect he saw behind it, and invited Rank to join his Vienna group. Freud persuaded Rank to get a university education, and assisted him financially. Rank became the secretary of the Vienna group and was Freud's closest associate during that time.

But Rank made the same mistake as Adler and Jung. He took seriously Freud's repeated reassurances as to the need for innovations in psychoanalysis, and proceeded to develop his own views of psycho-analytic theory, for which he too was expelled. The work which invited controversy amongst the true believers in the Vienna group was *The Trauma of Birth* (1924). If we allow ourselves a speculation, it might appear that when Rank published his *The Myth of the Birth of the Hero* in 1909, he was taking the first step toward his own evolution as the hero, and now his *Trauma of Birth* could be seen as a further stage in his realization of the role of the hero.

As we consider important links between Rank's psychological development and his theory, we may note that he suffered early and persistent emotional deprivation and neglect at the hands of both parents. Then there was the sense of inferiority and shame at hiding in his mother's skirt, so to speak, while his elder brother challenged the father. One of Rank's tenets was that individuals suffer from either the fear of death or the fear of life. This might be seen as Rank's counterpart to Jung's extrovert and introvert. The core psychological viewpoint that developed out of his *The Trauma of Birth*, was the role of the creative will in evoking a rebirth for the neurotic individual whom Rank spoke of as *l'artiste manqué*. The primary cultural attitude that seized him was the aesthetic. All this is consistent with his theory of the creative will and the goal of creative rebirth.

The most significant psychological impact of his childhood was emotional deprivation, the lack of love and nurturance which evokes the archetypal affect of sadness and may lead to depression. As we know, he was suicidal during his late teens. The image that evokes sadness is the void of loss, the compensatory symbol is rebirth.

After he was expelled by Freud, Rank moved to Paris where he wrote a series of volumes expounding his theory which came to be called 'will therapy'. These are wide-ranging, deeply-thoughtful analyses of Freud, Adler and Jung, and the development of depth psychology in general, including his own revisions. These works also express his views with respect to the practice of psychotherapy, education and the arts. When Rank travelled to America, he gave lectures, held classes, was well received and soon found adherents. As the first lay psychoanalyst, he was welcomed at the Philadelphia School of Social Work. This led indirectly to his influence on Carl Rogers, Harry Stack Sullivan and others. It can be said that in the United States, Rank was the initiator of the non-directive, 'client centred', self-transformative approach to psychotherapy. He also contributed to the emerging art psychotherapies which were inspired by his *Art and the Artist*, with its theory of the neurotic as the *'artiste manqué'*.

Carl Gustav Jung

What stands out in Jung's very early memories is the absence of siblings. Until the age of 9 Jung was an only child. Then his sister Gertrude was born. There were no other siblings. His memory of Gertrude when she was a new-born infant reveals highly-typical reactions, although they are tempered in expression by Jung's age.

> My father brought me to my mother's bedside, and she held out a little creature that looked dreadfully disappointing: a red, shrunken face like an old man's, the eyes closed, and probably as blind as a young puppy, I thought. On its back the thing had a few single long red hairs which were shown to me – had it been intended for a monkey? I was shocked and did not know what to feel. Was this how newborn babies looked?
>
> (Jung 1961: 25)

Now to Jung's earliest memories:

> One memory comes up which is perhaps the earliest of my life, and is indeed only a rather hazy impression. I am lying in a pram, in the shadow of a tree. It is a fine, warm summer day, the sky blue, and golden sunlight darting through green leaves. The hood of the pram has been left up. I have just awakened to the glorious beauty of the day, and have a sense of indescribable well-being. I see the sun glittering through the leaves and blossoms of the bushes. Everything is wholly wonderful, colorful, and splendid.
>
> (Jung 1961: 6)

This memory was followed by another pleasant one in which Jung was sitting in a high chair and spooning warm milk with bits of broken bread in it. However another memory a short time later reflects a more troubled time.

> I am restive, feverish, unable to sleep. My father carries me in his arms, paces up and down, singing his old student songs. I particularly remember one I was especially fond of and which always used to soothe me, 'Alles schweige, jeder neige. . .' The beginning went something like that. To this day I can remember my father's voice, singing over me in the stillness of the night.
>
> I was suffering, so my mother told me afterward, from general eczema. Dim intimations of trouble in my parents' marriage hovered around me. My illness, in 1878 [when Jung would have been 3 years of age], must have been connected with a temporary

separation of my parents. My mother spent several months in a hospital in Basel, and presumably her illness had something to do with the difficulty in the marriage.

(Jung 1961: 8)

As a consequence of his mother's absence, Jung says that he

always felt mistrustful when the word 'love' was spoken. The feeling I associated with 'woman' was for a long time that of innate unreliability. 'Father,' on the other hand, meant reliability and – powerlessness. That is the handicap I started off with.

(ibid.)

Jung now distinguishes between what he calls his 'outward memories', and 'more powerful, indeed overwhelming images', some of which he says he recalled only dimly:

At that time I also had vague fears at night. I would hear things walking about in the house. The muted roar of the Rhine Falls was always audible, and all around lay a danger zone. People drowned, bodies were swept over the rocks. In the cemetery nearby, the sexton would dig a hole – heaps of brown, upturned earth. Black, solemn men in long frock coats with unusually tall hats and shiny black boots would bring a black box. My father would be there in his clerical gown, speaking in a resounding voice. Women wept. I was told that someone was being buried in this hole in the ground. Certain persons who had been around previously would suddenly no longer be there. Then I would hear that they had been buried, and that Lord Jesus had taken them to himself.

(Jung 1961: 9)

The idea that death was associated with being 'taken' by Lord Jesus led Jung to the disturbing conclusion that Lord Jesus could not be trusted. An ordinary prayer that used to comfort him now began to stir feelings of dread: *Spread out thy wings, Lord Jesus mild, and take to thee thy chick, thy child. . .*

This sinister analogy had unfortunate consequences. I began to distrust Lord Jesus. He lost the aspect of a big, comforting, benevolent bird and became associated with the gloomy black men in frock coats, top hats, and shiny black boots who busied themselves with the black box.

These ruminations of mine led to my first conscious trauma. One hot summer day I was sitting alone, as usual, on the road in front of the house, playing in the sand. The road led past the house up a hill, then disappeared in the wood on the hilltop. So from the house you could see a stretch of the road. Looking up, I saw a figure in a strangely broad hat and a long black garment coming down from the wood. It looked like a man wearing women's clothes. Slowly the figure drew nearer, and I could now see that it really was a man wearing a kind of black robe that reached to his feet. At the sight of him I was overcome with fear, which rapidly grew into deadly terror as the frightful recognition shot through my mind: 'That is a Jesuit.' Shortly before, I had overheard a conversation between my father and a visiting colleague concerning the nefarious activities of the Jesuits. From the half-irritated, half-fearful tone of my father's remarks I gathered that 'Jesuits' meant something specially dangerous, even for my father. Actually I had no idea what Jesuits were, but I was familiar with the word 'Jesus' from my little prayer.

(Jung 1961: 10–11)

To review Jung's earliest memories: First he is alone and happy in his carriage in the garden. Around 3 years of age he experienced the trauma of his mother being away in the hospital. He suffered a general eruption of eczema. The innate affect of sadness had been constellated and the nucleus of a complex had formed which led to distrust of 'love' and women. Here we no doubt see the origins of his underlying depression which lasted up to the time of his university years, and occurred periodically thereafter. His early memories also reveal a developing distrust of Lord Jesus. (No doubt his anxious ruminations were magnified by the fact that his own father was a theologian, as were nine of his uncles, and as had been his maternal grandfather.) Surrounded by relatives who believed in a God that is only light and good, Jung could not express his concerns to anyone. Then came the terrifying experience of 'the Jesuit'. So terrified was Jung that he ran to the top of the house and hid on a beam in the forbidden attic. At this point Jung's imagination was potentiated by the innate affect of fear, a state of panic. This terrifying experience was closely followed by a nightmare. Jung dreamt of an underground monster in the form of a phallus on a golden throne. The nightmare too became linked with his ruminations about whether or not he could trust Lord Jesus.

Whatever the specific sibling complex may be that is generated for the first-born who is an only son or daughter, it is in part a function of the number of years that the first-born son or daughter is an only child.

Any complexes that may develop during that period are not a product of sibling relationships, since there are no siblings. Looked at the other way around it is obvious that the lack of siblings is the unique family experience so long as the child is an only child. If this period is a considerable number of years, nine in the case with Jung, we might therefore, expect that during the time that he was an only child he is likely to have experienced jealousy *and* envy of the parents in an intensified form. We might suggest that the only child is the Oedipal child *par excellence*. Oedipus was, after all, an only child.

To be sure, a first-born child with siblings and a second-born child may also experience jealousy and envy of the parents, particularly Oedipal/Electral jealousy of the parent of the same sex because of the parent's relationship to the parent of the opposite sex. However, for these children sibling rivalry goes on at the same time in a never-ending cycle throughout early childhood, no matter what emotions may be constellated in relation to the parents. The only child has no siblings to be rivalrous with. For the only child, jealousy and envy are experienced in relation to the parents, and there follows then the possibility of an ongoing cycle throughout childhood of the continuing constellation of these emotions in relation to the parents.

If we try to characterize what this is like for the only child it would likely be a more-or-less constant awareness of the need to appease or satisfy both parents. This comes about in part because of the conscious or unconscious rivalry that may arise between the parents for the child's favours. The only child, in contrast to any child with siblings, is constantly aware of the advantages and the disadvantages of being the only child that the parents have to love or hate, be jealous of or envy, and so on and on. This position in the family must potentiate a sense of power, and an equally deep sense of helplessness. The more closely one examines the relationship of the only child to its parents the more evident it becomes that a myriad of experiences of the opposites held in a precarious balance is the everyday life of the only child, as Jung notes:

> I began to see my parents with different eyes, and to understand their cares and worries. For my father in particular I felt compassion – less, curiously enough, for my mother. She always seemed to me the stronger of the two. Nevertheless I always felt on her side when my father gave vent to his moody irritability. This necessity for taking sides was not exactly favorable to the formation of my character. In order to liberate myself from these conflicts I fell into the role of the superior arbitrator who willy-nilly had to judge his

parents. That caused a certain inflatedness in me; my unstable self-assurance was increased and diminished at the same time.

(Jung 1961: 24–5)

Now, we may ask, is there an all encompassing emotion that characterizes the family experience of the only child? It would seem likely that a tendency to secretiveness develops; this was highly developed in Jung during his early childhood. To have a secret, something that no one else knows, gives one power. It fills a void; the void of loneliness? Loneliness is a complex family emotion, an emotion to which the only child is highly susceptible, as Jung was. Reflecting on his early childhood, Jung says that he 'played alone, and in my own way. . . I did not want to be disturbed. I was deeply absorbed with my games and could not endure being watched or judged while I played them' (ibid.: 17–18). Between the ages of 7 and 9 Jung says that he was 'fond of playing with fire'. In an old stone wall he built fires in the cracks, little 'caves'. No one was allowed to tend these fires but he himself. 'My fire', he says, 'was living and had an unmistakable sanctity.' Around the same time Jung became fond of a stone that was embedded in a slope. 'Often', he says, 'when I was alone, I sat down on this stone, and then began an imaginary game.' He would begin by saying to himself that he was sitting on the stone and it was underneath him, but then he thought: 'The stone also could say "I" and think: "I am lying here on this slope and he is sitting on top of me" '. Jung was left then with the very unsettling question. 'Am I the one who is sitting on the stone, or am I the stone on which *he* is sitting?' (ibid.: 19–20). Late in his life Jung summed up his thoughts about his loneliness:

> As a child I felt myself to be alone, and I am still, because I know things and must hint at things which others apparently know nothing of, and for the most part do not want to know. Loneliness does not come from having no people about one, but from being unable to communicate the things that seem important to oneself, or from holding certain views which others find inadmissible. The loneliness began with the experiences of my early dreams, and reached its climax at the time I was working on the unconscious. If a man knows more than others, he becomes lonely. But loneliness is not necessarily inimical to companionship, for no one is more sensitive to companionship than the lonely man, and companionship thrives only when each individual remembers his individuality and does not identify himself with others.

(Jung 1961: 356)

As Jung makes clear, secretiveness was for him an inseparable component of loneliness:

> It is important to have a secret, a premonition of things unknown. It fills life with something impersonal, a numinosum. A man who has never experienced that has missed something important. He must sense that he lives in a world which in some respects is mysterious; that things happen and can be experienced which remain inexplicable; that not everything which happens can be anticipated. The unexpected and the incredible belong in this world. Only then is life whole. For me the world has from the beginning been infinite and ungraspable.
>
> (Jung 1961: 356)

On the basis of these memories and Jung's own evaluations of his life, what can we say about Jung's theory of analytical psychology and his early memories? The basic sibling complex is that of loneliness, secretiveness. The synthetic propensity of the only child is apparent in Jung's description of his need to 'judge' his parents, that is to say, to attempt a broader view of the parents as a whole. His traumatic memory of the Jesuit and the dream of the 'underground phallus' foreshadow the period of his 'confrontation with the unconscious' in midlife. The potentiation of the archetypal imagination by the innate affect of terror that took place at the age of 4 to 5 years of age, unfolded in stages of creativity which required a lifetime's commitment.

There is another trauma that Jung experienced, but he says very little about it. As a boy he was sexually violated by a man he had once 'worshipped'. In an early letter to Freud (28 October 1907) Jung tries to explain the ambivalent feelings that come up in him around intimate relationships.

> My veneration for you has something of the character of a 'religious' crush. Though it does not really bother me, I still feel it is disgusting and ridiculous because of its undeniable erotic undertone. This abominable feeling comes from the fact that as a boy I was the victim of a sexual assault by a man I once worshipped. . . This feeling, which I still have not quite got rid of, hampers me considerably. Another manifestation of it is that I find psychological insight makes relations with colleagues who have a strong transference to me downright disgusting. *I therefore fear your confidence.* I also

fear the same reaction from you when I speak of my intimate affairs.
(Jung, in Freud and Jung 1974: 95)

The emotions Jung describes are disgust and fear. He must have also felt shame and humiliation, as well as terrible feelings of betrayal, but he does not speak of these directly. His fear seems to be somehow more bearable. He names the emotion and describes it in a forthright way. But when he tries to describe his feelings of disgust, it feels primitive, awkward. On one hand, he denies it ('it does not really bother me'), yet on the other hand, it doesn't go away ('I still feel it is disgusting and ridiculous').

I shall close with some of Jung's boyhood eruptions of anger. In his memoirs, Jung tells how he was accused of copying a composition he had turned in to a teacher. He was infuriated he says: 'I shot to my feet, as horrified as I was furious, and cried "I did not copy it!" ' (1961: 65). But the teacher did not believe him. Jung goes on to say that 'profoundly disheartened and dishonored, I swore vengeance on the teacher, and if I had had an opportunity something straight out of the law of the jungle would have resulted' (ibid). So moved by this experience was Jung that he commented on it some seventy years later when he was interviewed on BBC for the film *Face to Face*. He goes on to say:

My grief and rage threatened to get out of control. And then something happened that I had already observed in myself several times before: there was a sudden inner silence, as though a soundproof door had been closed on a noisy room. It was as if a mood of cool curiosity came over me, and I asked myself, 'what is really going on here? All right, you are excited. Of course the teacher is an idiot who doesn't understand your nature – that is, doesn't understand it any more than you do. Therefore he is as mistrustful as you are. You distrust yourself and others, and that is why you side with those who are naive, simple and easily seen through. One gets excited when one doesn't understand things.'
(Jung, in Freud and Jung 1974: 65–6)

As Jung's rage was transformed into curiosity and then thinking, there is a shift out of chaos toward an ordered cosmos. I tried to describe this kind of development in Chapter 5. Not long after this experience of rage, as well as other instances, and most particularly an ongoing frustration with his inability to engage his father in a discussion of his father's loss of faith, Jung became avidly devoted to reading all the books of philosophy he could put his hands on. This interest in philosophy persisted throughout his life. His philosophic cultural attitude was second in development only to his religious attitude, and, of course these two attitudes are intimately linked in Jung's works.

SUMMARY

To sum up what we learn from a comparison of the early memories of Freud, Adler, Rank and Jung: First of all it is apparent that they are different along a number of dimensions. For first-born Freud, jealous rage is evoked at 17 months of age, followed by remorse and guilt at 23 months. The seeds of a jealousy complex have been planted. Rage is an innate existential affect of the collective unconscious. When jealousy reaches an extreme intensity, rage may be constellated and potentiate a particular form of the archetypal imagination. The experience of rage is a psychosomatic state of chaos. The compensatory image that is then constellated in the unconscious is the opposite of chaos, that is, order, the ideal of the ordered cosmos. We know that jealousy, in the form of the Oedipus complex, eventually became a central dynamic of the 'family' romance in Freud's theory, and pursuit of the origins – the primal scene – became the reductive method that dispels Freud's primal chaos and restores a sense of order. The reductive focus is revealed in the detective-like story form of Freud's case histories, his cause and effect, theorizing and the like.

For second son Adler, an intermediate child, the innate affect of shame is evoked at around 2 years of age in the comparison of himself suffering from rickets, with a healthy, active older brother. The seeds of an envy complex are sown. As an innate existential affect, shame potentiates the archetypal imagination in a specific way. The affect of shame creates a psychosomatic state of alienation. The compensatory opposite is constellated in the unconscious as the archetypal imagination of relatedness, the ideal of Utopian communitas. Envy, then, becomes the central dynamic of Adler's theory of the 'ego's arrangements', while the 'as if' attitude becomes the teleological method of dispelling the sense of alienation. Adler constructs a 'style of life' that fosters the development of a social attitude. He came to the concept of 'social interest' as the necessary counter to feelings of inferiority and the striving for superiority.

From the perspective on the theories of Freud and Adler that I have sketched above, it is possible to see Freud's emphasis on sexual and jealousy theories as directly related to the 'family romance', and the expression of the Eros dimension of family relationships. Likewise, from this perspective we see that Adler focuses the other polar dimension of family relationships, power.

Rank, a last-born, was emotionally abandoned by both father and mother. Sadness was the primary existential affect that was constellated, along with fear and shame. The creative 'will', fashioned after Schopenhauer's will, was central to Rank's theory. It was the source of all creativity and the means of overcoming neurotic difficulties. Rank spoke of the neurotic as the *artiste manqué*. The cure of neurosis lay in the creative will which evokes a rebirth experience. This is the dynamic of the innate existential affect of sadness which is constellated by the experience of loss. The psychosomatic state created by the affect of sadness is a sense of emptiness, a void. The unconscious compensatory function of this form of the archetypal imagination is that of rebirth of the Great Mother, the abundance of Nature in all its beauty. This is the principle of the aesthetic cultural attitude.

Only son Jung's earliest traumas are related directly to the parents, without intervening experiences with siblings. He experiences an early constellation of the complex family emotions of secretiveness and guilt in relation to his mother's absence when he was 3, and the difficulties of the parents' marriage. This is followed closely by the terrifying experiences of the 'Jesuit' and the dream of an 'underground monster'. Terror is an innate existential affect that potentiates its specific form of the archetypal imagination. In terror, we are face to face with the unknown. The ground under our feet trembles and drops away as we fall into the abyss. The unconscious compensatory opposite is the image of the sacred, the symbol of the holy mountain. Jung's emphasis on religious symbolism can in part be inferred from this. From his memoirs we learn that the disruption of his ordinary religious attitude by the terrifying experiences described above left him struggling for the better part of his life to arrive at a satisfying reconstruction of a new religious attitude. This we know was not accomplished until late in his life in his works, 'The psychology of the transference' (1946a), 'Answer to Job' (1952), *Aion* (1951a), and *Mysterium Coniunctionis* (1963).

In conclusion I wish to acknowledge that the foregoing is not meant to be a comprehensive comparison of the theories of Freud, Adler, Rank and Jung. My intent has been to show that each of the pioneers was engulfed by emotions in early childhood, which were specific to the combination of their sibling position and family atmosphere. These early experiences foreshadowed important elements of their theories. The differences in the views espoused in their theories reflect the specific contributions each made to the overall cycle of creative change in depth psychology. I have also tried to show how the innate existential affects constellated in early childhood through the problematic, and mysterious atmosphere which permeated their families, eventuated for each of them in a potentiation of the archetypal imagination in one or more of its four basic forms. Over time the psyche seeks to recreate and transform the underlying early experiences that were at first overwhelmed by such influxes of emotion. This compensatory process, the dynamic tension of opposites, of conscious and unconscious, is intrinsic to the archetypal imagination.

It is important to realize that the ordinary situation for the child from infancy on is to have satisfying and illuminating experiences of each of the forms of the archetypal imagination. This normal expectation is due to the fact that the cultural forms have over the ages become innate functions of the psyche. Thus the cultural attitudes: the philosophic, the social, the aesthetic and the religious, are the innate counterparts, with respect to the spirit, of the innate functions of the ego: thinking, feeling sensation and intuition, with respect to the world. Over time everyone tends to develop certain preferences, or discovers a particular talent, for one or another of the cultural forms. This is due to a variety of innate and family influences, benign on the average so long as there is good enough parenting. But as with the pioneers of depth psychology, the family influences may stir deeper emotions and more problematic responses which, in the case of the field of psychology, can be traced back to its roots in the early Greek myth of Asclepius, the wounded healer.

As a consequence of their wounding, each of the pioneers of depth psychology was drawn to the field of psychological healing, and each was deeply involved, consciously and unconsciously, with the recreation in themselves of one or more particular cultural attitudes which had been potentiated by the archetypal imagination. Freud sought resolution through the reductive, sleuthing, truth-seeking method of the scientific/philosophic cultural attitude; Adler sought to restore a sense of relatedness through the social cultural attitude; Rank saw the neurotic as a 'failed artist' who must therefore find equilibrium in creative rebirth through the aesthetic cultural attitude; while Jung saw that modern man and woman suffer from a lack of 'wholeness' which can be restored through a transformative experience of the realized Self. For Jung, the image of the self, of wholeness, corresponds to the image of God, a complex of opposites, light and shadow, approached through the religious cultural attitude.

This is not to say that each of the four pioneers did not develop other, secondary, cultural attitudes as well. Freud, for example, had a strong aesthetic bent: he was a gifted writer. Late in his life he was given the Goethe prize. Jung, in addition to his highly-developed religious attitude, had a strong philosophic bent as a secondary cultural attitude. Adler whose social attitude was finely tuned, was also musically talented and in early life had wanted to pursue a musical career. Thus he may be seen as having the aesthetic as a secondary cultural attitude. It is difficult to identify for certain Rank's secondary cultural development, although it may well have been the social. Finally it is important to emphasize that there is no reason to believe that the family milieu is of necessity the same for everyone who develops a preference for a specific cultural attitude. We know too little yet about the process of being chosen by the spirit to make any such judgements.

It would seem then, that although the depth psychology pioneers were certainly culturally developed in many ways, there is nevertheless, at the very centre of their theories a *specific* cultural attitude. Is this just coincidence? To me it seems more likely that as we better understand the cycle of creativity and the psychological forces inherent in it, we shall come to see it as a mirror of the individuation process in the individual. It will eventually be understood, I believe, that the innate process of individuation follows a fourfold cycle which is recapitulated at every stage of human development in ways appropriate to the particular stage. In the course of psychotherapy it is necessary to revive, so to speak, the normal growth process of development which, for whatever reasons, has been thwarted by the individual's life experiences. The dialectical process of psychotherapy may then facilitate a recreation of the personality in accord with the psyche's normal, innate thrust toward individuation and wholeness. In a discussion of the symbolic cultural attitudes, Henderson suggests that they are intrinsic to the development of self-reflective consciousness. Another way of saying this: The aesthetic, religious, philosophic and social attitudes are fundamental to the realization of the self.

> I can imagine a group of future analysts teaching a new appreciation of old cultural attitudes not because they set out to do this on purpose in any missionarizing spirit but because this teaching would be an inevitable result of their way of working with their patients.
> (Henderson 1962: 14)

I would suggest as a further consequence, that any major change in society, such as the emergence of depth psychology, must of necessity involve creative individuals whose ideas reflect all of the basic cultural attitudes in order that the changes to be brought about may become as fully as possible representative of the fundamental nature of world and spirit.

NOTE

1 Galileo (**M1**MMFFF) was the first-born child in his family, but the order of his younger male and female siblings is in question.

Chapter 9

Jung's synthesis

Jung's synthesis of the stages of psychotherapy provides confirmation of the cycle of creative change. He creates a synthesis of the cathartic approach of the early mesmerists and hypnotists as consolidated in Charcot's school as the theory of abreaction; with Freud's theory of psychoanalysis; Adler's theory of individual psychology; and his own theory of analytical psychology. Jung's understanding of the stages of psychotherapy is of particular interest, since it is only in a field such as depth psychology that the outer, or world cycle of creative change could be compared with the inner-directed development of an individual in psychotherapy. What we see then in the stages of psychotherapy is the kind of circumambulation that Jung speculated about so much, particularly in his late writings on such subjects as the fourfold nature of the carbon atom and its innate circulatory process, as well as his fourfold figure of the pyramid structure of the evolution of life and consciousness. It seems to me highly likely that all of the world cycles of creative change, in science, politics, the arts, the religions and psychology, are of necessity projections of the innate individuation process on to the plane of society.

I shall begin with Jung's stages of psychotherapy and then turn to contempory reactions to Jung's synthesis.

EARLY HISTORICAL SOURCES

Jung's synthesis of depth psychology encompasses a wide range of concepts. There is the archetype as symbol and emotion, and as a pattern of behaviour; and psychological types, and the stages of psychotherapy; as well as his method of active imagination as a dialogue between the conscious ego and the unconscious and, of course, his concept of the self as the organizing principle of the collective unconscious – the archetype of meaning and orientation. Jung's broad perspective on all relevant developments in the fields of psychology, philosophy, science, archaeology and religion is impressive. He took the whole of human history and culture as the necessary background and source for his thought. The field of psychology provides a microcosm of his interests as a whole.

In the broadest sense, Jung draws from the knowledge of the ages, those ideas and observations of a psychological nature which in the Renaissance began to see the light of day again, and which in the eighteenth and nineteenth centuries began to take on a new empirical form. In an article titled 'Fundamental questions of psychotherapy' (1951b), Jung briefly reviews the history of depth psychology in this light. He gives high credit to Paracelsus as one of the first explorers of the 'psyche', but goes on to say, however, that:

> Not until two centuries later did a new altogether different kind of empiricism arise with [younger son] Mesmer's theory of animal magnetism, stemming partly from practical experiences which today we should attribute to suggestion, and partly from the old alchemical lore.
>
> (Jung 1951b: 111–12)

Jung says:

> The physicians of the Romantic Age then turned their attention to somnambulism, thus laying the foundations for the clinical discovery of hysteria. But then almost another century was to pass before Charcot and his school could begin to consolidate ideas in this field. Thanks are due Pierre Janet for a deeper and more exact knowledge of hysterical symptoms, and the two French physicians, Liebeault and Bernheim, later to be joined by August Forel in Switzerland, for a systematic investigation and description of the phenomena of suggestion.
>
> (Jung 1951b: 112)

The next major discovery was made by Breuer and Freud. With their recognition of the 'affective origins of psychogenic symptoms', Jung says,

> our knowledge of their causation took a decisive step forward into the realm of psychology. The fact that the affectively toned memory

images which are lost to consciousness lay at the root of the hysterical symptom immediately led to the postulate of an *unconscious* layer of psychic happenings.

(Jung 1951b: 112)

This layer proved not to be somatic as had been thought by academic psychologists, but rather psychic, 'because it behaves like any other psychic function from which consciousness is withdrawn, and which thus ceases to be associated with the ego'. Freud and Janet proved, at almost the same time, that this 'holds true of hysterical symptoms generally'. However, while Janet thought that the reason for 'the withdrawal of consciousness must lie in some specific weakness, Freud pointed out that the memory images which produce the symptoms are characterized by a disagreeable affective tone. Their disappearance from consciousness could thus easily be explained by *repression*' (Jung 1951b: 112). Jung then comments that an explorer in a new field must bear in mind that someone else may be approaching the same material in a different way. 'So it happened with Freud,' says Jung, 'his pupil Alfred Adler (MM2F[m]FMM) developed a view which shows neurosis in a very different light.' For Freud the root cause of neurosis has to do with sexuality. But for Adler, 'it is no longer the sexual urge, or the pleasure principle, that dominates the picture, but the urge to power, (self assertion, "masculine protest," "the will to be on top")' (Jung 1951b: 113).

THE FOUR STAGES OF PSYCHOTHERAPY

This is one of the most interesting and compelling of Jung's efforts to integrate the theories of Freud and Adler into a comprehensive whole; and to show how, and where, his theory of analytical psychology fits. 'I would venture', he says, 'to regard the sum total of our findings under the aspect of four stages, namely, confession, elucidation, education and transformation' (Jung 1931b: 55). Jung suggests that *confession* is the first and universal beginning, common to all psychotherapies. The stage of *elucidation* he assigns to Freud's psychoanalysis. The third stage, *education*, is related to Adler's individual psychology. The fourth stage, *transformation*, is his own contribution, analytical psychology. Jung's formulation of the stages of psychotherapy deserves special attention. It represents his most considered effort to draw the theories of Freud and Adler into a synthesis while at the same time giving them due respect. In addition, though, this fourfold scheme of the stages of psychotherapy is important for the insight it provides into the natural, self-directed processes of psychotherapy and individuation.

1 The stage of confession: catharsis

'The first beginnings of all analytical treatment of the soul', Jung says, 'are to be found in its prototype, the confessional. . . Once the human mind had succeeded in inventing the idea of sin, man had recourse to psychic concealment; or, in analytical parlance, repression arose. Anything concealed is a secret' (1931b: 55). In secrets, Jung sees both a medicament and a poison:

> The possession of secrets acts like a psychic poison that alienates their possessor from the community. In small doses, this poison may be an invaluable medicament, even an essential pre-condition of individual differentiation, so much so that even on the primitive level man feels an irresistible need actually to invent secrets: their possession safeguards him from dissolving in the featureless flow of unconscious community life and thus from deadly peril to his soul.
> (ibid.: 55–6)

Jung notes another form of concealment, 'the act of holding something back. What we usually hold back are emotions or affects' (ibid.: 57). For Jung, different forms of neurosis can be attributed to:

> The respective predominance of secrets or of inhibited emotions. . . At any rate the hysterical subject who is very free with his emotions is generally the possessor of a secret, while the hardened psychasthenic suffers from emotional indigestion held.
> (ibid.: 58)

Jung points out that nature visits us with illness when we keep secrets and hold back emotions in private. When emotions are expressed in communion with others, he says, 'they satisfy nature and may even count as useful virtues' (ibid.).

> There would appear to be a sort of conscience in mankind which severely punishes every one who does not somehow at some time, at whatever cost to his virtuous pride, cease to defend and assert himself, and instead confess himself fallible and human. Until he can do this, an impenetrable wall shuts him off from the vital feeling that he is a man among other men.
> This explains the extraordinary significance of genuine

straightforward confession – a truth that was probably known to all the initiation rites and mystery cults of the ancient world. There is a saying from the Greek mysteries: 'Give up what thou hast, and then thou wilt receive'.

(ibid.: 58–9)

In its beginnings psychoanalysis is nothing but a scientific rediscovery of an 'ancient truth'.

In concluding his discussion of the nature of confession, Jung makes the following caveat:

Now I am far from wishing to enunciate a general maxim. It would be difficult to imagine anything more unsavory than a wholesale confession of sin. Psychology simply establishes the fact that we have here a sore spot of first-rate importance. As the next stage, the stage of elucidation, will make clear, it cannot be tackled directly, because it is a problem with quite particularly pointed horns.

(ibid.: 60)

2   The stage of elucidation: Freud's psychoanalysis

Faced with the transference, mere confession is of no avail. Jung says,

Freud was driven to substantial modifications of Breuer's cathartic method. What he now practised he called the 'interpretative method.' This further step is quite logical, for the transference relationship is in especial need of elucidation. . . The result of the Freudian method of elucidation is a minute elaboration of man's shadow-side unexampled in any previous age. It is the most effective antidote imaginable to all the idealistic illusions about the nature of man; and it is therefore no wonder that there arose on all sides the most violent opposition to Freud and his school.

(ibid.: 63-4)

Jung goes on to point out that

Freud's interpretative method rests on 'reductive' explanations which unfailingly lead backwards and downwards, and it is essentially destructive if over done or handled one-sidedly. Nevertheless psychology has profited greatly from Freud's pioneer work; it has learned that human nature has its black side – and not man alone, but his works, his institutions, and his convictions as well. Even our purest and holiest beliefs rest on very deep and dark foundations; after all, we can explain a house not only from the attic downwards, but from the basement upwards, and the latter explanation has the prime advantage of being genetically the more correct, since houses are in fact built bottom-side first, and the beginning of all things is simple and crude.

(ibid.: 64)

In his discussion of elucidation, Jung suggests that 'the uproar over Freud's interpretation' is really our own problem. It is our childish naivety. We do not yet understand the relationship of the opposites, nor realize that 'les extremes se touchent really is one of the ultimate verities' (ibid.: 64). Our fundamental error, which according to Jung, Freud also fell into, 'lies in supposing that the radiant things are done away with by being explained from the shadow-side' (ibid.: 64). Jung does not lament the shock Freud's exposures caused. On the contrary he welcomes it. It is, he says,

an historic and necessary rectification of almost incalculable importance. For it forces us to accept a philosophical relativism such as Einstein embodies for mathematical physics, and which is fundamentally a truth of the Far East whose ultimate effects we cannot at present foresee.

(ibid.: 64–5)

In this last sentence we get another glimpse of the wide-ranging nature of Jung's synthetic bent. We shall see further evidence of his attempts to incorporate the standpoints of the East and the world of physics. This is further clarified in his following comments:

Nothing, it is true, is less effective than an intellectual idea. But when an idea is a *psychic fact* that crops up in two such totally different fields as psychology and physics, apparently without historical connection, then we must give it our closest attention. For ideas of this kind represent forces which are logically and morally unassailable; they are always stronger than man and his brain. He fancies that he makes these ideas, but in reality they make him – and make him their unwitting mouthpiece.

(ibid.: 65)

3   The stage of education: Adler's individual psychology

Continuing then with the discussion of the four stages of psychotherapy, Jung considers next the stage of education. The problem the patient now faces is the need for 'education as a social being' (ibid.: 65). This brings us to Adler. Here, for the first time, Jung draws a connection between the theories of Freud and Adler in terms of sibling position in their families. He does not *say* that he has Freud and Adler in mind, but from other sources it is clear that he is aware of their respective sibling positions. At any rate he compares the dominant tenets of their theories, that is to say, Freud's pleasure principle, and Adler's principle of the striving for power, as follows:

> On the average, all those who have no difficulty in achieving social adaptation and social position are better accounted for by the pleasure principal than are the unadapted who, because of their social inadequacy, have a craving for power and importance. The elder brother who follows in his father's footsteps and wins to a commanding position in society may be tormented by his desires; while the younger brother who feels himself suppressed and overshadowed by the other two may be goaded by ambition and the need for self-assertion.
>
> (ibid.: 66)

'Adler's method', he says, 'begins essentially at the stage of elucidation':

> Adler has shown convincingly that numerous cases of neurosis can be far more satisfactorily explained by the power instinct than by the pleasure principle. The aim of his interpretation is therefore to show the patient that he 'arranges' his symptoms and exploits his neurosis in order to achieve a fictitious importance; and that even his transference and his other fixations subserve the will to power and thus represent a 'masculine protest' against imaginary suppression. Obviously Adler has in mind the psychology of the underdog, or social failure, whose one passion is self-assertion. Such individuals are neurotic because they always imagine they are hard done by and tilt at the windmills of their own fancy, thus putting the goal they most desire quite out of reach.
>
> (ibid.: 66–7)

But, as Jung points out, Adler does not put too much reliance on understanding. He goes beyond that to recognition of the 'need for social education' (ibid.: 67). The distinction between Freud and Adler, as Jung sees it, is that 'Freud is the investigator and interpreter, Adler is primarily the educator' (ibid.). Adler seeks to make the patient a 'normal and adapted person' (ibid.). In the stages of psychotherapy the educational aims of the Adlerian school begin precisely where Freud leaves off; consequently they meet the needs of the patient who, having come to understand himself, wants to find his way back to normal life. . . The patient must be *drawn out* of himself into other paths, which is the true meaning of 'education,' and this can only be achieved by an educative will.

(ibid.: 67–8).

4 The stage of transformation: Jung's analytical psychology

In introducing the fourth stage, Jung comments that every stage of psychotherapy seems to be complete in itself. Whether we're in the midst of emotional discharge (confession), tracing the neurosis to its roots in childhood (elucidation), or learning adaptive social skills to develop greater self-esteem (education), each stage seems to be all that is needed. As he sees it:

This curious sense of finality which attends each of the stages accounts for the fact that there are people using cathartic methods today who have apparently never heard of dream interpretation, Freudians who do not understand a word of Adler, and Adlerians who do not wish to know anything about the unconscious. Each is ensnared in the peculiar finality of his own stage, and thence arise that chaos of opinions and view which makes orientation in these troubled waters so exceedingly difficult.

(ibid.: 68–9)

Attempting to explain this situation, Jung concludes that 'each stage does in fact rest on a final truth, and that consequently there are always cases which demonstrate this particular truth in the most startling way' (ibid.: 69). Jung turns to the doctor himself for the resolution of the problem. He says:

As a rule we take no account of the fact that the doctor who practises catharsis is not just an abstraction which automatically produces nothing but catharsis. He is also a human being, and although his thinking may be limited to his special field, his actions exert the influence of a complete human being. Without giving it a name and without being clearly conscious of it, he unwittingly does his share of explanation and education, just as the others do their share of catharsis without raising it to the level of a principle.

(ibid.: 69)

As for his own theory, Jung asserts that 'It too should not claim to be the finally attained and only valid truth. It certainly fills a gap left by the earlier stages, but in so doing it merely fulfils a further need beyond the scope of the others' (ibid.: 69–70). What could this psychic need be? What has not yet been addressed by the other stages? Jung asks: 'Can anything lead further or be higher than the claim to be a normal and adapted social being?' (ibid.: 70). His answer is that there are

> just as many people who become neurotic because they are merely normal, as there are people who are neurotic because they cannot become normal. That it should enter anyone's head to educate them to normality is a nightmare for the former, because their deepest need is really to be able to lead 'abnormal' lives.
>
> (ibid.: 70)

What this implies for Jung is a pluralistic view of the needs of human beings. In addition he notes that in psychotherapy one meets only individuals; and, 'there are no universally valid recipes and rules' (ibid.). From this standpoint he proposes that the personal relationship between two human beings, patient and doctor, is the healing factor. Jung says:

> In any effective psychological treatment the doctor is bound to influence the patient; but this influence can only take place if the patient has a reciprocal influence on the doctor. You can exert no influence if you are not susceptible to influence. It is futile for the doctor to shield himself from the influence of the patient and surround himself with a smoke-screen of fatherly and professional authority.
>
> (ibid.: 71)

'Between doctor and patient,' Jung says, 'there are imponderable factors which bring about a mutual transformation' (ibid.: 72).

For Jung, commitment to a deeper process of psychological development grounds the stage of transformation. First of all the analyst needs to be analysed. Beyond that 'the fourth stage of transformation requires the counter-application to the doctor himself of whatever system is believed in – and moreover with the same relentlessness, consistency, and perseverance with which the doctor applies it to the patient' (ibid.: 73). Jung points out that the step from education, the third stage, to self-education of the doctor at the stage of transformation, is a natural progression. He recognizes, however, that this is not a popular idea:

First, because it seems unpractical, second, because of the un-
pleasant prejudice against being preoccupied with oneself; and
third, because it is sometimes exceedingly painful to live up to
everything one expects of one's patient. The last item in particular
contributes much to the unpopularity of this demand, for if the
doctor conscientiously doctors himself he will soon discover things
in his own nature which are utterly opposed to normalization, or
which continue to haunt him in the most disturbing way despite
assiduous explanation and thorough abreaction.

(ibid.: 73–4).

The ultimate problem lies in the difficult recognition by the doctor that
the 'questions which worry him as much as his patients cannot be
solved by any treatment, that to expect solutions from others is childish
and keeps you childish, and that if no solution can be found the question
must be repressed again' (ibid.: 74):

What was formerly a method of medical treatment now becomes a
method of self-education and with this the horizon of our psychology is immeasurably widened. The crucial thing is no longer the
medical diploma, but the human quality. This is a significant turn of
events, for it places all the implements of the psychotherapeutic art
that were developed in clinical practice, and then refined and
systematized, at the service of our self-education and self-perfec-
tion, with the result that analytical psychology has burst the bonds
which till then had bound it to the consulting-room of the doctor. It
goes beyond itself to fill the hiatus that has hitherto put Western
civilization at a psychic disadvantage as compared with the civilizations of the East. We Westerners knew only how to tame and
subdue the psyche; we knew nothing about its methodical development and its functions.

(ibid.: 75)

In a later article, entitled 'Fundamental Questions of Psychotherapy'
(1951b), Jung expands further on the new developments. In particular
he explores further his conviction that 'any complicated treatment is an
individual, *dialectical* process, in which the doctor, as a person, partici-
pates just as much as the patient':

We could say, without too much exaggeration, that a good half of
every treatment that probes at all deeply consists in the doctor's
examining himself, for only what he can put right in himself can he
hope to put right in the patient. It is no loss, either, if he feels that

the patient is hitting him, or even scoring off him: it is his own hurt that gives the measure of his power to heal. This and nothing else, is the meaning of the Greek Myth of the wounded physician.

(Jung 1951b: 116)

In his discussion of the practice of psychotherapy in 'The psychology of the transference' (1946a) Jung re-emphasizes the importance of the psychotherapist's commitment to the dialectical process:

It is like passing through the valley of the shadow, and sometimes the patient has to cling to the doctor as the last remaining shred of reality. This situation is difficult and distressing for both parties; often the doctor is in much the same position as the alchemist who no longer knew whether he was melting the mysterious amalgam in the crucible or whether he was the salamander glowing in the fire. Psychological induction inevitably causes the two parties to get involved in the transformation of the third and to be themselves transformed in the process, and all the time the doctor's knowledge, like a flickering lamp, is the one dim light in the darkness.

(Jung 1916: 198–9)

Our discussion of the stages of psychotherapy leads in the end to the core of analytical treatment, the patient's 'transference' and the psychotherapist's 'countertransference'. Here we find the transformative process that, gods willing, may produce the synthesis of personality, the goal which the alchemists described as the *mysterium coniunctionis*, the *hierosgamos*.

CONTEMPORARY REACTIONS TO JUNG'S SYNTHESIS

Now for a brief review of some aspects of the growing interest shown by psychotherapists in Jung's synthesis. In *Jung and the Post-Jungians*, Andrew Samuels (1985) describes a dialectical process which he sees taking place between different schools of analytical psychology. This approach, he says, 'can enable us to see the discipline as a whole'. His basic schema highlights the developmental school and the archetypal school, which, he says, 'appear to be attacking the centre', defined as the basic tenets of 'classical analytical psychology'. When fleshed out with the interests of individual participants in this dialectical process, this schema serves a very useful purpose. Throughout the book Samuels identifies themes and pinpoints the areas of agreement or disagreement, while at the same time suggesting ways in which a synthesis might arise out of this process, or so I understand him.

Since in my view a synthesis of depth psychology was achieved by Jung in his analytical psychology, I am inclined to interpret the ongoing dialogue between individuals with differing perspectives as a process of extending and testing and questioning Jung's synthesis. This is comparable to a similar process that followed Newton's great synthesis in the field of physics. It required some fifty years of struggle between adherents and doubters before there was general acceptance of Newton's theory. Somewhere in the midst of such a dialogue the seeds are often sown for what will eventually be a new 'revolt' that will set in action a new cycle of creativity. This has already occurred in physics with the advent of Planck's quantum theory.

It may be that Samuels sees in what he calls 'classical analytical psychology', the same synthesis that I have been describing. If so, there are basic areas which still need to be addressed. In my view, an area of particular importance is the role of the family in the structuring of complexes which determine the form and direction of an individual's destiny. The family tends not to be considered in any great detail in the Jungian literature. Samuels takes up very briefly the fact that Jung had a theory of the influence of the family on the individual, but Samuels relegates its significance to the field of family therapy where similar attitudes have developed. As has been apparent from the beginning, I place the influences of the family at the centre of the psychological processes which shape and energize the individual's innate potentials. Nevertheless, on the whole Samuels's book is an important contribution, not only to the Jungian community, but also to the developing consciousness of Jung's theory which is gradually taking place in the broader field of depth psychology and psychotherapy, and in widening circles amongst the public at large.

From a certain perspective one can see that Freud's psychoanalytic theory and practice has in recent years been modified in ways which bring it closer to Jung's analytical psychology. There is, of course, the earlier history of modifications in Freud's views which first took the form of Adler's defection, followed by that of Jung and then Rank. Freud himself modified his theory throughout his lifetime, and some of his modifications can be seen as direct reactions to Adler, Rank and Jung. But Jung's defection was more of a blow to Freud than that of Adler or Rank. Jung was without a doubt the most creative and productive of all of Freud's early collaborators. Freud's response to Jung's divergent views as to the nature of libido and incest was to excommunicate him for his heresy.

This tendency toward dogmatism led Freud in the end to form a secret society, an inner circle of 'true' believers, each with a secret seal ring. Jung's ideas became anathema to the true believers, and this stance has been perpetuated into the present day amongst orthodox Freudians. The tragedy of this situation is that the followers of Freud were cut off from Jung's developing theory of analytical psychology. Of course, there have been many alterations in Freud's theory since his death. Some were initiated by his daughter Anna Freud and other women analysts, for example, Karen Horney and Melanie Klein. Now there are many variants of Freud's original psychoanalysis, although a central core of orthodoxy still persists. Adler's and Rank's ideas have been pretty well integrated into some of the divergent schools. And, of course, schools of Adlerians and offshoots of Rank are still active. But the incorporation of Jung's ideas has taken longer, and is only now clearly apparent in the writings of a few innovative individuals.

D. W. Winnicott and Heinz Kohut have made some of the most 'heretical' changes in Freudian theory. Winnicott, who was first a pediatrician, moved naturally enough into child analysis. It is, of course, impossible to analyse young children unless one is willing to allow them to play, a fact which both Anna Freud and Melanie Klein reluctantly recognized. Even so, they used the child's play primarily as a medium to be interpreted; they had little apparent understanding of the function of play and imagination as the transformative principle of both development and therapeutic change. At first Winnicott also tended to see play from just such a limited point of view, but he gradually recognized its central importance to child analysis, and himself became a true participant with young children. Nevertheless he still was inclined to see the interpretations he made as of primary significance. Later in his life he began to see more adults for analysis, and came to the conclusion that analysis itself is essentially play, that is, play with images (Winnicott 1971). As he moved towards this better understanding of play and imagination, he found himself becoming more aware of an inner core of the individual, that is private and nearly inaccessible. It comprises a masculine and a feminine element.

> I found myself greatly enriched by this way of thinking. . . I was no longer thinking of boys and girls or men and women but I was thinking in terms of the male and female elements that belong to each. . . In an attempt to formulate this I found myself in the position of comparing *being* with *doing*.
>
> (Winnicott 1966: 190–1)

To be sure, Freud had recognized the bisexuality of human nature, but he had not arrived at an adequate conceptualization. What we see in Winnicott's developing view is something much closer to Jung's conception of the anima and the animus as the contra-sexual aspect of the individual which has an important and ongoing psychological role in the personality.

Kohut's modifications of Freudian theory have to do with the transference and counter-transference and with a conception of the self as an inner core of the personality. He introduced the idea to Freudian analysts that it is natural to have empathy for a patient, and that it is even therapeutic (Kohut 1977). Kohut's ideas were only being fully expressed at the time of his death in 1981, but they clearly begin to approach aspects of the concept of the Self that Jung articulated in the 1920s, although, as has been usual amongst Freudian analysts, Kohut does not refer to Jung's work. Jung had, of course, recognized the importance of a natural human relation to the analysand, which is why he gave up the practice of using a couch and sitting behind the patient. His reasoning was that the patient should be able to see the analyst's face and vice versa, so that each could tell what the other was feeling. Thus, for Jung, analysis became a dialectical, emotionally alive, human relationship. It is unfortunate that Kohut did not refer to Jung's work. But whether the source is acknowledged or not, contemporary psychoanalytic thought is finally catching up with Jung.

These convergences toward Jung indicate that the artificial barrier set up by Freud, and concurred in by his orthodox followers, will ultimately be breached. This should prove to be a gain for all psychotherapists. The free interchange of ideas is essential to the continuing development of any field of endeavour. It has been somewhat easier for analysts who have grown up, so to speak, in the community of Jungian analysts, to incorporate ideas from other schools of thought, but that is relative. On one hand, a counter-reaction did take place within the Jungian community. Among the most orthodox followers of Jung, Freud's theory became a focus of criticism, and gradually was ignored. On the other hand, there have always been Jungian analysts who understand that Jung was a Freudian before he developed his own approach, and that much of his work rests on the contributions of Freud. These analysts remained open to the ideas of those Freudians who were initiating modifications of Freud's theory as, for example, the English school of Jungian psychology with its close relationships with Klein, Winnicott and others. In Germany too, there has been a developing dialogue and co-operative exchange between the

Freudian and Jungian schools. This openness has begun to spread to the younger members of other Jungian communities, particularly in the United States.

With all that said, I should like to express the opinion that Jung's analytical psychology is the most comprehensive theory now available. This is, of course, a tribute to Jung's genius. But there are other reasons. First of all, when the break came with Freud Jung did not cut himself off from the ideas of Freud or Adler. Instead he saw his developing theory as a synthesis that included the perspectives of both. In addition he saw his theory carrying forward the essential ideas they had espoused. Thus Jung had the advantage of an open and free interest in, and engagement with, the works of both Freud and Adler, as well as Rank, Ferenczi and others whom he cited numerous times. The end result was that Jung's view was not clouded by an irrational rejection of any viable idea in the field of psychology. It could be said then that the convergence of other views toward Jung's analytical psychology, is evidence that his views represent a paradigm, in the sense that Kuhn uses the term (1962, 1977) to describe a period in the history of science when a synthesis of a field is achieved. The present phase of this development can be seen then as the further clarification and testing of the validity of Jung's ideas, as well as the extension of his ideas and their application in new ways. At any rate, this is how I understand the creative ferment that is stirring in depth psychology today.

Chapter 10

Epilogue – the family of nations

As I have been writing this book the world has been engulfed in a whirlwind of change. These changing events reflect new developments in the world order, but they also offer an extraordinary opportunity to validate, or invalidate, conclusions reached, and questions raised, in this book, particularly the relationship of sibling position and political leadership, and the urgent problem of good and evil.

THE CONTEMPORARY WORLD IN CHANGE

Like everyone else, I have been fascinated by the wildfire of change that has taken place in Eastern Europe. The Iron Curtain has been drawn back by Mikhail Gorbachev and the Berlin Wall has been dismantled and sold for souvenirs. All the countries that were absorbed into the Russian hegemony after the Second World War are now in the process of replacing the domination of the communist regimes with proposed democratic parliaments and governments.

What is most intriguing about these contemporary events is how sharply they seem to focus the problem of good and evil. It is crystal clear that two kinds of change are occurring almost simultaneously. One is driven by *perestroika* and *glasnost* – the other is driven by dreams of empire and absolute power. Scarcely was the 'cold' war declared over by Mikhail Gorbachev, before Saddam Hussein's 'hot' war erupted as Iraq invaded Kuwait, and the spectre of Hitler appeared once again on the horizon. Democracy and dictatorship appear to be locked in a fateful struggle.

These are precarious times, more precarious than ever experienced in the past. The holocaust, as well as our possession of atomic weapons, are constant reminders of the frightening potential for destruction. Yet is it possible that this period of extraordinary change may also hold out the possibility for a new inspiriting of family and society? Such a 'revolution' if it were to come about, would of necessity be based in a new world-wide community of nations and peoples, the 'global village' we hear so much about these days. For that to happen, however, there will have to be a new vision of the universe, a new 'pageant of the spheres' to potentiate the imagination as once occurred in the ancient land of Sumer. As Neumann and Jung have advocated, a new ethic would have to be fostered which encompasses the old one, but creates a further demand on self-reflective consciousness, that is, awareness of the inseparable oppositions within the human psyche.

How this could come about is difficult to imagine. However, in a letter written to Victor White, 10 April 1954, Jung proposes that such a new kind of consciousness will come into the collective when a prominent individual surprises everyone by showing a degree of psychological maturity when it is least expected.

> There is need of people knowing about their shadow, because there must be somebody who does not project. They ought to be in a visible position where they would be expected to project and unexpectedly they do not project! They can thus set a visible example which would not be seen if they were invisible.
>
> (Jung 1975: 168)

Even more astounding than Jung's idea is the possibility that this process may have already happened. It surely began to stir when Mikhail Gorbachev took power in Russia. But is it conceivable that the meeting of Ronald Reagan and Mikhail Gorbachev in Moscow in 1988 was just such a moment as Jung refers to? On that occasion, visible to all the world on television, the most unlikely person, President Ronald Reagan, dropped his inflammatory rhetoric about the 'evil empire', and described Gorbachev as a 'friend' (Doder and Branson 1990: 319).

With the foregoing in mind, I shall try to capture the spirit of some of these recent events and their potential consequences. We shall explore the dynamics in terms of Jung's analytical psychology, taking up the apparent stand-off between the opposites of democracy and dictatorship, and the related problem of the sources of good and evil. To illustrate these issues, we shall take up the lives of some well-known individuals, especially political leaders. We begin with Mikhail Gorbachev on the one hand, who evokes comparisons with Franklin Delano Roosevelt, and Saddam Hussein on the other, who compares himself to Stalin.

Mikhail Sergeyevich Gorbachev

Around the world the issue of human rights is gaining a higher profile. To be sure it has taken the activism of many courageous individuals who have suffered for their outspokenness. But now something that could not have been imagined a few years ago has happened in Russia. A new leader for the times, Gorbachev (**M1**[17]**M**),[1] is attempting to bring to fruition the earlier efforts of Krushchev (**MFM3**) to reveal the horrors of the Stalin era, and accomplish the reforms of the dissidents who have been so persecuted. Who is this Mikhail Gorbachev, the man of the hour, who appears to have been 'chosen' for just such an existential task?

Although I had long been unable to find any reliable information about the childhood and background of Mikhail Gorbachev, I had anticipated, however, that he would be an only child. This because he has risen to the peak of the Russian political hierarchy at a critical moment in the history of his country, a moment which calls for a leader who can identify with society as a whole – left and right, liberal and conservative – and who can speak to the failure of economic policies and the increasing deprivation, in this case of the Soviet citizen, as well as the oppressive surveillance by the KGB which made social life a constant dissociative experience, and the demoralization that is everywhere evident.

What is it that makes such a leader? On the one hand he must have acquired from his family and its relationship to the collective a thorough knowledge of the political apparatus and a demonstrated competence within the 'system' as it existed. On the other hand he must have acquired from the family atmosphere a self-confident ability to think for himself and to re-evaluate the accepted view of things in the light of the developing *Zeitgeist*.

If we knew enough about Gorbachev's family background, the experience of his ancestors, and the way in which their experience was passed down, in part through conscious memory, but most significantly through the unconscious memory of the parents' ancestral complexes, we would be better equipped to say something about the way in which Gorbachev has been chosen by the spirit, so to speak, to bring to fruition the changes in the attitude toward Stalin that were initiated by Nikita Krushchev, and secretly fostered by Yuri Andropov, and others whose names we do not know, but who must have existed. To succeed in the present situation Gorbachev must be capable of holding the opposites of the political situation in consciousness and in balance and to somehow achieve a synthesis which unites the opposites in a new vision of the society. As we have seen, this ability to hold the opposites and achieve a synthesis is the natural talent of the only child.

Comparisons have been made between Gorbachev and Franklin Delano Roosevelt. This is not unexpected in view of the similar circumstances that were prevalent in the USA during the great depression of the 1930s when Roosevelt became president. However, it is the similar characteristics and behaviour of the two men that is noticed by astute observers. Here are some of the ways in which they have been compared:

1 Gorbachev uses TV like Roosevelt used the radio for his fireside chats. He speaks directly to all of the people.
2 Like Roosevelt, Gorbachev has managed to lead both the incumbent regime and the opposition – an authoritarian in the pursuit of democracy.
3 And also like Roosevelt he has staked out the political centre.

> 'It is, as Soviets say, no accident that Gorbachev permits Boris Yeltsin – the purged politburo member turned populist to attack him from the left, while hard-liner Yegor Ligachev snipes at him from the right. The dance between left and right is astounding,' says the Harriman Institute's Robert Legvold.
>
> (*Time Magazine*, January 1990)

These comparisons highlight qualities which are part of the political repertoire of the only child. Roosevelt (**M1**), like Gorbachev (**M1**[17]M), was an only child. As we have seen earlier, it is an only child who is called to leadership at a time of great social unrest and the collapse of basic support systems, as in the depression of the 1930s and as is now true in the Soviet Union. One of the reasons that the only child is leader of choice in such situations is in part the fact of the triadic family constellation of mother, father and child. The only child has the experience of keeping a balance between the attention and expectations of the parents, first in childhood experience, and then as inner objects of the psyche. That is a prominent factor in establishing the only child's synthetic propensity and the balancing of opposites.

Saddam Hussein

Saddam Hussein has been compared with Hitler. Is this a fair comparison? Probably this question cannot be answered with the facts at hand. In the early period of Hitler's rise to power, it would have been very difficult to predict his ultimate behaviour. But since we now have the advantage of hindsight with regard to Hitler's life, it may be possible to draw some limited comparisons with Hussein.

Hussein has been an opportunist of the first water and has used Machiavellian tactics of a savage nature in order to acquire the power he now holds. During the war with Iran he turned to the use of poison gas. He also gassed the Kurds who form a part of Iraq, and he threatened others, especially Israel. In addition he has threatened the use of biological warfare. He held hostages and threatened to put them in the line of fire if Iraq were attacked. All in all he seems to have little compunction against using whatever weapons are at his disposal, that is, if he thinks he can get away with it. This has created considerable anxiety since it is known that he is not far from being able to produce atomic weapons. Without a doubt he is capable of doing things that others would be quick to call evil. On the other hand, in the past he may have done some things for his country which have benefited the Iraqi people, just as Hitler was able to say he had done much for the Germans when the country was in such serious economic trouble when he came to power.

Although Hussein proclaimed a holy war against Israel and the western allies, his statements did not reveal such thoroughgoing policies of death and destruction as Hitler's plans for the annihilation of the Jews, the psychiatrically ill, and others. But did Hitler reveal his long-range plans early on? Whether or not Hussein is as dangerous as Hitler, he is without a doubt dangerous. The question that remains then is, how does such a person come to be?

Saddam Hussein was born in poor circumstances in a remote village. There is a report that while his mother was pregnant with him, she was overwhelmed by two tragic losses: Her husband died and their one-year-old son died of cancer. She was grief stricken, perhaps a major depression. There is a story that she was suicidal and that she tried to abort Saddam (Waldman 1991). Neither of these occurred and Saddam was born in April 1937, in the home of Khairallah Talfah, his mother's brother. The mother, Sabha, then married Hassan, her late husband's brother, forcing him first to divorce his wife. Sabha left her infant Saddam to be raised by her brother, Khairallah Talfah. Saddam seems to have lived in his maternal uncle Khairallah's household until he was 3. Then his cousin Adnan was born, and around the same time his uncle Khairallah was arrested by the British and imprisoned for five years. At that time Saddam went to live with his mother and her husband Hassan.

Although we don't know the years of their birth, one or more of his three younger half-brothers may have already been born. They lived in primitive conditions and Hassan, a rough illiterate peasant, put Saddam to work tending sheep. He was not allowed to go to school. At the age of 10 he ran away, back to his uncle Khairallah's home. He and his cousin Adnan (three years his junior) went to school together and became best friends. Khairallah also had a daughter, Sajidah, who may have been older than Saddam, or younger. When they grew up, Saddam and Sajidah were married. She is his first cousin. Later in life Saddam feuded with Adnan, who was at once cousin, friend, and brother-in-law. In 1989 Adnan died mysteriously in a helicopter crash.

At the age of 18 Saddam followed his uncle to Baghdad. In 1956 he participated in a violent mass demonstration of the Ba'ath Party. In 1957 at the age of 20 he became a member of Ba'ath. In 1958 he was arrested for the first time and served six months in jail for killing his brother-in-law or uncle (if true). By the age of 22 he was one of ten young Ba'ath Party guerillas assigned to assassinate Abdal-Karum Qassim, the dictator who had overthrown the monarchy a year before. The plan was botched, but Saddam escaped. He spent the following five years in Egypt under Nasser's protection. In 1963 several Ba'ath army officials were killed and Saddam hurried back to Iraq. The party lost power, however, and in 1964 Saddam was arrested in a second coup attempt and spent two years in prison.

Saddam was a distant cousin of Ahmed Hasan al Bahr, a Tikrite, who became president of the Ba'ath Party in July 1968. He treated Saddam (who was twenty-three years younger) as a son. From the scanty information available, I have conjectured that Saddam Hussein is either a first-born or an only child/only son. This is supported in my view by the fact that Saddam was *not* the leader of the Ba'ath party revolution. The leader of the revolution appears to have been Ahmed Hassan al Bakr. Comparable in many ways to Stalin, Saddam worked his way up through the ranks using strongarm methods in the service of the ruling members of the party. As soon as he was able to command power he was ruthless, assassinating many who had been loyal to him. Stalin undertook similar tactics when he took control of the communist revolution, and he continued a horrifying reign of terror until he died in 1953. Saddam Hussein exercises power in the same way.

It is important to keep in mind that both Stalin and Hussein rose to power through a hierarchy of revolutionary leaders, and then consolidated personal control of the party, the military and the country as a whole. They became dictators of the most imperial stripe. They clearly had no compunctions about ruthless behaviour of any kind. They fit Harry Stack Sullivan's diagnostic category of the 'malevolent transformation of personality'. In this respect both Stalin and Saddam Hussein can be compared with Hitler.

With regard to family atmosphere, it would seem that the qualities of character, or rather lack of character, that Stalin, Hitler and Hussein show, are to be traced to the demoralizing situations within their families. They were ill cared for, brutalized, and abandoned. Stalin and Saddam had no consistent fathering. Saddam's father died before his birth and he was turned over to an uncle who left him at the age of 3 when he, the uncle, was imprisoned. Saddam then went to live with his mother and stepfather. The stepfather is described as 'a brutish man who used to amuse himself by humiliating Saddam. His common punishment was to beat the youth with an asphalt-covered stick, forcing him to dance around to dodge the blows' (Karsh and Rautsi 1991: 10). Stalin's father was a drunkard who left home when Stalin was about 3. He is said to have returned occasionally thereafter. The mother, however, took Stalin to a Catholic boarding school where it appears they both lived. Very little more is known about Stalin's childhood. He was educated to some extent at the Catholic school.

Regarding sibling position, Stalin was an only child. Saddam Hussein has three younger half-brothers, but is most likely an only child/son psychologically, passed from one family to another. Yet as I have said above, the other possibility is that he has the experience of a first-born. Hitler, in contrast, was a younger son. This fits the expectations of my earlier studies. Hitler promulgated a revolution and eventually took over the government. Stalin and Saddam Hussein each worked up through the ranks during the consolidation of a revolution. And each came to power at a time when their particular personalities served them well in containing the divergent elements of the revolutionary group, while at the same time moving toward total dictatorial control. They gained support of the common people in their respective countries during difficult times through the projection of a public image of the great, benevolent father protector.

DEMOCRACY OR DICTATORSHIP

Dickens's well-worn phrase is strangely apropos again: these are the best of times; these are the worst of times. It is as if the spirit of the French Revolution was once more in the air. The similarity of what has been happening in the countries of Eastern Europe, as well as in the

Philippines, and most recently South Africa, to the period of the French Revolution is striking – masses of people in the streets bringing down the Bastille again and again. Central to all of these revolutionary movements is the sense of a new era of freedom and support for the rights of the individual citizen. But will this euphoria be followed by the atmosphere of the tribunal as in the French Revolution, the desperate attempt to preserve the 'purity' of the revolution by purging those who dissent, thus creating the very instrument of god-given vision and authority which the revolution had sought to transform?

In the revolution of the American colonies this self-destructive enantiodromia was avoided, through what mysterious mix of good will and luck we shall never know. Was it the background of British history and its struggle toward democracy, or perhaps the separateness on a new continent, or the high quality of the founders of the new republic, or was it the creation of a constitution and bill of rights which allowed for a democratic transfer of power at regular intervals, as well as establishing inalienable rights of the individual citizen?

To be sure, the new republic was soon put to the test of its high ideals in the secession of the southern states over the issue of slavery. The Civil War was won by the northern states and slavery was abolished, yet the issue of full rights for all citizens had not been settled. In the south, economic slavery replaced the old form of slavery. The non-violent civil rights movement of the 1960s led to considerable improvement in the rights of African Americans and other minorities, but full equality for all citizens has not yet been achieved. In the USA women did not win the right to vote until 1920. The struggle still goes on.

Democracy

The psychological origins of democracy are surely to be found in the inner dialogue of individuation – becoming oneself – the dialectic between conscious and unconscious. As Jung (1916) has put it:

> It is technically very simple to note down the 'other' [inner] voice . . . and to answer its statements from the standpoint of the ego. It is exactly as if a dialogue were taking place between two human beings with equal rights.
>
> (Jung 1916: 88–9)

This statement conveys the essence of Jung's method of active imagination, which is a reactivation in psychotherapy of the innate process of individuation. If we look to the socio-political world for the projection of this process, it would appear to be democracy. 'A dialogue . . . between two human beings with equal rights' is the essence of democracy. It is also the essence of true friendship and of true marriage.

We need only look to ourselves, to our friends, our spouses, our family, to realize how imperfect is our commitment to 'true' democracy. Nevertheless, the ideal exists, and we are often painfully aware when we fail its requirements. This, of course, is the human condition. To strive for an ideal makes us vulnerable to a potentiation of the opposite in the unconscious which will eventually have its due. With this we are made aware that the individuation process does not lead to perfection, but rather to a circumambulation of the self. As Jung put it, the goal is wholeness. The goal is also the process itself. It requires a lifelong engagement in an intrapsychic dialogue between conscious and unconscious, ego and shadow.

Speaking to the nature of political democracy, Jung characterizes the Swiss experience of some four hundred years of struggle with a commitment to democracy.

> We came to the conclusion that it is better to avoid external wars, so we went home and took the strife with us. In Switzerland we have built up the 'perfect democracy,' where our warlike instincts expend themselves in the form of domestic quarrels called 'political life.' We fight each other within the limits of the law and the constitution, and we are inclined to think of democracy as a chronic state of mitigated civil war. Thus far we have succeeded, but we are still a long way from the ultimate goal.
>
> (Jung 1946b: 224)

Jung concludes that a further step, an introversion of the dialectic of conscious and unconscious, is yet to be taken.

> We still have enemies in the flesh, and we have not yet managed to introvert our political disharmonies. We still labour under the unwholesome delusion that we should be at peace within ourselves. Yet even our national, mitigated state of war would soon come to an end if everybody could see his own shadow and begin the only struggle that is really worth while; the fight against the overwhelming power drive of the shadow. We have a tolerable social order in Switzerland because we fight among ourselves. Our order would be

perfect if only everybody could direct his aggressiveness inwards, into his own psyche.

(Jung 1946b: 224)

Then in discussion of the tragic world situation following the Second World War, Jung comments on his hopes and fears for the future:

> The marked tendency of the Western democracies to internal dissension is the very thing that could lead them into a more hopeful path. But I am afraid that this hope will be deferred by powers which still believe in the contrary process, in the destruction of the individual and the increase of the fiction we call the State. The psychologist believes firmly in the individual as the sole carrier of mind and life. Society and the State derive their quality from the individual's mental condition, for they are made up of individuals and the way they are organized.

(Jung 1946b: 225)

This puts us in mind of the urgent need to better understand what it is in human nature, or human circumstances, that thwarts the normal individuation process and leads to authoritarianism and evil. The major issue would appear to be a failure to 'inspirit' the dialogue of inner and outer, unconscious and conscious, personified as ego and shadow in Jung's terminology.

Dictatorship

The question is still open as to what leads to dictatorship. Jung has also addressed this problem. His ideas of how an individual becomes a leader is illuminating. It is not just the will to power of the individual, he says, but rather a combination of the individual's will and the desire of the community to be led.

> One could easily assert that the impelling motive in this development is the will to power. But that would be to forget that the building up of prestige is always a product of collective compromise: not only must there be one who wants prestige there must also be a public seeking somebody on whom to confer prestige. That being so, it would be incorrect to say that a man creates prestige for himself out of his individual will to power; it is on the contrary an entirely collective affair. Since society as a whole needs the magically effective figure, it uses this need of the will to power in the individual, and the will to submit in the mass, as a vehicle, and

thus brings about the creation of personal prestige. The latter is a phenomenon which, as the history of political institutions shows, is of the utmost importance for the comity of nations.

(Jung 1928a: 150–6)

The foregoing offers a useful perspective on the question of leadership and authoritarianism. In fact this essentially grounds our understanding of dictatorship since it postulates that there must be a common need shared by a potential leader and the society. But we have not yet satisfactorily understood dictatorship from a psychological perspective. For that we must try to understand good and evil.

GOOD AND EVIL

To explore the nature of good and evil, I begin with an effort to identify the psychological dynamics which account for our experience of good and evil. This leads directly to the innate archetypal affects, contempt and shame. Contempt/shame seems to have evolved from the inherited affective reflex, disgust, which is present in infants from birth. The survival function of disgust is to identify noxious, potentially poisonous substances and avoid them. For example, using the senses of smell and taste, we turn away from rotten food, or reject it by spitting it out of the mouth. In the extremity of disgust we may still experience the primal reaction of vomiting. At this fundamental level, the life stimulus is rejection; the inner (inherited) image/imprint is alienation. The life stimulus and the innate image/imprint are two halves of the symbol: when the two halves unite, the emotion is constellated. The process is similar to the 'innate releasing mechanism' described by the ethologist Tinbergen, or the 'key tumbler' structures that release prototypical patterns of behaviour (Stevens 1983: 56–8). When the affect contempt/shame is released, we humans experience the terrible, withering feeling of rejection, either toward the other (contempt), or toward the self (shame).

> In Disgust, lips curl, noses wrinkle. We pull away from a dirty, smelly object. In Humiliation we writhe and squirm and may even retch, because the dirty, smelly object we want to get away from is ourself.
>
> (Chodorow 1991: 131)

As consciousness is engulfed by contempt/shame, it is as if one is banished, driven into the wilderness, far from human community.

Whether one experiences contempt or shame, one is alienated. When a state of profound alienation is in consciousness, the opposite is constellated in the unconscious, that is, the moral idea of the 'good', Utopian *communitas*, the highest ideal of the social cultural attitude. On the plane of the emotions, the dialectic of joy and interest and their dynamisms of imagination and exploration fall into the unconscious where they begin to interweave with unconscious compensatory fantasies around inclusion and exclusion: the imagination of human relationship. Here we find the incipient forms of Utopian fantasies. Such fantasies may be about dictatorial power, as well as the democratic ideal.

The foregoing would seem to describe roughly the dynamics of what comes to be seen in its extreme forms as good or evil. Evil is the rejection of relatedness; it creates a state of alienation from oneself and from others. Good on the other hand is acceptance of the demands of relatedness. It is an intrinsic form of the imagination that is shaped by the ideal of *communitas*.

To recapitulate, we could say that the striving for 'good' in the social-political realm is fostered by the archetypal imagination of the Utopian society with freedom and justice for all. This is based in understanding the archetypal affect of contempt/shame as the source of both the ego function of feeling, and the symbolic cultural attitude of the social. These two functions have presumably evolved over the ages from the two aspects of the archetypal affect: the impressive which manifests as the feeling function of the ego, and the expressive which manifests as the social cultural attitude. This may be seen in the psychosomatic experience of the psyche when the archetypal affect is constellated. That is to say, an extreme state of alienation – a loss of relatedness to oneself and to others – which is felt as dreadful shame: a turning away, hanging one's head, wishing to fall through the floor; or as the equally alienating feeling of contempt: pulling back, looking down one's nose and sneering in disdain of the other, which of course alienates oneself from others and from one's own 'better', or social side. All of the above refers to the social cultural attitude, the ideal of the good/*communitas*, and to family and society, the social realms of human relationships.

A related question is whether or not infants are born who are immoral, or amoral? This could occur, presumably, only if there are genes of immorality or amorality which can be inherited. Is it possible that there are such genes? Following out the discussion above, it would seem that if there are they would have to be related to the social aspect of human nature. Perhaps when the encyclopedia of the human genome is completed we shall be able to answer this question. At the present time there is no verifiable evidence of the inheritance of acquired characteristics of such a nature. Nor does it seem likely that there will be, since such genetic development would seem to fly in the face of the survival of the species. This brings us then to the difficult task of sorting out, if possible, the aspects of family life which lead to the kind of behaviour we think of as good or evil.

First some further thoughts on the relationship of the innate cultural form of the social/moral with its ideal of the good, and its compensatory opposite, the innate affect contempt/shame. When constellated, contempt/shame drives the conscious attitude of social relatedness into the unconscious and creates the psychosomatic state of alienation. Alienation is a very painful state. If it becomes chronic and is reinforced over time it leads to isolation and withdrawal. An extreme state of alienation is paranoia. One solution is to identify a scapegoat. This is what Hitler did.

Adolph Hitler

Hitler was severely shamed in his childhood by his father and by the general degradation of his family. Later he faced other shaming defeats in his efforts to make a living as an artist. His service in the First World War seems to have given him his first satisfying sense of achievement. From the time when he entered politics he dressed himself in a uniform. He discovered his gift for oratory, and realized the power it gave him over others. His first efforts at fomenting a revolution failed, and he was imprisoned. But prison gave him an opportunity to formulate his message and to see it published, as *Mein Kampf*. When released from prison he had greater prestige than when he went in. He had transformed himself from a failed artist to a political visionary. And no longer need he blame himself, he had identified the scapegoat – the Jew. He registers in *Mein Kampf* the moment on the street in Vienna when he realized that he could be an anti-Semite. This decision was transformative, a seizure by the spirit, an evil spirit, Jung would say. Now he would build a new society of blond, blue-eyed Germans devoted to the Fatherland. Then he would conquer the world. His was a megalomania perfectly tuned to the needs of the masses of Germans who were shamed by the defeat of the First World War, and who suffered from the humiliating loss of parts of their homeland and the various restrictions of the armistice agreement.

Hitler was capable of committing evil of an enormity that had not been experienced since the days of the Ottoman empire, and Genghis Khan. The Jews, the weak and the ill were to be exterminated. To assure his own power, he was willing to execute his loyal fellow revolutionaries, as well as anyone else who stood in his way. He was totally untrustworthy, using lies and trickery to achieve his surprise attacks on other countries, and on any other occasion that suited him. All this and more is well known. Redeeming features are hard to find. Perhaps he was good to his mother, and to the woman he married just before his suicide. However, it is known that intimacy and ordinary sexual experience was for him impossible.

The question that still remains open is: how does someone regress to such a primitive, archaic identification with an archetypal vision of such destructiveness? To talk of the constellation of the ancient Norse God Wotan, as Jung has done, may be instructive of the archetypal qualities of his identification, but this leaves unaddressed the question of how this came about. We know that there was historical preparation for Hitler's recourse to the term Aryan and the swastika symbol as well as those who pressed a course of return to the primitive gods of the Norse, Wotan in particular. However, as I have said, to see Hitler's reaction as a purely archetypal situation does little for our understanding of the human situation. Who was Hitler? How did he come to be the way he was? All of this did not happen overnight. His life is not a myth. He did not wake up one day suddenly transformed. His transformation was a process of years, and his early development from infancy to adulthood was an equally long period. It is extremely important to see that Hitler was seized by the spirit and what the consequences were. Jung has tried to make these clear. It was an evil spirit, he says. But how does an evil spirit acquire the upper hand in a person's life? Not by chance, not by accident, is it perhaps by infection?

How, then, was Hitler infected? To be infected there must be a 'psychological' virus or bacteria in the surrounding atmosphere. Can we identify the psychological infection and the bacteria or virus that it sprang from? What comes to mind first is the intense humiliation of the German people following their defeat in the First World War. When the archetypal affect of shame is constellated there follows an unconscious constellation of the compensatory symbol of the ideal, Utopian society. To recover from deep humiliation one must come to grips with an ethical conflict; was the war itself justified on moral grounds? If this approach proves unacceptable, then one seeks to blame someone other than oneself and one's country. Here is where the infection occurs. This is what happened to Hitler. He had been shamed as a child, not only by the brutality of his home where his drunken father would beat him and his brother, but also because of the suspicion that existed for his father, and was communicated to Hitler, that there was a Jewish relative in the background of the family. Anti-Semitism was the virus that infected Hitler's father and his son, and that had infected a large proportion of Germans. Anti-Semitism was prevalent in most, if not all of the European countries, and others as well. It was highly virulent in Germany.

The virus of anti-Semitism is a significant quality of the 'evil' spirit that seized Hitler, as he himself noted in *Mein Kampf*.

> Since I had begun to concern myself with this question and to take cognizance of the Jews, Vienna appeared to me in a different light than before. Wherever I went, I began to see Jews, and the more I saw, the more sharply they became distinguished in my eyes from the rest of humanity. Particularly the Inner City and the districts north of the Danube Canal swarmed with a people which even outwardly had lost all resemblance to Germans. . .
>
> All this could scarcely be called very attractive; but it became positively repulsive when, in addition to their physical uncleanliness, you discovered the moral on this 'chosen people'. . .
>
> Was there any form of filth or profilgacy, particularly in cultural life, without at least one Jew involved in it?
>
> If you cut even cautiously into such an abscess, you found, like a maggot in a rotting body, often dazzled by the sudden light—a kike!
>
> Gradually I began to hate them. . .
>
> For me this was the time of the greatest spiritual upheaval I have ever had to go through.
>
> I had ceased to be a weak-kneed cosmopolitan and become an anti-Semite. . .
>
> Hence today I believe that I am acting in accordance with the will of the Almighty Creator: *by defending myself against the Jew, I am fighting for the work of the Lord.*
>
> (Hitler 1927: 56–65)

Deep down he feared that he himself might be Jewish; he needed to establish beyond all doubt that he was 'pure' Aryan. What better way than to persecute, and eventually attempt to destroy the whole Jewish race. Moreover, he knew that this approach would gain him the support of a large part of the German people, those who were virulently anti-Semitic, and who would welcome a scapegoat to alleviate their humiliation.

Hitler became a powerful orator and created a *participation mystique* when he spoke to the masses. And it was always the masses he spoke to. Masses assembled by constant propaganda and by threats and innuendos and sometimes forceful persuasion. But it must be acknowledged that there were indeed masses of people in Germany at that time who were only too willing to hear the kinds of things Hitler had to say. This, as I have suggested, was in large part due to the great humiliation the German people experienced in the First World War and its harsh legacy of lost territory and reparations. Hitler spoke to the lowest common denominators of decency, but always in terms that exalted the ideas he proposed to a mystical level of justification for the God-given destiny of the German soul.

How Hitler came to power is now well documented. It began with an unsuccessful coup attempt, followed by organizational work to develop a core of ruthless supporters. Using all the tactics of persuasion, threats and intimidation, as well as lies and deceit, Hitler edged his way into the government, and then, as the ageing Hindenburg began to give him some credence, he acted swiftly and decisively to achieve a non-violent coup, cloaked in the apparent processes of democracies, but in fact utilizing the most manipulative means to get the aged man to appoint him to the position of chancellor. This was immediately followed by a supposed referendum which was nothing but a means of eliminating the power of the legislators and taking full power into his own hands. He was then dictator.

Pursuing further our question of what makes for dictatorship, a valuable comparison can be made between Bernt Engelmann, a German who resisted the Nazi regime; and Hitler. Engelmann's experience speaks directly to the differences in family atmosphere.

Bernt Engelmann

Studs Terkel, in his foreword to Bernt Engelmann's *In Hitler's Germany* (1986), concludes with the following evocative thoughts:

> It was so easy. Nobody was more surprised than Adolph Hitler himself. It was the evil of banality as much as the banality of evil that was the challenge there and then. It may possibly be the challenge here and now. Bernt Engelmann's account is more than memoir; it is a cautionary tale.

Adolph Hitler and Bernt Engelmann were both Germans, Engelmann by birth and in heritage, Hitler by decision to change his citizenship from Austrian to German. Hitler was of an earlier generation; Engelmann was a teenager when Hitler came to power. All around him Engelmann saw a majority of the German youth his age and younger joining Hitler's youth groups, while he, at his grandfather's urging, joined a socialist group of the working class. Obviously Engelmann was not alone, but nevertheless in the minority. It would seem that Jung is right; it is the masses that give over their own consciousness and act in thoughtless unison to bring about the kinds of evil that Hitler exemplified. The questions then are: What are the differences between Hitler, the Hitler youth, and Engelmann? Was Engelmann born with genes of a higher moral potential? Or was he fortunate in having a family that was not infected by anti-Semitism, and other virulent attitudes of contempt for other humans – the aliens? Clearly the evidence is far more persuasive for the latter conclusion than the former. A comparison of the family life of Hitler and Engelmann reveals the vast chasm that separates them. To summarize briefly some of the most salient differences.

Engelmann himself sought to understand the reasons for his lack of 'infection' by the spirit of the times as embodied in Hitler and his policies. In the introduction to his book Engelmann seeks to determine the parameters of the 'causes' of Hitler's Germany and its disastrous consequences. He gives various reasons for his own immunity to the Nazi state. In conclusion he attempts to characterize his fears and his concerns for the future.

> My own bitter experiences during the Nazi years explain why I cannot agree with those intellectuals in present-day Germany who view the twelve years of Nazi domination as the 'work of sinister demons,' as 'the product of a grim fate' for which no one can be held accountable. I am convinced that one must seek to understand the factors that made individuals and groups vulnerable to the lure of militarism and totalitarianism, and that one must continue to resist them whenever they appear in the world today. It is in the hope of contributing to such an understanding that I offer this book to the reader.
>
> (Engelmann 1986: xiii)

Engelmann's 'immunity' to Nazism is readily understandable when one reads what he has to say about his family. He was a schoolboy of 12 when Hitler came to power in 1933. 'Much depends', he says, 'on how each individual viewed the Nazi regime at the time, and how he chose to respond to it.'

> As a blindly loyal supporter; as an opportunistic fellow traveller who saw only his own gains; as a docile, apolitical citizen, who obeyed the authorities and did what he considered his duty; as one who kept quiet and shut his eyes but was 'privately against it all'; as an innocent victim; as someone who resisted the regime as best he could, cautiously and rather passively; or even as someone who repeatedly risked his life by resisting boldly and actively, like my 'Uncle Erich,' alias Major von Elken.
>
> (Engelmann 1986: ix-x)

Engelmann himself became aware of the political situation while he was quite young.

> I knew where I stood, and even as a child participated in clandestine resistance to Hitler's lawless regime. My lively interest in what was going on can be ascribed to my immediate environment: my parents and relatives and their closest friends.
>
> (Engelmann 1986: x)

This is a vitally important statement, which Engelmann elucidates with great clarity and depth. His father was an exemplary man who was closely involved with his son and determined to see that he understood everything that was going on in the world. Engelmann remembers with delight the 'marvellous stories' his father told him as a little boy:

> Later, when I developed into a rather precocious youth, avid to learn and to understand the world, he answered all my questions patiently and thoroughly. He followed the politics of the Weimar Republic attentively, though from a distance. He was a staunch advocate of democracy to whom Nazism appeared as a dangerous sickness – he could only hope that the patient, Germany, would survive.
>
> (Engelmann 1986: x)

His mother he describes as a hard-working, strong-minded woman, who was not much interested in politics. She was, however, 'quick to recognize practical steps that could be taken to assist the victims of an obviously inhuman policy'.

Comparing his parents, Engelmann says: 'from my father I learned to analyse things logically, from my mother to draw practical conclusions and to act on them'. Both abilities were essential to him since when he was 16 his parents had him 'declared of legal age' and transferred to him the remains of their own fortune and what was left of the resources of relatives and friends, 'who by then had fled the country'.

> My family, was split up by the outbreak of the war. The plan had been to leave Germany by the autumn of 1939 and wait in England for the fall of Hitler. My father was already in London, but my mother and I were unable to join him.
>
> (Engelmann 1986: x)

In his grandparents, he also found admirable qualities. His maternal grandfather was a self-made and self-taught man who from the age of 17 remained a trade unionist even though in later life he had become a wealthy man:

> He greeted the Nazis' propaganda with mockery and scorn. From my grandfather I received not only a sense for the value of fine old things, a receptivity to art, and a love of books, but also certain fundamental political views. It was he, the solid businessman with a house on the elegant Kurfürstendamm, who advised me when I was eleven to join Red Falcon, the organization for the youngest members of the Socialist Workers' Youth.
>
> (Engelmann 1986: xi)

His maternal grandmother was an extraordinary person who had a great influence on him. A tiny woman, not pretty but 'sharp-witted and splendidly educated', his grandmother was a 'walking encyclopedia'. In addition, he says, his grandmother was significant in developing his immunity to 'Fascism, militarism, and reactionary politics, my grandmother implanted in me an ineradicable commitment to democracy'. 'With this sort of family background,' he says, 'I might have been expected to resist the contagion of Nazi ideology, as well as the ultra-conservative nationalism that raged through Germany during my school years' (ibid.: xii).

Finally he attributes the 'fact that I never dreamed of yielding to the Nazis' propaganda and indoctrination not only to my origins, my education, my family and their friends, but also in great measure to the books these people gave me to read'. He then proceeds to list the books, beginning with Jack London and ending with Arnold Zweig. With these books he says,

> it was impossible for me to become a Nazi, or even a militarist. And when the books of most of these authors were banned and burned by

the Nazis, I knew beyond any doubt that Hitler and his henchmen were my enemies; how else could they do such a thing to the books I loved?

(Engelmann 1986: xii–xiii)

During the war Engelmann demonstrated his convictions in an ongoing participation in the underground railway which helped Jews to escape to other countries. Toward the end of the war he was imprisoned in Dachau. He survived and was liberated by the allies.

The contrast between Engelmann's childhood and Hitler's is as extreme as one can imagine. It would be very difficult to believe that Engelmann could have become a Hitler, or that Hitler could have become an Engelmann. Is this just an isolated case which proves nothing? I believe not. Everything we now know about the childhood experiences of battered children who grow up to batter their own children, or of sexually-abused children whose only defence against the degradation and the cruelty of their homes is to dissociate into a multitude of personalities, suggests that Engelmann's character and Hitler's character are in the largest part due to the atmospheres of their respective families.

But Engelmann's story is not a unique one. There are now available many stories of the heroism of ordinary people who cared enough to help and protect the potential victims of the Nazis terror. And the stories they tell of their own homes and why they acted the way they did have a common core of morality and ethical values learned from caring parents and relatives and friends.

Jung on evil

In the end we are all caught in the dilemma of imperfection and the further fact that the psyche is a *complexio oppositorum*. Every conscious reaction has its unconscious counterpart, and vice versa. Trying his best to arrive at a clear position with respect to good and evil, Jung takes up first the question of 'conscience'. After an examination of the differences between a 'conscious moral code' as is acquired in Freud's concept of the 'superego', versus an unconscious 'conscience' which finds expression often in unconscious acts and in dreams, Jung notes that the unconscious cannot be totally dependent upon consciousness.

Without at least some degree of autonomy the common experience of the complementary or compensatory function of the unconscious would not be possible. If the unconscious were really dependent on the conscious, it could not contain more than, and other things than, consciousness contains.

(Jung 1958: 441)

From this Jung argues that 'morality as such is a universal attribute of the human psyche', but he also points out that this is not true of any moral code. Even though conscience often coincides with the conscious moral code, it just as often is in contradiction of it. From this situation Jung draws the following conclusion.

> The concept and phenomenon of conscience thus contains when seen in a psychological light, two different factors: on the one hand a recollection of, and admonition by, the *mores*; on the other, a conflict of duty and its solution through the creation of a third standpoint. The first is the moral, and the second the ethical, aspect of conscience.

(Jung 1958: 455)

It is the concept of a 'conflict of duty' that gives the final meaning to Jung's view of good and evil. We are left with the difficult and inescapable fact that as human beings we are incapable of being certain of our judgements of good and evil. What does Jung offer as a solution? Self-knowledge and psychology. Speaking directly, then, to the issue of self-knowledge, Jung asserts:

> The problem of evil, as it is posed today, has need, first and foremost, of *self-knowledge*, that is, the utmost possible knowledge of his own wholeness. He must know relentlessly how much good he can do, and what crimes he is capable of, and must beware of regarding the one as real and the other as illusion. Both are elements within his nature, and both are bound to come to light in him, should he wish – as he ought – to live without self-deception or self-delusion. . . Such self-knowledge is of prime importance, because through it we approach that fundamental stratum or core of human nature where the instincts dwell. Here are those pre-existent dynamic factors which ultimately govern the ethical decisions of our consciousness. This core is the unconscious and its contents, concerning which we cannot pass any final judgment. Our ideas about it are bound to be inadequate, for we are unable to comprehend its essence cognitively and set rational limits to it. We achieve knowledge of nature only through science, which enlarges consciousness; hence deepened self-knowledge also requires science, that is psychology. No one builds a telescope or microscope with

one turn of the wrist, out of good will alone, without a knowledge of optics.

(Jung 1961: 330–1)

Jung goes even further in his exhortation for increased interest in the psyche:

Today we need psychology for reasons that involve our very existence. We stand perplexed and stupefied before the phenomenon of Nazism and Bolshevism because we know nothing about man, or at any rate have only a lopsided and distorted picture of him. If we had self-knowledge, that would not be the case. We stand face to face with the terrible question of evil and do not even know what is before us, let alone what to pit against it. And even if we did know, we still could not understand 'how it could happen here'.

(Jung 1961: 331)

FAMILY OF NATIONS

I speak of a family of nations for several reasons. The first is in response to what is happening in Europe with the formation of a community of nations who are seeking to reach agreement on many economic and military issues. They aim for a common market by 1992. At the same time, the French and the English, traditional enemies in the more distant past, and still viewing each other with suspicion, are tunnelling beneath the English Channel between France and England. This is a historic event primarily because the English isolationist policy is finally giving way to a more co-operative stance. These are good reasons for using the term, a family of nations, but there is a deeper need to be met which has been discussed by many concerned leaders, as well as others. In previous chapters I have shown how sibling position in the family and the atmosphere of the family, along with the *Zeitgeist*, have significant impact on the destiny of the individual and the future of society. This has been illustrated in greatest depth through studies of political leadership, and through the evolution of depth psychology. However, it has also been shown that similar developments occur in all fields of endeavour. In physics, the Copernican revolution, and the subsequent Planckian revolution, were prime sources for understanding the creative cycle in the field of science. The history of the arts and religion reveal similar cycles of revolutionary change which arrive at a new synthesis through the cycle of creative individuals of particular sibling positions, and with particular family backgrounds. Thus, the cycle of creativity goes on in all of the symbolic cultural forms: art, religion, science (philosophy), and society.

Most of the examples I have presented lead us to perceive the change in these cycles as having a salutary result. However, a more doubting attitude turns up some stubborn questions. It is an undeniable fact that in the face of the seemingly-impossible situation of Hitler's attempts to conquer the world, as well as Japan's assault in the Second World War, the United States felt the need to develop, and then use, atomic weapons. The efforts to save ourselves and the rest of the world from the horrors of Hitler's Germany and Tojo's Japan led us to develop the very weapons which now make it possible to destroy all life on the globe. It behoves us then to take seriously the means by which we can contain those weapons, and eventually do away with them. This is obvious to every thoughtful individual.

It needs to be emphasized, though, that the family of nations does now exist and has existed in varying degrees of comity for ages. Before the 'nation' became a conscious reality, there was a 'family of families' in the old tribal societies. The tribes may have been at odds with one another much of the time, but they nevertheless maintained at least a wary eye on each other and must have felt some sense of potential relationship other than constant warfare. There is after all a psychological reason for the drawing together of peoples into groups and tribes, and then larger constellations of nations and empires. Humans like all mammals are basically social creatures. Survival is ultimately dependent on a sufficiently secure group which can protect the vulnerable process of birth and the nurturance of infants, and their survival into adulthood. Obviously this need may often run counter to other needs.

One of the other consequences of this social nature of humans and other mammals, is a finely-tuned responsiveness to the differences and similarities of emotional tone and modes of behaviour. In humans this leads inevitably to diversity in friendships, in love relationships and in animosities as well. Sensitivity to one another is largely an unconscious process of feelings and emotional complexes. There is nothing particularly new in what I am saying, but I should like to extend our awareness of this deep layer of feeling and emotional responsiveness into areas that seem far more difficult to understand. I am thinking here of certain curious shifts in political leadership that take place as the social-political situation varies. I have already shown how sibling position and the family atmosphere as well as the *Zeitgeist* have profound effects on the destiny of individuals. We have seen that there is a matching of leaders of particular sibling positions with shifts in the *Zeitgeist*. But there is another layer of arrangements going on all the time in the family of nations. This appears in the relationships between the leaders of different countries. Frequently there is a matching of sibling rank among leaders whose countries are going through similar situations. For example, in 1945 there was the meeting in Yalta of Churchill (**M1**[7 years]M), Roosevelt (**M1**) and Staling (**M1**). In recent years, heads of state in the USA (Reagan, Bush), Britain (Thatcher, Major), Germany (Kohl), France (Mitterrand), Poland (Walesa), The Phillipines (Aquino), and South Africa (de Klerk), are all younger siblings.

What are we to make of this shifting about of leadership throughout an area of common concern to several nations? It is difficult enough to understand how a single leader of a particular sibling position and family atmosphere comes to power at any one time in a nation, let alone to try and imagine the situation when individuals of the same sibling position come to power at the same time in other countries. When several nations are governed by individuals of the same or closely related sibling positions, we may expect that an unconscious level of kinship will exist between them. At best, this should have a salutary effect on the comity of nations. But such an unconscious state can also swing the other way. Our growing awareness of the human condition must lead us to confront these deeply unconscious issues so that they may begin to come to consciousness.

Depth psychology

In closing I wish to follow up on Jung's exhortation above on the great need for psychology in these times. What if anything can depth psychology contribute? Our work with individual patients is primary, but a secondary task is to foster the development of a point of view which emphasizes the seriousness of the world situation, economically, ecologically and politically, and encourages the idea of a global village as a solution to the fragmentation of the present time. Finally, it is essential to keep attention focused on the individual, family and society, in that order, as the sources and the resources of change. The most urgent priority is finding a way to understand better the sources and manifestations of good and evil. This leads to the need for individuals to become aware of the opposites in themselves and seek to hold the opposites in consciousness.

In closing, I wish to express my advocacy of a working hypothesis that has been formulated in this book; namely, that libido, as the instinct of life, or the life force - psychic energy - is primarily experienced through the innate archetypal affects of joy and interest, and their twin dynamisms, play/imagination and curiosity/exploration. Further I suggest that these inherited affects and their dynamisms, come to represent in their ultimate realized forms, what is meant by the cosmogonic principles, Eros and Logos, or the Yin and Yang of the Tao. It seems to me that this conception of libido as the intertwining of two primal affects with their dialectical dynamisms, gives some psychological grounding to the archetypal images of incest; the hierosgamos of the gods, and that third and final stage of the alchemical process, the chymical marriage.

The following comments by Jung on the culmination of the alchemical process appear to bear on the foregoing notions:

> After the hostility of the four elements has been overcome, there still remains the last and most formidable opposition, which the alchemist expressed very aptly as the relationship between male and female. . . Our reason is often influenced far too much by purely physical considerations, so that the union of the sexes seems to it the only sensible thing and the urge for union the most sensible instinct of all. But if we conceive of nature in the higher sense as the totality of all phenomena, then the physical is only one of her aspects, the other is pneumatic or spiritual. The first has always been regarded as feminine, the second as masculine. *The goal of the one is union, the goal of the other is discrimination.* [my italics]
>
> (Jung 1963: 89)

This dialectical opposition may also be viewed as the eternal, and ever unrequited romance, of two kinds of memory - fantasy, the memory of being; and memory, the memory of becoming. The two kinds of memory spring from an original irrepresentable unity, symbolized in the mythical images of Purusha, the Atman, the Rotundum, and the like, which when divided into heaven and earth, male and female, become the source of all creation. Jung describes that moment as

> The first morning of the world, the first sunrise after the primal darkness, when that inchoately conscious complex, the ego, the son of the darkness, knowingly sundered subject and object, and thus precipitated the world and itself into definite existence. . . Genesis 1:1–7 is a projection of this process.
>
> (Jung 1963: 108)

If this is evidence of the potential for healing the 'great split', then it would provide substance to Erich Neumann's hoped for 'emergence of the new ethic'. The new ethic demands that we humans take responsibility for our complex nature and stop projecting the shadow on to each other. 'The time has now come for the principle of perfection to be sacrificed on the altar of wholeness' (Neumann 1969: 133).

> Our growing insight into the limitations of the human condition must inevitably lead, in the course of the next few centuries, to an increasing sense of human solidarity and to a recognition of the fact that, despite all differences, the structure of human nature is everywhere, in essence, the same. The common rootedness of all religion and philosophy in the collective unconscious of the human race is beginning to become obvious.
>
> But just as this solidarity of our species accounts for the inner history of mankind, so the unity of the planet earth will determine the history of the future. . . Slowly but surely, the human race is withdrawing the psychological projections by means of which it had peopled the emptiness of the world with hierarchies of gods and spirits, heavens and hells; and, with amazement, for the first time, it is experiencing the creative fullness of it own primal psychic Ground.
>
> And yet, out of the midst of this circle of humanity, which is beginning to take shape from the coming-together of every part of the human species – nations and races, continents and cultures – the same creative Godhead, unformed and manifold is emerging within the human mind, who previously filled the heavens and spheres of the universe around us.
>
> (Neumann 1969: 133–5)

NOTE

1 Gorbachev (**M1**[17]M) is essentially an only child. In an article in the *Washington Post*, David Remnick, foreign correspondent in Moscow, asked the following question: 'What does it mean to history . . . that Gorbachev grew up almost as an only child? His one sibling, his brother Alexander, was born 17 years after Gorbachev' (Remnick 1989). Most biographies either lack early family history, or they agree with Remnick's report that Mikhail Sergeyevich Gorbachev has but one sibling, a much younger brother named Alexander (Sasha), who was born 16 or 17 years later, around the time Mikhail left home to go away to school (Sheehy 1990: 52). One biographical source cites a conversation with an anonymous senior official who said

Gorbachev had an older brother (no name) who died on the front in the Second World War (Doder and Branson 1990: 440). But since I have found no other report of an older brother, and since Gorbachev's psychology clearly seems to be that of an only child, I am inclined to think that there has been a misunderstanding. Gorbachev's father, Sergei Andreyevich had brothers and other male relatives who fought in the war and died (Sheehy 1990: 45). Perhaps the older brother who died was a brother of Sergei. Or, if there was an older brother, he must have been many years older and/or grown up in another household. In addition to my search of standard biographical sources, I have written Gorbachev asking for clarification of these questions. I look forward to his answer.

Bibliography

Adler, A. (1927) *Understanding Human Nature*, New York: Perma Books, 1949.

Adler, A. (1956) *The Individual Psychology of Alfred Adler*, H. L. Ansbacher and R. R. Ansbacher (eds) New York: Harper & Row, 1964, second printing, 1967.

Adler, A. (1959) *The Practice and Theory of Individual Psychology*, Totowa, New Jersey: Littlefield-Adams.

Adler, A. (1964) *Superiority and Social Interest*, H. L. Ansbacher and R. R. Ansbacher (eds) New York: Viking Press, 1973.

Al-Khalil, S. (1989) *Republic of Fear, the Inside Story of Saddam's Iraq*, New York: Pantheon Books.

Axline, V. (1964) *Dibs in Search of Self*, New York: Ballantine Books, 1976.

Bachelard, G. (1938) *The Psychoanalysis of Fire*, Boston: Beacon Press, 1968.

Barber, J. D. (1972) *The Presidential Character: Predicting Perfomance in the White House*, Englewood Cliffs, New Jersey: Prentice Hall.

Beaverbrook, Lord (1926) *Politicians and the War*, Garden City, NY: Doubleday.

Beebe, J. (1987) 'Discussion: Original morality', in M. A. Mattoon (ed.) *The Archetype of Shadow in a Split World*, 84–9, Einsiedeln, Switzerland: Daimon Verlag.

Berkeley, H. (1968) *The Power of the Prime Minister*, London: Allen & Unwin.

Bingham, C. (1920) *The Prime Ministers of Britain 1721–1921*, London: Murray.

Blake, J. (1989) 'Number of siblings and educational attainment', *Science*, 245 (4913), 32–6.

Bolen, J. S. (1984) *Goddesses in Everywoman*, New York: Harper & Row.

Bottome, P. (1957) *Alfred Adler: A Portrait from Life*, New York: Vanguard.

Caillois, R. (1958) *Man, Play and Games*, New York: Schocken Books, 1979.

Campbell, J. (1949) *The Hero with a Thousand Faces*, New York: Bollingen Foundation, Meridian edn, 1956.

Campbell, J. (1951) *The Flight of the Wild Gander*, South Bend, Indiana: Regnery Gateway, 1979.

Campbell, J. (1959) *The Masks of God: Primitive Mythology*, New York: Viking Press, Penguin Books, 1977.

Cassirer, E. (1953) *The Philosophy of Symbolic Forms*, 1, *Language*, New Haven & London: Yale University Press, fifth printing, 1965.

Cassirer, E. (1955) *The Philosophy of Symbolic Forms*, 2, *Mythical Thought*, New Haven & London: Yale University Press, fifth printing, 1966.

Chodorow, J. (1991) *Dance Therapy and Depth Psychology; The Moving Imagination*, London: Routledge.

Conquest, R. (1991) *Stalin: Breaker of Nations*, New York: Viking Penguin.

Current Biography. (Monthly except December) New York: H. H. Wilson.

Current Biography Cumulated Index, 1940–1985. New York: H. H. Wilson.

Current Biography Yearbook. (Yearly) New York: H. H. Wilson.

Darwin, C. (1872) *The Expression of the Emotions in Man and Animals*, Chicago and London: University of Chicago Press, 1965, fifth impression, 1974.

de Mille, A. (1951) *Dance to the Piper*, Boston: Little, Brown & Co.

Denton, L. (1988) 'Biosocial theory sees many roads to emotion: genetic, cultural, personal factors weighed', *The APA Monitor*, 19(10), 16.

Dietrich, B. C. (1974) *Origins of Greek Religion*, Berlin/New York: Walter de Gruyter.

Dictionary of American Biography, 10 vols with 8 supplements and index. New York: Charles Scribner's Sons. (First published in 1929.)

Dictionary of National Biography (1885–1900), 21 vols with supplement. London: Oxford University Press.

Doder, D. and Branson, L. (1990) *Gorbachev: Heretic in the Kremlin*, New York: Penguin Books, 1991.

Dunham, B. (1963) *Heroes and Heretics: A Social History of Dissent*, New York: Dell Publishing Co.

Dunn, J. and Plomin, R. (1990) *Separate Lives: Why Siblings are so Different*, USA: Basic Books.

Edinger, E. (1974) *Ego and Archetype*, Baltimore, Maryland: Penguin Books.

Eibl-Eibesfeldt, I. (1972) 'Similarities and differences between cultures in expressive movements', in R. A. Hinde (ed.) *Non-Verbal Communication*, Cambridge: Cambridge University Press.

Ekman, P. (1972) 'Universal and cultural differences in facial expression in emotion', in J. K. Cole (ed.) *Nebraska Symposium on Motivation, 1971*, Lincoln: University of Nebraska Press.

Ekman, P. (ed.) (1982) 'Emotion in the human face', 2nd edn, Cambridge: Cambridge University Press.

Eliade, M. (1963) *Myth and Reality*, New York: Harper & Row, 1975.

Eliade, M. (1967) *From Primitives to Zen: A Thematic Sourcebook of the History of Religions*, New York: Harper & Row, 1977.

Ellenberger, H. F. (1970) *The Discovery of the Unconscious*, New York: Basic Books.

Ellis, H. (1926) *A Study of British Genius*, New York: Houghton Mifflin.

Engelmann, B. (1986) *In Hitler's Germany*, New York: Pantheon Books.

Erikson, E. H. (1963) *Childhood and Society*, New York: W. W. Norton & Co.

Erikson, E. H. (1969) *Gandhi's Truth*, New York: W. W. Norton & Co.

Ernst, C. and Angst, J. (1983) *Birth Order: Its Influence on Personality*, Berlin/Heidelberg/New York: Springer-Verlag.

Fox, R. (1967) *Kinship and Marriage*, Baltimore: Penguin Books.

Freud, S. (1900) *The Interpretation of Dreams*, New York: Basic Books, 1955.

Freud, S. (1909) 'Analysis of a phobia in a five-year-old boy', *Collected Papers*, 3, 149–289, London: Hogarth Press, 1948.

Freud, S. (1954) *The Origin of Psychoanalysis: Letters to Wilhelm Fliess, Drafts and Notes, 1897–1902*, M. Bonaparte, A. Freud and E. Kris (eds) New York: Basic Books.

Freud, S. (1985) *The Complete Letters of Sigmund Freud to Wilhelm Fliess, 1887–1904*, J. M. Masson (ed.) Cambridge, MA: Harvard University Press.

Freud, S. and Jung, C. G. (1974) *The Freud/Jung Letters*, W. McGuire (ed.) Princeton: Princeton University Press.

Galton, F. (1869) *Hereditary Genius*, Cleveland and New York: Meridian Books, 1962.

Gipson, L. H. (1962) *The Coming of the Revolution*, New York: Harper & Row.

Goleman, D. (1990) 'The link between birth order and innovation'. Science section, *The New York Times*, 8 May 1990, B5 and B9.

Goodall, J. (1990) *Through a Window: My Thirty Years with the Chimpanzees of Gombe*, Boston: Houghton Mifflin Company.

Graves, R. (1955) *The Greek Myths*, 1, Baltimore: Penguin Books.

Graves, R. and Patai, R. (1963) *Hebrew Myths: The Book of Genesis*, New York: McGraw-Hill, 1966.

Grosskurth, P. (1987) *Melanie Klein*, Cambridge, MA: Harvard University Press.

Harris, I. D. (1964) *The Promised Seed*, Glencoe, Ill.: Free Press of Glencoe.

Heidel, A. (1942) *The Babylonian Genesis*, Chicago and London: The University of Chicago Press, 1956.

Henderson, J. L. (1962) 'The archetype of culture', *The Archetype, Proceedings of the 2nd International Congress of Analytical Psychology, Zurich*, New York: S. Karger, 1964, 3–15.

Henderson, J. L. (1964) 'Ancient myths and modern man', in C. G. Jung and M. L. von Franz (eds) *Man and his Symbols*, 104–57, New York: Doubleday & Co.

Henderson, J. L. (1967) *Thresholds of Initiation*, Middletown, Connecticut: Wesleyan University Press.

Henderson, J. L. (1977) 'Individual lives in a changing society', *Psychological Perspectives* 8(2), 126–42.

Henderson, J. L. (1984) *Cultural Attitudes in Psychological Perspective*, Toronto: Inner City Books.

Henderson, J. L. (1985) 'The origins of a theory of cultural attitudes', *Psychological Perspectives* 16(2), 210–20.

Henderson, J. L. (1991) 'C. G. Jung's psychology: additions and extensions', Memorial lecture in London, 1 March 1991.

Henderson, S. (1991) *Instant Empire*, San Francisco: Mercury House.

Hillman, J. (1961) *Emotion: A Comprehensive Phenomenology of Theories and their Meanings for Therapy*, Evanston: Northwestern University Press.

Hillman, J. (1983) *Healing Fiction*, Barrytown, New York: Station Hill Press.

Hitler, A. (1927) *Mein Kampf*, trans. R. Manheim. Boston: Houghton Mifflin Co., 1971.

Huizinga, J. (1950) *Homo Ludens: A Study of the Play Element in Culture*, Boston: The Beacon Press, 1955/64.

Izard, C. E. (1977) *Human Emotions*, New York: Plenum Press.

Jones, H. E. (1933) 'Order of birth in relation to the development of the child', in C. Murchison (ed.) *A Handbook of Child Psychology*, 204–41, Worcester, Mass.: Clark University Press.

Jung, C. G. (1902) 'On the psychology and pathology of so-called occult phenomena', *Collected Works* 1, 1–88, Princeton: Princeton University Press, 1975.

Jung, C. G. (1907) 'The psychology of dementia praecox', *Collected Works* 3, 1–151, Princeton: Princeton University Press, 1972.

Jung, C. G. (1909) 'The family constellation', *Collected Works* 2, 466–79, Princeton: Princeton University Press, 1973.

Jung, C. G. (1910) 'Psychic conflicts in a child', *Collected Works* 17, 1–35, Princeton: Princeton University Press, 1954.

Jung, C. G. (1911) 'On the doctrine of complexes', *Collected Works* 2, 598–604, Princeton: Princeton University Press, 1973.

Jung, C. G. (1912a) 'Two kinds of thinking', *Collected Works* 5, 7–33, Princeton: Princeton University Press, 1967.

Jung, C. G. (1912b) 'The concept of libido', *Collected Works* 5, 132–41, Princeton: Princeton University Press, 1967.

Jung, C. G. (1912c) 'The transformation of libido', *Collected Works* 5, 142–70, Princeton: Princeton University Press, 1967.

Jung, C. G. (1912d) 'The origin of the hero', *Collected Works* 5, 171–206, Princeton: Princeton University Press, 1967.

Jung, C. G. (1916) 'The transcendent function', *Collected Works* 8, 67–91, Princeton: Princeton University Press, 1975.

Jung, C. G. (1917/1926/1943) 'On the psychology of the unconscious', *Collected Works* 7, 1–119, Princeton: Princeton University Press, 1966.

Jung, C. G. (1919) 'Instinct and the unconscious', *Collected Works* 8, 129–38, Princeton: Princeton University Press, 1975.

Jung, C. G. (1920) 'The psychological foundations of belief in spirits', *Collected Works* 8, 300–18, Princeton: Princeton University Press, 1975.

Jung, C. G. (1921) *Psychological Types*, *Collected Works* 6, Princeton: Princeton University Press, 1974.

Jung, C. G. (1924) 'Analytical psychology and education', *Collected Works* 17, 63–132, Princeton: Princeton University Press, 1954.

Jung, C. G. (1926) 'Spirit and life', *Collected Works* 8, 319–37, Princeton: Princeton University Press, fourth printing, 1978.

Jung, C. G. (1927) 'The structure of the psyche', *Collected Works* 8, 139–58, Princeton: Princeton University Press, 1975.

Jung, C. G. (1927/31) 'Introduction to Wickes's "Analyse der kinderseele" ', *Collected Works* 17, 39–46, Princeton: Princeton University Press, 1954.

Jung, C. G. (1928a) 'The relations between the ego and the unconscious', *Collected Works* 7, 121–241, Princeton: Princeton University Press, 1966.

Jung, C. G. (1928b) 'The spiritual problem of modern man', *Collected Works* 10, 74–94, 2nd edn, Princeton: Princeton University Press, 1970.

Jung, C. G. (1929a) 'Commentary on "The secret of the golden flower" ', *Collected Works* 13, 1–56, Princeton: Princeton University Press, 1976.

Jung, C. G. (1929b) 'Problems of modern psychotherapy', *Collected Works* 16, 53–75, Princeton: Princeton University Press, 1975.

Jung, C. G. (1930) 'Introduction to Kranefeldt's "Secret Ways of the Mind" ', *Collected Works* 4, 2nd edn with corrections, 324–32, Princeton: Princeton University Press, 1970.

Jung, C. G. (1930–34) 'The visions seminars', from the *Complete Notes of Mary Foote*, books 1 and 2, Zurich: Spring Publications, 1976.

Jung, C. G. (1931a) 'The aims of psychotherapy', *Collected Works* 16, 36–52, Princeton: Princeton University Press, 1975.

Jung, C. G. (1931b) 'Problems of modern psychotherapy', *Collected Works* 16, 53–75, Princeton: Princeton University Press, 1954/1975.

Jung, C. G. (1933) 'Brother Klaus', *Collected Works* 11, 316–23, Princeton: Princeton University Press, 1975.

Jung, C. G. (1934a) 'A review of the complex theory', *Collected Works* 8, 92–104, Princeton: Princeton University Press, 1975.

Jung, C. G. (1934b) 'A study in the process of individuation', *Collected Works* 9(1), 290–354, Princeton: Princeton University Press, 1977.

Jung, C. G. (1935) 'The Tavistock lectures: on the theory and practice of analytical psychology', *Collected Works* 18, 5–182, Princeton: Princeton University Press, 1976.

Jung, C. G. (1936a) 'Individual dream symbolism in relation to alchemy', *Collected Works* 12, 41–223, Princeton: Princeton Univeristy Press, 1974.

Jung, C. G. (1936b) 'The concept of the collective unconscious', *Collected Works* 9(1), 42–53, Princeton: Princeton University Press, 1977.

Jung, C. G. (1936c) 'Yoga and the west', *Collected Works* 11, 529–37, Princeton: Princeton University Press, 1975.

Jung, C. G. (1938a) 'Psychological aspects of the mother archetype', *Collected Works* 9(1), 75–110, Princeton: Princeton University Press, 2nd edn, 1968.

Jung, C. G. (1938b) *Dream Analysis*, W. McGuire (ed.) Princeton: Princeton University Press, 1984.

Jung, C. G. (1940) 'The psychology of the child archetype', *Collected Works*, 9(1), 151–81, Princeton: Princeton University Press, 1977.

Jung, C. G. (1945) 'The phenomenology of the spirit in fairytales', *Collected Works* 9(1), 207–54, Princeton: Princeton University Press, 1977.

Jung, C. G. (1946a) 'The psychology of the transference', *Collected Works* 16, 163–323, Princeton: Princeton University Press, 1975.

Jung, C. G. (1946b) 'The fight with the shadow', *Collected Works* 10, 218–26. Princeton: Princeton University Press, 1978.

Jung, C. G. (1947) 'On the nature of the psyche', *Collected Works* 8, 159–234, Princeton: Princeton University Press, 1975.

Jung, C. G. (1948) 'Address on the occasion of the founding of the C. G. Jung Institute, Zurich, 24 April 1948', *Collected Works* 18, 471–6, Princeton: Princeton University Press, 1976.

Jung, C. G. (1951a) *Aion: Researches into the Phenomenology of the Self*, *Collected Works* 9(2), Princeton: Princeton University Press, 1968.

Jung, C. G. (1951b) 'Fundamental questions of psychotherapy', *Collected Works* 16, 111–25, Princeton: Princeton University Press, 1975.

Jung, C. G. (1952) 'Answer to Job', *Collected Works* 11, 355–470, Princeton: Princeton University Press, 1975.

Jung, C. G. (1956) 'Symbols of transformation', 2nd edn, *Collected Works* 5, Princeton: Princeton University Press, 1968.

Jung, C. G. (1958) 'A psychological view of conscience', *Collected Works* 10, 437–55, Princeton: Princeton University Press, 1978.

Jung, C. G. (1961) *Memories, Dreams, Reflections*, New York: Random House – Vintage Books, 1965.

Jung, C. G. (1961/64) 'Symbols and the interpretation of dreams', *Collected Works* 18, 185–264, Princeton: Princeton University Press, 1976.

Jung, C. G. (1963) *Mysterium Coniunctionis*, Princeton: Princeton University

Press, 1974.

Jung, C. G. (1973) *Letters*, 1, Princeton: Princeton University Press.

Jung, C. G. (1975) *Letters*, 2, Princeton: Princeton University Press.

Kalff, D. (1980) *Sandplay*, Santa Monica: Sigo Press.

Kane, J. N. (1959) *Facts About the Presidents*, New York: Wilson.

Karsh, E. and Rautsi, I. (1991) *Saddam Hussein, a Political Biography*, New York: Free Press.

Kerenyi, C. (1947) *Asklepios*, New York: Pantheon, 1959.

Kerenyi, C. (1959) *The Heroes of the Greeks*, New York: Grove Press.

King, N. L. (1960) *Lincoln's Manager David Davis*, Cambridge, MA: Harvard University Press.

Koch, H. L. (1958) 'Some emotional attitudes of the young child in relation to characteristics of his sibling', *Child Development* 27, 293–426.

Kohut, H. (1977) *The Restoration of the Self*, New York: International Universities Press.

Koyre, A. (1965) *Newtonian Studies*, Chicago: University of Chicago Press, first Phoenix edn, 1968.

Kramer, S. N. (1959) *History Begins at Sumer*, Garden City, New York: Doubleday Anchor Books.

Kramer, S. N. (1961) *Sumerian Mythology*, New York: Harper & Brothers.

Kramer, S. N. (1963) *The Sumerians*, Chicago: The University of Chicago Press.

Krüll, M. (1986) *Freud and his Father*, New York/London: W. W. Norton & Co.

Kuhn, T. S. (1957) *The Copernican Revolution: Planetary Astronomy in the Development of Western Thought*, Cambridge, MA and London, England: Harvard University Press, ninth printing, 1977.

Kuhn, T. S. (1962) 'The historical structure of scientific discovery', *Science* 136, 760–64.

Kuhn, T. S. (1977) *The Essential Tension: Selected Studies in Scientific Tradition and Change*, Chicago and London: University of Chicago Press.

Lagercrantz, H. and Slotkin T. (1986) 'The "stress" of being born', *Scientific American*, 254, 100–7, April.

Laing, R. D. (1972) *The Politics of the Family*, New York: Vintage Books.

Langer, W. L. (1948) *An Encyclopedia of World History*, Boston: Houghton Mifflin.

Lasko, J. K. (1954) 'Parent behavior towards first and second children', *Genetic Psychological Monographs*, 49, 96–137.

Layard, J. (1942) *Stone Men of Malekula*, London: Chatto & Windus (cite pp 62ff).

Layard, J. (1945) 'The incest taboo and the virgin archetype', 254–307, in *The Virgin Archetype: Two Essays*, Zurich: Spring Publications, 1972.

Lévi-Strauss, C. (1973) *From Honey to Ashes*, New York: Harper & Row.

Levy, D. M. (1937) 'Sibling rivalry', *American Orthopsychiatric Association Research Monograph* no. 2.

Lynd, H. (1958) *On Shame and the Search for Identity*, New York: Harcourt, Brace.

Machtiger, H. G. (1983) 'Reactions on the transference and countertransference process with borderline patients', in N. Schwartz-Salant and M. Stein (eds) *Chiron 1984*, 101–29.

Masson, J. M. (1984) *The Assault on Truth: Freud's Suppression of the Seduction Theory*, New York: Penguin Books, 1985.

Mathiot, A. (1967) *The British Political System*, Palo Alto: Stanford University Press.

Miller, A. (1983) *For Your Own Good: Hidden Cruelty in Child Rearing and the Roots of Violence*, New York: Farrar, Straus, Giroux.

Monte, C. F. (1977) *Beneath the Mask*, New York: Holt, Rinehart & Winston, 1980.

Nathanson, D. L. (ed.) (1987) *The Many Faces of Shame*, New York: Guilford Press.

Neumann, E. (1954) *The Origins and History of Consciousness*, Princeton: Princeton University Press, 1973.

Neumann, E. (1966) 'Narcissism, normal self-formation, and the primary relation to the mother', *Spring 1966*, 81–106.

Neumann, E. (1969) *Depth Psychology and a New Ethic*, Boston: Shambhala Publications, 1990.

Neumann, E. (1973) *The Child*, Boston: Shambhala Publications, 1990.

Osterman, E. (1965) 'The tendency toward patterning and order in matter and in the psyche', in J. B. Wheelwright (ed.) *The Reality of the Psyche*, 14–27, New York: G. P. Putnam's Sons, 1968.

Otto, R. (1923) *The Idea of the Holy*, Oxford/New York: Oxford University Press, 1981.

Perera, S. B. (1981) *Descent to the Goddess*, Toronto: Inner City Books.

Perera, S. B. (1986) *The Scapegoat Complex: Toward a Mythology of Shadow and Guilt*, Toronto: Inner City Books.

Perry, J. (1974) *The Far Side of Madness*, Englewood Cliffs, New Jersey: Prentice-Hall.

Petchkovsky, L. (1982) 'Images of madness in Australian aborigines', *Journal of Analytical Psychology*, 27, 21–39.

Piaget, J. (1952) *The Origins of Intelligence in Children*, New York: W. W. Norton & Co., 1963.

Piaget, J. (1954) *The Construction of Reality in the Child*, New York: Basic Books, 1971.

Piaget, J. (1962) *Play, Dreams and Imitation in Childhood*, New York: W. W. Norton & Co.

Plato (n.d./1952) 'Timaeus 90.C-D', in *Plato's Cosmology*, trans. F. M. Cornford, New York/London: Humanities Press.

Post, J. M. (1990) 'Saddam Hussein of Iraq: A Political Psychology Profile', testimony prepared for Hearings on Gulf Crisis of House Armed Services Committee on 5 December and House Foreign Affairs Committee on 11 December 1990.

Raglan, Lord (1956) *The Hero*, New York: Vintage Books.

Rank, O. (1907) *Der Künstler*, rev. and trans. edns, became *Art and Artist*, 1932.

Rank, O. (1909) *The Myth of the Birth of the Hero*, New York: Vintage Books, 1959.

Rank, O. (1924) *The Trauma of Birth*, New York: Harper & Row, 1973.

Rank, O. (1931) *Technik der Psychoanalyse*, I, 1926; II, 1929; III, 1931; English trans. *Will Therapy*, 1936.

Rank, O. (1941) *Beyond Psychology*, New York: Dover.

Rank, O. (1945) *Will Therapy and Truth and Reality*, New York: Alfred A. Knopf.

Remnick, D. (1989) 'Young Gorbachev', *Washington Post*, Friday 1 December 1989.

Riordan, M. (1987) *The Hunting of the Quark: A True Story of Modern Physics*, New York: Simon & Schuster.

Roberts, J. and Sutton-Smith, B. (1970) 'The cross-cultural and psychological study of games', in G. Luschen (ed.) *The Cross-cultural Analysis of Games*, 100–8, Champaign, Illinois: Stipes.

Roseboom, E. H. (1957) *A History of Presidential Elections*, New York: Macmillan.

Russell, D. (1986) *The Secret Trauma: Incest in the Lives of Girls and Women*, New York: Basic Books.

Rustow, D. A. (ed.) (1970) *Philosophers and Kings: Studies in Leadership*, New York: Braziller.

Samuels, A. (1985) *Jung and the Post-Jungians*, London and New York: Routledge & Kegan Paul.

Samuels, A. (1987) 'Original morality in a depressed culture', in M. A. Mattoon (ed.) *The Archetype of Shadow in a Split World*, 69–83, Einsiedeln, Switzerland: Daimon Verlag.

Samuels, A. (1989) *The Plural Psyche*, London and New York: Routledge.

Samuels, A., Shorter B. and Plaut, F. (1986) *A Critical Dictionary of Jungian Analysis*, London: Routledge & Kegan Paul.

Sandner, D. (1979) *Navaho Symbols of Healing*, New York: Harcourt, Brace, Jovanovich.

Sayers, D. (1955) *Dante: The Divine Comedy, II: Purgatory*, trans. and introduction, Harmondsworth, Middlesex: Penguin Books, 1959.

Schaya, L. (1971) *The Universal Meaning of the Kaballah*, Baltimore: Penguin Books, 1973.

Schooler, C. (1972) 'Birth order effects: not here, not now', *Psychological Bulletin* 78, 161–75.

Schwartz-Salant, N. (1982) *Narcissism and Character Transformation*, Toronto: Inner City Books.

Schwartz-Salant, N. (1986) 'On the subtle body concept in clinical practice', in N. Schwartz-Salant and M. Stein (eds) *The Body in Analysis*, 19–58, Wilmette, Illinois: Chiron Publications.

Sciolino, E. (1991) *The Outlaw State*, New York: John Wiley & Sons.

Sears, P. S. (1951) 'Doll play aggression in normal young children. Influence of sex, age, sibling status, father's absence', *Psychological Monographs* 65 (whole no. 323).

Sheehy, G. (1990) *The Man who Changed the World*, New York: HarperCollins.

Singer, J. (1976) *Androgyny*, Garden City, NY: Anchor Press/Doubleday.

Slater, P. E. (1968) *The Glory of Hera*, Boston: Beacon Press.

Smelser, W. and Stewart, L. H. (1968) 'Where are the siblings? A re-evaluation of the relationship between birth order and college attendance', *Sociometry* 31(3), 294–303, September 1968.

Stein, M. (1983) 'Power, shamanism, and maieutics in the countertransference', *Chiron 1984*, N. Schwartz-Salant and M. Stein (eds).

Stein, M. (1988) 'Sibling rivalry and the ego's envy of the self', in L. H. Stewart and J. Chodorow (eds) *The Family: Personal, Cultural and Archetypal Dimensions. Proceedings of the National Conference of Jungian Analysts*, 1–12, San Francisco: C. G. Jung Institute.

Stevens, A. (1983) *Archetypes: A Natural History of the Self*, New York: Quill.

Stewart, C. T. (1981) 'Developmental psychology of sandplay', in G. Hill (ed.) *Sandplay studies: Origins, Theory and Practice*, 39–92, San Francisco: C. G. Jung Institute of San Francisco.

Stewart, C. T. and Stewart, L. H. (1981) 'Play, games and stages of development: a contribution toward a comprehensive theory of play', presented at the 7th annual conference of The Association for the Anthropological Study of Play (TAASP), Fort Worth, April 1981.

Stewart, L. H. (1961) 'Birth order and political genius', presented at the 1961 conference of the California State Psychological Association.

Stewart, L. H. (1962) 'Oedipus was an only child', presented at conference of the Mount Zion Hospital Psychiatric Service, San Francisco.

Stewart, L. H. (1970) 'The politics of birth order', Proceedings of the 78th Annual Convention of the APA, 5, 365–6, Washington D.C.: American Psychological Association.

Stewart, L. H. (1976) 'Kinship libido: toward an archetype of the family', Proceedings of the Annual Conference of Jungian Analysts of the United States, 168–82, San Francisco: C. G. Jung Institute of San Francisco.

Stewart, L. H. (1977a) 'Sand play therapy: Jungian technique', in B. Wolman (ed.) *International Encyclopedia of Psychiatry, Psychology, Psychoanalysis and Neurology*, 9–11, New York: Aesculapius Publishers.

Stewart, L. H. (1977b) 'Birth order and political leadership', in M. Hermann with T. Milburn (eds) *A Psychological Examination of Political Leaders*, 206–36, New York: Free Press.

Stewart, L. H. (1978) 'Gaston Bachelard and the poetics of reverie', in G. Hill *et al.* (eds) *The Shaman from Elko*, San Francisco: C. G. Jung Institute of San Francisco.

Stewart, L. H. (1981a) 'Play and sandplay', in G. Hill (ed.) *Sandplay Studies: Origins, Theory and Practice*, 21–37, San Francisco: C. G. Jung Institute of San Francisco.

Stewart, L. H. (1981b) 'The play-dream continuum and the categories of the imagination', presented at the 7th annual conference of The Association for the Anthropological Study of Play (TAASP), Fort Worth, April 1981.

Stewart, L. H. (1982) 'Sandplay and analysis', in M. Stein (ed.) *Jungian Analysis*, 204–18, La Salle: Open Court Publishing Co.

Stewart, L. H. (1984) 'Play-eros', in *Affects and Archetypes II*, paper presented at active imagination seminar in Geneva, Switzerland in August 1984.

Stewart, L. H. (1985) 'Affect and archetype: a contribution to a comprehensive theory of the structure of the psyche', in the Proceedings of the 1985 California Spring Conference, 89–120, San Francisco: C. G. Jung Institute.

Stewart, L. H. (1986) 'Work in progress: affect and archetype', in N. Schwartz-Salant and M. Stein (eds) *The Body in Analysis*, 183–203, Wilmette, Illinois: Chiron Publications.

Stewart, L. H. (1987a) 'A brief report: affect and archetype', *Journal of Analytical Psychology* 32(1), 35–46.

Stewart, L. H. (1987b) 'Affect and archetype in analysis', in N. Schwartz-Salant and M. Stein (eds) *Archetypal Processes in Psychotherapy*, 131–62, Wilmette: Illinois: Chiron Publications.

Stewart, L. H. (1987c) 'Kinship libido: shadow in marriage and family', in M.

A. Mattoon (ed.) *The Archetype of Shadow in a Split World*, 387–99, Einsiedeln, Switzerland: Daimon Verlag.

Stewart, L. H. (1989) 'Jealousy and envy: complex family emotions', in L. H. Stewart and J. Chodorow (eds) *The Family: Personal, Cultural and Archetypal Dimensions*, Proceedings of the national conference of Jungian analysts, 13–21, San Francisco: C. G. Jung Institute.

Stewart, L. H. (1990) Foreword to Neumann's *The Child*, Boston: Shambhala.

Stewart, L. H. and Stewart, C. T. (1979) 'Play, games and affects: a contribution toward a comprehensive theory of play', in A. T. Cheska (ed.) *Play as Context*, 42–52, *Proceedings of The Association for the Anthropological Study of Play* (TAASP), Westpoint, NY: Leisure Press, 1981.

Sulloway, F. J. (n.d.) 'Orthodoxy and innovation in science: the influence of birth order in a multivariate context', paper presented at the annual meeting of the American Association for the Advancement of Science, February 1990.

Sutton-Smith, B. (1975) 'Play as adaptive potentiation', *Sportwissenschaft* 5, 103–18.

Sutton-Smith, B. (1978) *The Dialectics of Play*, Schorndorf, West Germany: Verlag Karl Hofman.

Sutton-Smith, B. and Rosenberg, B. G. (1970) *The Sibling*, New York: Holt, Rinehart & Winston.

Taft, J. (1958) *Otto Rank, a Biographical Study Based on Notebooks, Letters, Collected Writings, Therapeutic Achievements and Personal Associations*, New York: Julian Press.

Taylor, R. L. (1952) *Winston Churchill*, Garden City, NY: Doubleday.

Tomkins, S. S. (1962) *Affect Imagery Consciousness*, I, New York: Springer Publishing Company.

Tomkins, S. S. (1963) *Affect Imagery Consciousness*, II, New York: Springer Publishing Company.

Tomkins, S. S. (1982) 'Affect theory', in P. Ekman (ed.) *Emotion in the Human Face*, 2nd edn, 353–95, Cambridge: Cambridge University Press.

Trotter, R. J. (1983) 'Baby face', *Psychology Today*, August, 14–20.

Vanendonck, J. (1921) *The Psychology of Daydreams*, New York: Macmillan.

Verba, S. (1961) *Small Groups and Political Behavior: A Study of Leadership*, Princeton: Princeton University Press.

Vitz, P. C. (1988) *Sigmund Freud's Christian Unconscious*, New York: Guilford Press.

Volkogonov, D. (1988) *Stalin: Triumph and Tragedy*, transl. Harold Shukman, New York: Grove Weidenfeld.

Wagner, M. E. and Schubert, H. J. P. (1977) 'Sibship variables and United States Presidents', *Journal of Individual Psychology*, 3(1), 78–85.

Waldman, P. (1991) 'A tale emerges of Saddam's origins that even he may not have known', *The Wall Street Journal*, February 7.

Walesa, L. (1987) *A Way of Hope, an Autobiography*, New York: Henry Holt & Co.

Watson, J. D. (1968) *The Double Helix: A Personal Account of the Discovery of the Structure of DNA*, New York and Scarborough, Ontario: A Mentor Book, 1969.

Whitney, D. C. (1967) *The American Presidents*, Garden City, NY: Doubleday.

Winnicott, D. W. (1964/68) 'The squiggle game', *Psychoanalytic Explorations*, 299–317, Cambridge, MA: Harvard University Press, 1989.

Winnicott, D. W. (1966) 'On the split-off male and female elements', *Psychoanalytic Explorations*, 168–92, Cambridge, MA: Harvard University Press, 1989.

Winnicott, D. W. (1971) *Playing and Reality*, New York: Basic Books.

Winnicott, D. W. (1975) *Through Paediatrics to Psycho-analysis*, New York: Basic Books.

Winnicott, D. W. (1977) *The Piggle: an account of the psychoanalytic treatment of a little girl*, I. Ramzy (ed.), New York: International Universities Press, Inc., 1979.

Yeltsin, B. (1990) *Against the Grain*, New York: Summit Books.

Name index

The Name index includes only authors from whose works extracts are quoted.

Subject index

The Subject index also includes individuals as subjects.